9/EP

A Dictionary
of Days

A Dictionary of Days

Leslie Dunkling

Facts On File Publications
New York, New York ● Oxford, England

A Dictionary of Days

Library of Congress Catalog Card Number: 88-3825
CIP data available on request
British CIP data available on request

ISBN 0-8160-1416-9 (HC)
ISBN 0-8160-2138-4 (PB)

Printed in the United States of America

10 9 8 7 6 5 4 3 2

CONTENTS

Which is the properest day to drink

Saturday, Sunday, Monday?

Each is the properest day, I think.

Tell me but yours,

I'll mention my day,

Let us but fix on some day:

Why should I name but one day?

       Dr Thomas Arne (1770–1778)

ACKNOWLEDGEMENTS

The seeds of this book were sown in the 1970s in the pages of *Viz.*, the newsletter of the Names Society. Letters from members of the society first made me aware that there were more days in the year with names than I had realized. Eventually Mr Alec Mowbray, of Bognor Regis, sent me a calendar-chart on which he had indicated days with names. There were rather more blank spaces than names, and it was in an attempt to fill those blanks that I began to collect further examples of named days.

In 1983 I was able to renew a long-standing friendship with Dr Terrence Keough, of Ottawa. The generous hospitality of Terry (and his partner Barbara Dyroff) enabled me to make use of the facilities of both the National Library of Canada and the University of Ottawa. The staffs of both libraries were very helpful. I later made use of other university libraries, such as those of the University of Michigan and the State University of New York at Fredonia. Once again the library staffs were cooperative in every way. At Fredonia Professor Edwin Lawson was not only hospitable, but later went to the trouble of sending me many photocopied items.

Subsequently the people I was most to plague with queries were those who work in the reference library of the BBC's External Services at Bush House. I have great admiration for both their knowledge and their patience. I would also like to thank friends and colleagues who have helped me in one way or another with this book, especially Philip Dodd, John Foley, Rochelle Chernikoff, Caroline Dunton, Gordon Wright, Francis Hallawell, Albert Jones, Bob Marsden, Sue Cokyll and Andrew Delahunty. Writing is essentially a lonely occupation, and the support and encouragement of friends is therefore especially valuable and much appreciated.

INTRODUCTION

Some years ago I had occasion to write to the late Eric Partridge. I asked him for some information, and mentioned in passing that I was compiling a reference book. 'Make sure you entertain as well as instruct the reader', was his comment when he replied. It was something that he himself was well able to do, of course. In several previous books, and now in this one, I have tried to follow both his advice and example. This book therefore contains what might be called the 'usual' reference information and facts about named days in English-speaking countries, but I have also made it more personal. That will be evident in both my selection of named days, and in the comments made about them.

As far as straightforward information is concerned, it seems to me that there is an obvious need for a kind of Reader's Guide to Named Days. Shakespeare, to take one example, refers in his plays to Twelfth Night, St Lambert's Day, Hallowmas, Holy-rood Day, St Davy's Day, Feast of Crispin (St Crispin's Day, the day of Crispin Crispianus, etc.), All-Souls' Day, St Valentine's Day, Ascension Day and Martlemas, as well as chair days, dancing days, salad days, halcyon days, dog days, doomsday, love-day, etc. Many of these references are far more obscure to the modern reader than they would have been to an Elizabethan audience, and even those which seem familiar are not necessarily as simple as they appear to be. When is Twelfth Night, for example? The answer to that will tend to vary according to the dictionary you happen to consult. At least there will be a brief entry for Twelfth Night in any reasonable dictionary. St Lambert's Day, St Davy's Day, Feast of Crispin, etc., are unlikely to be mentioned.

Readers of more recent literature are just as likely to run into problems when particular days are mentioned. In her novel *The Group*, for example, the American writer Mary McCarthy mentions Commencement Day, Class Day, Washington's Birthday, Lincoln's Birthday, May Day, Hallowe'en, Feast of Stephen, Thanksgiving Day, Mother's Day. She also refers to Blue Monday, uses the word 'day' at one point in a very special sense and is consciously archaic with her use of 'yestreen'. British readers, especially, would be hard put to it to explain the significance of some of these, just as American readers might have difficulties when reading *Abbie*, by Dane Chandos. Abbie has a tendency to head her highly entertaining letters with titles such as Waterloo Day, Maundy Thursday, Candlemas, Lady Day, Lammas Day, Empire Day.

Difficulties are not always caused by the cultural differences between Americans and the British. Many Americans would be bemused by F. Scott Fitzgerald's mention of Tap Day in *Tender is the Night*, while British readers might well not understand James Joyce's short story about Ivy Day. Once again, normal English dictionaries will prove to be unhelpful with such terms.

It would be pleasant, incidentally, if the fictional Aunt Abbie's habit of naming the day in correspondence was more widely observed. Dr R. J. Brumpton once drew my attention to the published diary of the Reverend Francis Kilvert. The curate made full use of any named day, using the system May Day, preceded by May Eve and followed by May Morrow. The correspondence columns of newspapers would surely have an extra interest if letter-writers added such touches.

I have talked of named days in literature, but in real life such days are often of great importance as focal points within the year. They are especially important, perhaps, when they are holidays and provide a break from routine, or when they inspire traditional practices. Traditions are somehow comforting. 'They kept up the Christmas carol,' says Oliver Goldsmith's Vicar of Wakefield, referring to his rural parishioners, 'sent true-love knots on Valentine morning, ate pancakes at Shrovetide, showed their wit on the first of April, and religiously cracked nuts on Michaelmas Eve.' As for the city workers in later times, a few special days in the year must have seemed like gold dust. Elmer Rice described an office-worker of the 1920s in his play *The Adding Machine*. The man worked a six-day week, with a half-holiday on Saturdays in July and August. He had a week's paid holiday a year, 'an' legal holidays. I nearly forgot them. New Year's, Washington's Birthday, Decoration Day, Fourth o' July, Labor Day, Election Day, Thanksgivin', Christmas. Good Friday if you want it. An' if you're a Jew, Young Kipper (Yom Kippur) an' the other one.'

All the days I have mentioned so far merit an entry in this book, of course. There are many others, of a more local nature, which I have excluded. The public swimming pool in my area, for instance, advertises Saturday as Funday for children. Similarly, a London theatre offers children Jumbo Days and Double Decker Days. These are copy-writers' inventions, able to be used in publicity material but probably never used in speech. Another kind of named day is sometimes hinted at in novels. 'It was 'Roy Hobbs Day' . . .', says Bernard Malamud, in *The Natural*, meaning that it was a day when proceeds from a baseball game would go to a player of that name. 'Monday, Rubenstein Day, dawned cold and disgusted,' writes Richard Bissell in *The Pajama Game*. It is the day when Rubenstein, the union representative, will visit the factory.

Such localized, ad-hoc naming of the day occurs frequently in real life. 'Yesterday was official Putting-A-Brave-Face-On-It-Day,' wrote Simon Barnes in *The Times* (February, 1987). The names may well be used in speech by particular groups of people, if only for a short time. It would clearly be impossible to collect all such names, and doing so would in any case serve little purpose. I have nevertheless drawn on a very wide range of sources for the days which I do list. The areas covered are indicated below:

National events: Australia Day, Canada Day

Historical events: Admission Day, VJ-Day

Christian events: Easter Day, Christmas Day

Sporting events: Grey Cup Day, Derby Day

Calendar events: New Year's Day, Midsummer Day

Royal events: Coronation Day, Royal Oak Day

Regional events: Up-helly-A, Old Man's Day

Family events: Family Day, Mother's Day

University events: Gaudy Day, Encaenia Day

School events: Sports Day, Speech Day

Military events: Trafalgar Day, K-Day

Institutional events: Thinking Day, Kid's Day

Local community events: Mayoring Day, Charter Day

Folkloric events: All Fools' Day, May Day

Political references: Ivy Day, Primrose Day

Ethnic events: Acadian Day, American Indian Day

Personal commemoration: Washington's Birthday, Martin Luther-King Day

Fund raising: Flag day, Lifeboat Day

Business life: Contango Day, Settling Day

Jewish feasts: Yom Kippur, Rosh Hashanah

Generic terms: yesterday, Wednesday

Verbal expressions: lack-a-day, welladay

Technical terms: sidereal day, solar day

Food and Drink: Pancake Tuesday, Fig Sunday

Personal events: birthday, name day

Fictional: Durin's Day, Ford's Day

Biographical: Beer Day, First Sunday after the Derby

I have also dealt with some days which are very difficult to categorize. I am very fond of Belagcholly Day, for instance, and it seems to defy classification.

As one who has rather a weakness for word-play I would have liked to call this book *Naming the Day*. Book-sellers would probably then have assumed that it dealt with wedding etiquette and shelved it accordingly. The subject of the book does at least allow me one dreadful pun. Surely, in bringing this Introduction to an end, I can truly say that it is time to call it a day?

Leslie Dunkling
Candlemas, or Groundhog Day, 1987

BIBLIOGRAPHIC NOTE

I have, of course, referred to a great many reference books while compiling this dictionary. I have preferred to mention them under the appropriate entries rather than list them in a separate Bibliography. References will be found *passim* to certain well-known source books, such as the *Oxford English Dictionary*, to which I am greatly indebted, Eric Partridge's *Dictionary of Historical Slang*, Brewer's *Dictionary of Phrase and Fable*, the Opies' *Lore and Language of Schoolchildren*, Weekley's *Etymological Dictionary of Modern English*, and so on.

A

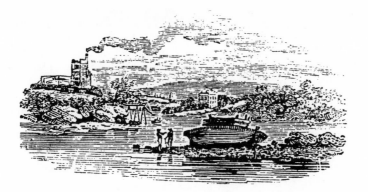

Acadian Day

The Acadians were originally the French colonists of the seventeenth century who lived in the area known in French as *Acadie* and in English as Acadia. This area was centred on what is now Nova Scotia, but included Prince Edward Island and parts of Maine and Quebec. In modern times Acadians, or Cajuns as they are popularly known, are the French-speaking inhabitants of the Maritime Provinces. They have often maintained a folk culture which remains separate from that of the English-speaking inhabitants, and this is displayed each year in many local Acadian Day celebrations, usually in July or August. The most famous literary reference to the Acadians occurs in Longfellow's poem 'Evangeline'. This deals with the expulsion of some of the early Acadians from their territories. The poem contains such well-known lines as:

Silently one by one, in the infinite meadows
of heaven
Blossomed the lovely stars, the forget-me-
nots of the angels.

Account Day

A typical announcement in the London *Times*, on the page which lists Stock Exchange prices, reads: 'Account days – dealings began May 12. Dealings end May 30. Contango Day June 2. Settlement Day June 9.' 'Account day' in this context simply refers to one of the four important days associated with any period of trading, but the term is also used as a synonym for **Settlement Day** (or **Settling Day**), the day on which payment becomes due in respect of deals made during that period. Religious writers of the past have pointed out that there will be a 'great day of accounts' on the final Day of Judgement.

Actday See TAP DAY.

Adelaide Cup Day See MELBOURNE CUP DAY.

Admission Day

Some American states celebrate the anniversary of their admission to the Union with a public holiday on or near the actual day. California (September 9th, 1850) and Hawaii (August 21st, 1959) still use the term 'Admission Day'. Others refer to the day by the name of their state: **Colorado Day** (August 1st, 1876), **Indiana Day** (December 11th, 1816), **Nevada Day** (October 31st, 1864), **West Virginia Day** (June 20th, 1863). In Vermont the date of the state's admission (March 4th, 1791) coincides with **Town Meeting Day**, when such matters as budgets, teachers' salaries, etc., are decided on. The remaining states, which do not seem to mark the day with any special celebrations, were admitted to the Union as follows: Alabama – December 14th, 1819; Alaska – January 3rd, 1959; Arizona – February 14th, 1912; Arkansas – June 15th, 1836; Connecticut – January 9th, 1788; Delaware – December 7th, 1787; Florida – March 3rd, 1845; Georgia – January 2nd, 1788; Idaho – July 3rd, 1890; Illinois – December 3rd, 1818; Iowa – December 28th, 1846; Kansas – January 29th, 1861; Kentucky – June 1st, 1792; Louisiana – April 30th, 1812; Maine – March 15th, 1820; Maryland – April 28th, 1788; Massachusetts – February 6th, 1788; Michigan – January 26th, 1837; Minnesota – May 11th, 1858; Mississippi – December 10th, 1817; Missouri – August 10th, 1821; Montana – November 8th, 1899; Nebraska – March 1st, 1867; New Hampshire – June 21st, 1788; New Jersey – December 18th, 1837; New Mexico – January 16th, 1912; New York – July 26th, 1788; North Carolina – November 21st, 1789; North Dakota – November 2nd, 1889; Ohio – March 1st, 1803; Oklahoma – November 16th, 1907; Oregon – February 14th, 1859; Pennsylvania – December 12th, 1787; Rhode Island – May 29th, 1790; South Carolina – May 23rd, 1788; South Dakota – November 2nd, 1889; Tennessee – June 1st, 1796; Texas – December 29th, 1845; Utah – January 4th, 1896; Virginia – March 4th, 1791; Washington – November 11th, 1889; Wisconsin – May 29th, 1848; Wyoming – July 10th, 1890.

Advent Sunday

The Sunday nearest to November 30th. 'Advent' is from Latin *adventus* 'arrival' and is used of the period which precedes Christmas, beginning either on ST ANDREW'S DAY (November 30th) or the Sunday nearest to it. Advent includes four Sundays, each of which is an Advent Sunday, but used without further reference the term means the first Sunday of the Advent season. This marks the beginning of the Church Year, except in the Greek Church. The Advent season was formerly, and for many Christ-

ians remains, a time of fasting and prayer. For modern children it is mainly associated with the excitement of opening the 'doors' on an Advent calendar. There is ultimately a connection between the words 'Advent' and 'adventure'. The earliest sense of the latter word was something that 'arrived' by chance, without being planned.

Air Force Day

September 10th. This was inaugurated in 1953 in Canada 'to mark the importance of the Royal Canadian Air Force'. A less reverent tribute is paid by the weekly radio show, *The Royal Canadian Air Farce*.

alack-a-day

Also **alack-the-day**. An archaic expression of regret, dissatisfaction or surprise. The original meaning was something like 'Shame or reproach to the day!' Its full force is seen in Shakespeare's *Romeo and Juliet* (IV.v), where the nurse exclaims 'O lamentable day!' and 'O heavy day!' before announcing that Juliet is 'dead, deceas'd, she's dead; alack-the-day!' By the eighteenth century the normal form of the expression was **lack-a-day**. This led to the adjective 'lackadaisical', used of someone who was affectedly sentimental and languishing, given to uttering 'Lack-a-day!' on frequent occasions. 'Lackadaisical' in its turn gave rise to another variant of the exclamation – 'Lackadaisy!' It is tempting to see the modern exclamation 'Oops-a-daisy!' as yet another development.

Alamo Day

March 6th. The Alamo was originally a Franciscan mission built in 1722 at San Antonio, Texas. It took its name from the grove of cottonwood, or poplar, trees (*alamo* in Spanish) in which it stood. By the end of the eighteenth century the Alamo was being used as a fort, and in 1836 it was occupied by a garrison of Texans who were in revolt against the Mexican government, Texas at that time being part of Mexico. Davy Crockett, the hunter and folk-hero, was with the Texans, having gone to the Alamo to help them. Colonel James Bowie, who gave his name to the bowie knife, was also present. The fort was subjected to a thirteen-day siege by some 3,000 Mexicans led by Antonio Santa Anna. The Texans were hopelessly out-numbered but refused to surrender. The Alamo was taken by assault on March 6th and the men who had defended it were slaughtered. When Sam Houston led the Texans to victory against the Mexicans at San Jacinto six weeks later he exhorted his men to 'Remember the Alamo'. Most Texans remember it still.

Alaska Day

October 18th, 1867 marked the formal transfer of the Territory of Alaska from Russia to the United States after its purchase. A holiday is celebrated in America's largest state on or near that date.

Alexandra Rose Day

Also **Alexandra Day**, **Rose Day**. Queen Alexandra, the Danish-born wife of Edward VII, inaugurated Alexandra Rose Day on June 26th, 1912. Rose emblems were sold to raise money for hospitals. The original day commemorated the fiftieth anniversary of the queen's arrival in England. Queen Alexandra died in 1925, but the rose emblems are still sold each year in Britain on a day in June.

Alholland Eve

An early variant of HALLOWE'EN. In Stow's *Survey of London* (1698) we find: 'These lords (of misrule) beginning their rule on Alholland Eve continued the same till the morrow after the Feast of the Purification, commonly called Candlemas Day.' Another variant, **All-halland eve**, is found in Shakespeare's *Measure for Measure*, II.:

Pompey   ... And, I beseech you, look into Master Froth here, sir, a man of fourscore pound a year; whose father died at Hallowmas – was't not at Hallowmas, Master Froth?
Froth   All-hallond eve.

Alice Springs Show Day See HOBART REGATTA DAY.

All Fools' Day

See APRIL FOOLS' DAY. The form All Fools' Day was probably a deliberate joke, meant to link it with ALL SAINTS' DAY and ALL SOULS' DAY.

All Hallows' Day

November 1st. An early name for ALL SAINTS' DAY. 'Hallow' has the basic meaning 'holy', in this case 'a holy person, a saint'. In the Lord's Prayer the phrase 'hallowed be thy name' means 'may thy name be honoured as holy'. Another former name for this day was All Hallow-mass, which became Hallowmas. Shakespeare seems to have thought that it was the shortest day of the year, judging by the king's remark in *Richard II*, referring to his wife's banishment:

My wife to France, from whence set forth
                              in pomp,
She came adorned hither like sweet May,
Sent back like Hallowmas or short'st of
                              day. (V.i)

The 'hallow' reference has been retained in the popular name for All Hallows' Eve – Hallowe'en.

All Saints' Day

November 1st. The day when all the saints, especially those whose individual feast days tend to pass unnoticed, are honoured. Wordsworth dedicated one of his sonnets to a man who was presumably born on this day, since he was named Toussaint (French 'all saints') Louverture. The day was earlier known as ALL HALLOWS' DAY. In countries like France, Germany, Italy, Spain and Portugal, it is a public holiday, but in the English-speaking world, only the state of Louisiana seems to recognize it, making it an optional public holiday.

All Souls' Day

November 2nd. The day when prayers are offered for all the pious dead. The evening of November 1st is also called **All Souls' Eve**, and is subject to superstitious beliefs. In John Steinbeck's *To a God Unknown* we find: ' "This is a strange time", she said softly. . . . "It's like an All Souls' Eve, when the ghosts are loose".' In Cheshire and Shropshire many still go out 'souling' on All Souls' Day, though they are unlikely in modern times to be given the specially made 'soul cakes' which were once distributed. The Opies reported that in the 1950s children still referred to the apples, biscuits and coins they received as 'soul cakes'. Shakespeare has the Duke of Buckingham comment on the day in a poignant fashion:

Buckingham	This is All Souls' day, fellow, is it not?
Sheriff	It is, my lord.
Buckingham	Why, then, All Souls' day is my body's doomsday.

He is soon afterwards led off to the executioner's block.

Amami Night

In the 1920s the manufacturers of a hairwash almost managed to make 'Amami Night' a synonym for 'Friday night' by means of an intensive advertising campaign. It featured the slogan: 'Friday night is Amami night.'

American Indian Day

In 1914 Red Fox James of the Blackfoot Indian tribe rode some 4,000 miles on a pony to urge Americans to celebrate American Indian Day once a year. Such a day is now commonly observed in many different states, but usually on a local basis. A Friday in late September seems to be a popular time for it.

Anniversary

The annual celebration of any day of particular importance. 'Anniversary' is ultimately from Latin *annus versus* 'returning yearly'. **Anniversary Day** was an earlier name for AUSTRALIA DAY.

Annual Day

The day on which a society or club has its annual meeting. Mordecai Richler, in *Joshua Then and Now*, makes much of the Annual Day of the William Lyon Mackenzie King Memorial Society. All the members of the Society are Jewish and are very well aware that the former Canadian prime minister was decidedly anti-Semitic. He was also, in their opinion, 'the most vile of men, mean-spirited, cunning, somewhat demented, and a hypocrite on the grand scale.' On the Annual Day the Society members mock their 'hero' in a number of ingenious ways.

Annunciation

March 25th. A church festival, also known as LADY DAY, commemorating the annunciation ('announcement') made by the angel Gabriel to the Virgin Mary that she would give birth to Christ. The Annunciation was a favourite subject of religious painters.

Anzac Day

April 25th. A national holiday in Australia and New Zealand. 'Anzac' is an acronym formed from the initial letters of 'Australian and New Zealand Army Corps'. It was coined in January 1915, for telegraphic use. Shortly afterwards, on April 25th, 1915, Anzac troops stormed Gallipoli, the Turkish peninsula, during the First World War. The day has been observed as a holiday since about 1920, and in modern times honours the war dead of both world wars, as well as those who died in Vietnam and Korea.

Apple and Candle Night

A local name for HALLOWE'EN amongst children in the Swansea area of Wales. The game of Apple and Candle is played by suspending a stick from the ceiling and attaching an apple to one end, a lighted candle to the other. Players try to eat the apple, while avoiding the candle which constantly swings towards them. In the game's more sadistic forms, the player is blindfolded and the stick is twirled around at the beginning of the game.

Apple Pie Day

The Thursday following the first Tuesday in December for the boys at Winchester College during the nineteenth century. Apple pies were served on large pewter dishes, called gomers.

Apple Tuesday

The third Tuesday in October. The New York Fruit Growers Association attempted to get Apple Tuesday adopted on a national basis in 1905. The idea was that every citizen should eat at least one apple on that day. It was duly celebrated in New England in 1907, and in Indiana in 1913.

April Day

Since the first day of each month can be referred to as its 'day', this expression could mean April 1st, just as MAY DAY is May 1st. (Similarly **April Eve** could refer to the previous day, and **April Morrow** to April 2nd, and so on throughout the year.) In more general terms, an April day seems to have been a Shakespearean favourite. For example, in *The Two Gentlemen of Verona* (I.iii) Proteus says: 'O, how this spring of love resembleth/ The uncertain glory of an April day.' In *The Merchant of Venice* ((II.ix) the servant tells Portia of a young man's arrival:

A day in April never came so sweet
To show how costly summer was at hand
As this fore-spurrer comes before his lord.

April Fools' Day

April 1st. This day is also known by various other names, including **All Fools' Day**, **April Noddy Day**, **Gowkie Day**, **Gowkin' Day**, etc. It is the day on which practical jokes of one kind or another are both permitted and expected. At the simplest level, children tell one another that their shoe-laces are undone, then shout 'April fool' when the victims glance towards their feet. More elaborate jokes include those played by the media, at least one spurious 'news' item being the order of the day. There have been references to April fools since at least the seventeenth century, but the tradition no doubt goes back much further. A similar day is known to many different nations.

Literary references to this day include an essay by Charles Lamb on 'All Fools' Day'. Lamb says he is rather fond of fools. The more blunders a man commits in your company, he says, the more he proves that he is unlikely to betray you in any way. He is revealing that he is not on his guard, carefully watching what he says and does, but is behaving in a relaxed and natural way. Perhaps the finest literary comment on the day is made by Mark Twain, in *Pudd'nhead Wilson's Calendar*: 'April 1. This is the day upon which we are reminded of what we are on the other three hundred and sixty-four.'

April Noddy Day

April 1st. This is a dialectical variant of APRIL FOOLS' DAY. The origin of 'noddy' in the sense of 'fool, simpleton' is unclear, though Professor Weekley draws attention to Dickens's *Our Mutual Friend*, where Noddy is a pet form of Nicodemus.

Arbor Day

A day set aside for the planting of trees (Latin *arbor* 'tree'). Nebraska celebrates such a day (usually April 22nd) as a public holiday. Arbor Day was first proclaimed in that state in 1872, when over a million trees were planted. President Harding urged the national adoption of the day in 1922. The legislature of California had earlier made March 7th **Bird and Arbor Day**.

Armed Forces Day

The third Saturday in May. This supplanted the US Army, Navy and Air Force Days after 1950.

Armistice Day

November 11th. The former name of VETERANS DAY in the US and REMEMBRANCE DAY in Britain, Canada, etc. The armistice ending World War I was signed at eleven o'clock on November 11th, 1918, and a two-minute silence was observed at that time. There are two chapters in *Abbie*, by Dane Chandos, which amusingly describe how Abbie bullies everyone into buying poppies on Armistice Day, though she gives them away to ex-servicemen.

Army Stitch Day
A US slang expression for ARMISTICE DAY.

Ascension Day
Also known as **Holy Thursday**. The day on which Jesus Christ is said to have ascended to heaven, forty days after Easter Sunday. The day is of great significance in Shakespeare's *King John*. Peter of Pomfret (Pontefract) predicts that 'ere the next Ascension day at noon, Your Highness shall deliver up your crown.' John orders the hermit Peter to be imprisoned 'and on that day at noon whereon he says I shall yield up my crown, let him be hang'd.' Peter is duly hanged, though John later admits that, in a sense, the prediction was a true one. On the eve of Ascension Day John had been obliged to do homage to the Pope for his kingdom.

Ascot Sunday
The Sunday before Royal Ascot week in June, according to the actor David Niven in *The Moon's a Balloon*. It was a Sunday when the chapel at Niven's school was filled to capacity with parents who were staying at nearby country houses, ready to attend the race-meeting. He recounts that, at the age of nine, he was singing a solo part in chapel on Ascot Sunday when his voice broke. 'Suddenly, on the word 'wall' a fearful braying sound issued from the angelic face of the soloist. I tried for the note again: this time it sounded like a Rolls-Royce klaxon of the period.' The result of all this was general uproar in the chapel, followed later by a caning for Niven. His headmaster was convinced that he had deliberately made trouble. Niven still considered this unfair when writing of the incident decades later, since what happened was genuinely beyond his control. He

admits, however, that he had already worked quite hard at being 'something of a clown'.

Ash Wednesday
The first day of Lent. The name derives from the custom in the Roman Catholic Church (since the time of Pope Gregory the Great (590–604)) of sprinkling ashes that day on the heads of those who show sorrow for their sins. 'Ash Wednesday' is also the title of an important poem by T. S. Eliot, published in 1930 after he had become a member of the Anglican Church. The name has also been given to a variety of rose.

Asia Day
August 9th, 1987. A cultural festival held in Bradford, England, reflecting the city's large Asian population.

Assumption
August 15th. A feast day in the Roman Catholic Church honouring the reception into heaven of the body of the Virgin Mary, there to be reunited with her soul. The Feast of the Assumption dates from the sixth century. In 1950 Pope Pius XII declared that the Corporal Assumption was an official dogma of the Church. (The original meaning of 'to assume' was 'to take to oneself, to receive, to adopt'. By the sixteenth century the verb had already acquired its meaning of 'to take for granted as the basis for further discussion'.)

Astronomical day See DAY.

at-home day
A day set aside by a person of rank for the receiving of visitors at home. Individuals would often announce their at-home days in the newspapers for the benefit of their acquaintances.

August Bank Holiday
Sometimes known also as **Summer Bank Holiday**. This was one of the national

holidays instituted in England and Ireland by Sir John Lubbock's Act, passed in 1871. It was formerly observed on the first Monday in August but has been transferred in modern times to the last Monday of the month. See also BANK HOLIDAY.

Australia Day

January 26th or the following Monday. The day commemorates the landing of the British at Sydney Cove in 1788. Until 1935 it was known as **Anniversary Day** or **Foundation Day** in some states, having first been celebrated in Sydney in 1817.

Autumnal equinox See EQUINOX.

Autumn Daze

The 'daze' for 'days' joke is found in various parts of the US, attached to local festivals. Autumn Daze, where 'daze' can be interpreted rather pleasantly as 'dazzled by the light', is used locally in Branson, Missouri.

Four days of craft fairs and similar activities take place in late September.

Aviation Day

December 17th. This was the day on which the Wright brothers made the first sustained flight in 1903. In 1934 the Secretary of the US Navy, Claude A. Swanson, announced that it would be celebrated as Aviation Day. He directed that 'all the available airplanes of the Navy Department should take to the air at 10.30 in the morning and remain in flight for half an hour.'

Awayday

A word coined by a clever advertising agent to describe a special excursion ticket issued by British Rail. It hints at 'getting away from it all', while recalling that a sports team which plays an 'away' match contrasts with the 'home' team. The word has not entered into general usage, but could easily do so.

B

Bachelors' Day
Another name for LEAP DAY. 'Bachelor Days' was a series of articles by A. A. Milne which appeared in the magazine *Punch*. They were later reprinted in book form as *The Day's Play*, enjoying a considerable success.

Back Badge Day
March 21st. Celebrated by the Gloucestershire Regiment of the British Army, whose men wear a badge on the back as well as the front of their caps. They have done so since March 21st, 1801, when the Battle of Alexandria was fought. The men were ordered to stand back to back, facing away from the charging French cavalry, until the enemy were almost upon them. They then turned and fired, causing the French to retreat in disorder.

Balaclava Day
This was an Army slang term, during the Crimean War, for 'pay-day'. The small port of Balaclava was a supply base for the British troops, who would go there after being paid to make their purchases. Balaclava was also the scene, on September 26th, 1854, of the infamous Charge of the Light Brigade, celebrated in Lord Tennyson's poem. The port also gave its name to the warm woollen head-covering which was later issued to troops.

Ball Monday
Formerly in Oxfordshire an alternative name for EASTER MONDAY because games such as stool-ball, trap-ball, etc., were played that day. However, the remark in Smollett's *Peregrine Pickle*, to the effect that 'the careful matron on the ball day feigned herself extremely ill', refers to the day on which a formal ball, or dance, was to be held.

Banian Day
This was originally a nautical term in the early nineteenth century for a day on which no meat was served. The allusion was to the Banians, Hindu vegetarians. In Jamaica the term came into general use, applied to any day of austerity or fasting, especially the day before pay-day. It was sometimes written **Banyan Day**, and in modern times has been corrupted into, or has merged with, BEN JONSON DAY.

Bank Holiday
In Britain this term refers to an official public holiday, not a Saturday or Sunday, when the banks are closed. Typical bank holidays are NEW YEAR'S DAY, GOOD FRIDAY, EASTER MONDAY, AUGUST BANK HOLIDAY, CHRISTMAS DAY, BOXING DAY. A traditional activity on a bank holiday is to spend some time at a fairground. The fair on Hampstead Heath is especially well-known. John Galsworthy describes the scene there

at the time of a Whitsuntide bank holiday in *A Modern Comedy*.

Bank night

A ploy introduced by American cinema owners in the 1930s and 40s, designed to attract paying customers during the week. On a bank night members of the audience were eligible for cash prizes drawn by lottery.

Bannock Day

In some parts of Scotland, an alternative name for PANCAKE DAY, or SHROVE TUESDAY. It can also be applied, sometimes as **Bannocky Day**, to any day on which bannocks are traditionally eaten. The exact nature of a 'bannock' varies from place to place, but it is a flat cake made of oatmeal, barley or pease-meal, baked on a griddle. Currant-bannocks are also found.

Banyan Day See BANIAN DAY.

Barbecue Day

A day on which an open-air barbecue is a principal entertainment. 'Fourth of July was always barbecue day in Georgia,' writes Margaret Walker in *Jubilee*. 'Barbecue' adapts an American-Spanish word *barbacoa*, itself representing a word used by a now-extinct people who lived in the Bahamas. Washington Irving used the word in its modern sense in 1809, though he thought it necessary to explain the word to his readers.

Barnaby Day

June 11th. Also known as **Barnaby Bright** or **Long Barnaby**. By the Old Style reckoning of the calendar this was the longest day of the year, hence the saying: 'Barnaby bright, Barnaby bright, the longest day and the shortest night.' 'Barnaby' is an English form of 'Barnabas', this being ST BARNABAS' DAY.

Bartholomew Day

August 24th. Saint Bartholomew, about whom very little is known, was one of the twelve apostles, perhaps to be identified with Nathanael. In 1572, in France, the great massacre of the Huguenots (Protestants) occurred on this day. It was also the day on which a famous London fair was held for over seven hundred years, until 1855. It was celebrated by Ben Jonson in *Bartholomew Fayre* (1614), a light comedy which presents a picture of the ballad-singers, stall-holders, bawds and cut-purses of the time:

> Here's master Bartholomew Cokes, of Harrow o' the Hill, in the County of Middlesex, esquire, takes forth his license to marry mistress Grace Wellborn, of the said place and county: and when does he take it forth? today! the fourth and twentieth of August! Bartholmew-day! Bartholomew upon Bartholomew! (I.i)

Bash-a-Pom Day, Melbourne See DOTTY DAY.

Bastille Day

July 14th. A national holiday in France, the equivalent of INDEPENDENCE DAY in the US. The Bastille was a notorious state prison in Paris, dating from the fourteenth century. Its reputation was at its worst in the time of Richelieu's ministry (1624–42). On July 14th, 1789, the Bastille was stormed by a Parisian mob who eventually forced De Launey, the commandant, to surrender. He was killed, and his head mounted on a pike. A year later the building was razed. Charles Dickens deals with this period in *A Tale of Two Cities*.

bath day See VISITING DAY.

Battle of New Orleans Day

January 8th. An optional public holiday in Louisiana. The reference is to a battle which took place on January 8th, 1815. Andrew Jackson and 6,000 Americans defeated a force of some 12,000 British soldiers. The British suffered the loss of their General Packenham and over 2,000 men. American losses were 8 dead and 13 wounded. Also known as JACKSON DAY, **Old Hickory's Day.**

Battleship Day
February 15th. A colloquial reminder of the blowing up of the US battleship *Maine*, which occurred in Havana Harbour on February 15th, 1898. Separate enquiries by US and Spanish authorities were unable to fix responsibility for the explosion, which caused the loss of 260 men. 'Remember the Maine' nevertheless became an American catchphrase in the Spanish-American War. 'One of the late jokes of the summer,' writes Sara Jeanette Duncan in *Those Delightful Americans*, 'was "What did the horse say when they clipped his tail?" "Remember the Maine." '

Becket's Day
Tuesday, according to Dr Brewer in *The Reader's Handbook*, was a special day for Saint Thomas à Becket, the martyred Archbishop of Canterbury. He was born on a Tuesday and assassinated on a Tuesday. Amongst other events that occurred on the same day were Becket's baptism, his vision of martyrdom, his flight from Northampton, the removal of his body from the crypt to a shrine, etc. Brewer remarks chattily that Henry VII regarded Saturday as his lucky day, while Napoleon favoured the second of every month.

Beer Day
A particular memory for the actress Doris Day, who describes in her autobiography what she missed about her father when he separated from her mother. One special memory was 'the frequent aroma of my father's homemade beer. Hops have a peculiarly satisfying smell, and on "beer days" I loved to have their pungent odour greet me when I came home from school.'

Belagcholly Day
A day on which one feels melancholy because one is suffering from a heavy cold. 'Belagcholly Days' is the title of an anonymous poem which is reprinted in *A Whimsey Anthology* by Carolyn Wells. It begins:

Chilly Dovebber with his boadigg blast

Dow cubs add strips the beddow add the
     lawd,
Eved October's suddy days are past –
Add Subber's gawd!

Washington Irving caught the mood of such a day, if not its accompanying cold, when he visited Westminster Abbey:

> On one of those sober and rather melancholy days, in the latter part of autumn, when the shadows of morning and evening almost mingle together, and throw a gloom over the decline of the year, I passed several hours in rambling about Westminster Abbey (*The Sketch Book*).

Belgian-American Day
Mid-August. Celebrated in Ghent, Minnesota, where the name of the town was bestowed by the original Belgian immigrants.

Bell Belt Day See WAKES SUNDAY.

Beltane Day
May 1st (Old Style). 'Beltane' is from a Gaelic word of disputed meaning, though 'bright fire' is a popular explanation. This may be a folk-etymology suggested by the custom of lighting bonfires on the hills at this time, though bonfires were also lit at Lammas and Hallowmas, which like Beltane Day were formerly Scottish QUARTER DAYS. An early attempt was made to link the name to Baal, but this is not worth serious consideration.

Benefit Day
In modern times more likely to be **Benefit Night**. The day on which the receipts of a theatrical performance are given to a particular actor, playwright, etc. Steele refers in *The Spectator* 288 to 'the benefit days of my plays and operas'. The day on which the unemployment benefit cheque arrives has apparently become MONEY DAY in the Liverpool area.

Ben Jonson Day

In Jamaica a 'day of reckoning' or one of austerity, enforced by lack of money. The day of reckoning allusion is apparently to one Ben Jonson, not the seventeenth-century dramatist, but an eighteenth-century negro slave-trader. He kidnapped a young girl and sold her into slavery, only to be kidnapped in turn by the girl's brothers, who exchanged him for her. There is probable confusion, however, with BANIAN DAY.

Bennington Battle Day

August 6th. It was near the town of Bennington, in Vermont, that American forces led by General Stark inflicted a heavy defeat on the British forces in 1777. The day is still celebrated as a state holiday, though most banks remain open.

Big Bang Day

October 27th, 1986. A day of significant change at the London Stock Exchange. It marked the end of fixed commissions on stock exchange transactions, the removal of the distinction between stockbrokers acting purely as agents and stock-jobbers operating only as principals, together with what one newspaper (the *Independent*) referred to on the day itself as 'the invasion of well-capitalised foreign securities houses into the London market'. 'Many people seem to see Big Bang day as an end in itself', wrote Sir Kenneth Berrill, in the same newspaper, 'risking a definite sense of anti-climax when it becomes clear that the City is still standing, relatively undevastated.' The *Guardian*, amidst its serious comments on the event, also poked fun at the idea of everyone in the City of London spending countless hours playing with computers. 'It's Big Bang Day at the Stock Exchange,' said Steve Bell, in his *If* cartoon strip.

> Basically it means that from now on anyone can partake in the great electronic future of the Financial Services Industry. All you have to do is take your money for a short walk down to your nearest amusement arcade, find a machine that you can really relate to on a cheery personal level, and Bob's your uncle.

big day

A day of special importance or significance. 'Big' has been used in this sense since the seventeenth century, as a variant of 'great.'

Big Feast Sunday See FEAST SUNDAY.

Binding Tuesday

Another name for HOCK TUESDAY, the second Tuesday after EASTER DAY. The day before was also called **Binding Monday**, it being the custom in rural England for the women to bind the men on that day, demanding a forfeit of money, used for church or parish purposes, in order to release them. On Binding Tuesday the men bound the women in a similar way. The good-humoured victims were usually coach-passengers and the like who were passing through the villages.

Bird and Arbor Day See ARBOR DAY.

birthday

The day on which a person is born, or the annual observation of that day. It is a special, individual day, especially for children. Robert Louis Stevenson realized how disappointing it must be for a child to have to share it with a more general celebration, such as Christmas Day, and therefore presented his own birthday to one such sufferer. He drew up a convincingly formal document in 1891, which read in part:

> In consideration that Miss Annie H. Ide . . . was born out of all reason upon Christmas Day, and is therefore out of all justice denied the consolation and profit of a proper birthday; And considering that I have attained an age when, O, we never mention it, and that I have no further use for a birthday of any description. . . . Have transferred . . . to the said Annie H. Ide, all and whole my rights and privileges in the thirteenth day of November, formerly my birthday, now,

hereby, and henceforth; the birthday of the said Annie H. Ide to have, hold, exercise and enjoy in the customary manner, by the sporting of fine raiment, eating of rich meats, and receipt of gifts, compliments and copies of verse, according to the manner of our ancestors.

Stevenson said that if Annie violated the terms of his deed then his birthday was to pass to the President of the United States. The lady concerned died in 1945 at the age of sixty-eight, at which time her family assured Harry S Truman that she had indeed observed the terms and that he was not therefore entitled to assume November 13th as his birthday. The reference to 'fine raiment' in Stevenson's deed is interesting, since it recalls that the phrase 'birthday suit' once meant the suit of fine clothes worn, especially by courtiers, on the sovereign's birthday. The humorous use of the phrase to denote nudity is credited to Smollett, in the eighteenth century. Of the many books that deal with the subject, *Birthdays*, by Linda Rannells Lewis, probably says most that is worth reading.

Birthday of Martin Luther King Jr See MARTIN LUTHER KING'S BIRTHDAY.

Black Friday
A description applied to various Fridays on which some disastrous event has occurred, but especially perhaps to Friday, September 24th, 1869. Clarence Day refers to it in *These Were the Days*, speaking of his father: 'He had gone through the panic of '69 and Black Friday, and had begun to make money.' It was the day on which Jay Gould and James Fisk Jr precipitated the infamous Wall Street Panic. A rather similar Black Friday occurred on May 11th, 1866, when the great bankers Overend, Gurney & Co stopped all payments and caused a commercial panic. The partners were subsequently committed for trial as conspirators to defraud, but were acquitted. In Labour Party circles a reference to Black Friday may mean May 12th, 1926 when the General Strike was broken

up. In school slang it was once applied to any Friday on which an examination took place.

Black Monday
The Monday on which school re-opened after the Summer vacation. Henry Fielding remarks in *Tom Jones* that eighteenth-century schoolboys referred to the day in this way. In modern times this awful day is rarely a Monday: educational authorities usually try to make the first week mercifully short. Black Monday has also been applied to certain Easter Mondays on which disastrous events are said to have occurred. In prison slang the phrase was also applied to the Monday on which an execution was carried out.

Black Sabbath
Also called a **Witches' Sabbath**. An annual meeting of demons, sorcerers and witches, presided over by the Devil, and occurring at midnight. It is sometimes referred to as a Sabbat. The origin appears to be a special application of French *sabbat* 'Sabbath', probably reflecting early anti-Semitism, though it may merely use 'sabbath' in the sense of 'time of worship'. 'Don't you like the fiesta?' asks a character in John Steinbeck's *To a God Unknown*. The reply is: 'It reminds me of witchcraft and the Black Sabbath.'

Black Saturday
In the English workman's slang of the late nineteenth and early twentieth centuries, this was a Saturday on which no pay was received, because it had all been paid as advances. The term was also applied to September 10th, 1547, the date of the Battle of Pinkie, near Edinburgh, where the English totally defeated the Scots.

Black Sunday
The title of a novel by Thomas Harris. It concerns an attempt to assassinate the President of the United States on New Year's Eve, when he attends the Sugar Bowl Football Classic in New Orleans.

Black Tuesday

October 29th, 1929. The worst day of the Wall Street Crash, which began on October 23rd. Over 17 million shares were sold on the Tuesday on the New York Stock Exchange. Many banks and companies subsequently closed, leading to mass unemployment and an economic depression which affected Europe as well as the USA. One of the 'incidents of the day', according to *The Times* on October 30th, 'was the fatal fall from one of the upper storeys of an apartment house building in which he lived, of the president of a company whose stock a few months ago sold at 113, and yesterday sold at 4.'

Blind Man's Holiday

A fairly common expression in the seventeenth and eighteenth centuries referring to twilight, when it was too dark to read or work, but too soon to light the candles. The phrase became rare in the nineteenth century.

Bloody Monday

A phrase used by English schoolboys in the eighteenth century to refer to the first day of vacation. This would normally have been a time of rejoicing, but for those who offended during the term it was a day of detention and punishment. 'Bloody' at the time would have referred literally to bloodshed: use of the word as a colloquial intensifier came later. See also BLACK MONDAY.

Bloody Sunday

A name applied first to November 13th, 1887, when a political demonstration in London was broken up by the police. Two of the crowd died. The name was later applied to January 30th, 1972, when anti-internment marchers in Londonderry were dispersed by British troops. Thirteen civilians died.

Bloomsday

June 16th, 1904. The novel *Ulysses* by James Joyce, first published in 1922, deals with the events of this one day in Dublin. Leopold Bloom, his wife Molly, and Stephen Dedalus are the three main characters in the book, corresponding roughly to Odysseus, Penelope and Telemachus in Homer's *Odyssey*. Bloom and Dedalus wander through the city and eventually meet. The last chapter is Molly Bloom's famous monologue.

Blue Bird Day

'At eleven a bright sun burned off the haze, making what hunters called a "blue-bird day", and any hope of bagging a goose during the middle hours was lost.' This explanation of the term is given in *Chesapeake*, by James A. Michener, which is set in Maryland. The blue bird is a small perching bird seen in the US from Spring to early Autumn. In Britain the fieldfare is sometimes referred to as a blue-bird.

Blue Cross Day

The last day of a 'sale' period in a shop or store, when items still unsold are marked with a blue cross and are reduced to half the marked price. This expression was noted in 1986 in places as far apart as Kingston, Surrey and Huntly, Aberdeenshire.

Blue Monday

Originally the Monday before Lent, later any Monday which a workman used for drinking rather than working. 'Blue' was at one time a synonym for 'drunk'. It was said that if one drank enough, everything acquired a blue tinge. In modern times a blue Monday is any Monday when one returns reluctantly to work after a pleasant weekend and suffers to some extent from a fit of the blues (or 'blue devils', as it was in the original version). Fats Domino's hit single of the 1950s, 'Blue Monday', increased the use of the phrase. In *The Group*, Mary McCarthy writes: 'It seemed to her that she could not face another "blue Monday" watching Mr LeRoy scratch his moustache as he looked through her reports.'

Boat Race Day

Normally a reference to the day in March or April when the annual boat-race between Oxford and Cambridge University eights is rowed on the Thames. The race begins at Putney and ends 4¼ miles later at Mortlake, unless something interesting, such as the sinking of one of the boats, occurs *en route*.

Bob Apple Night

A regional name amongst children for HALLOWE'EN because the game of Bob Apple (also known as Snap Apple and Apple on the Line) is played. Basically the game consists of trying to eat an apple which is suspended from a height on a piece of string. As a bite is taken the apple swings away and returns to hit the player in the face. Players may also be blind-folded and have their hands tied behind their backs.

Bobby Ack Day

May 29th. A local name (Ulverston) for ROYAL OAK DAY. The 'bobby' refers to the knob-like oak-apple; 'ack' represents an older pronunciation of 'oak'. In Ulverston, the children's punishment for those who forget to wear an oak leaf or oak apple on this day is to pull the offender's hair.

Bonfire Night

An alternative name for GUY FAWKES DAY in some parts of England. In Scotland the name is applied to the Monday nearest May 24th, the former EMPIRE DAY. Modern bonfires are lit for amusement; they were originally bone-fires, in which the bones of animals or human beings were burnt, not for amusement. Traditional nights for festive bonfires, apart from those already mentioned, are MIDSUMMER EVE and ST PETER'S EVE. They are also likely to form part of any JUBILEE celebrations.

Booster Days

Days devoted to the boosting of a town's prosperity. In *Babbitt*, by Sinclair Lewis, there is a full description of The International Organization of Boosters' Clubs, to which George F. Babbitt belonged, and its importance in the 1920s:

> Of a decent man in Zenith it was required that he should belong to one, preferably two or three, of the innumerous 'lodges' and prosperity-boosting lunch-clubs; to the Rotarians, the Kiwanis, or the Boosters; to the Oddfellows, Moose Masons, Red Men, Woodmen, Owls, Eagles, Maccabees, Knights of Pythias, Knights of Columbus, and other secret orders characterized by a high degree of heartiness, sound morals, and reverence for the Constitution.

Lewis describes a typical meeting of the Boosters, where there is a fine for calling a fellow Booster by anything but his nickname.

Born days

'Such a complete disguise as never you see in all your born days,' writes Charles Dickens, in *David Copperfield*. The use of 'one's born days' to refer to one's lifetime dates back to at least the eighteenth century.

Borrowed Days

Also called **Borrowing Days**. The last three days of March, which are said to have been borrowed from April, according to Scottish folk-lore. Chambers, in *The Book of Days*, suggests that changes in the weather at this time may have given rise to the notion. In the Highlands of Scotland there was also an ancient belief that February 12th, 13th and 14th had been borrowed from January. It was thought that if the weather was stormy on those days it was a good omen for the rest of the year. If they were fine, then they might be the only fine days in the year.

Boston's Fourth of July See BUNKER HILL DAY.

Bounds Thursday

An occasional name for ASCENSION DAY or HOLY THURSDAY. It was the custom in many English parishes to 'beat the bounds' on this day, to walk around the parish boundaries in solemn procession.

Box Car Day

A parade, horse show, etc., held at Tracy, Minnesota, on LABOR DAY, in honour of the box-cars (freight wagons, covered and with sliding doors) used to carry grain. They are of great importance to the local economy. The first Box Car Day was held in 1927.

Box Day

An occasional synonym for BOXING DAY. Also a day during the vacation appointed in the Scottish Court of Session for the lodgement of papers which the Court had ordered to be deposited. The papers were placed in a box for each judge, who examined them privately.

Boxing Day

December 26th. The name used in England, Canada, Australia, etc., for the day following CHRISTMAS DAY, unless that day is a Sunday, when Boxing Day is moved to the Monday. The name derives from the custom of giving Christmas boxes to tradesmen, postmen, servants and the like on this day. 'Christmas box' now indicates a present, usually of money, no longer associated particularly with a 'box' of any kind. The original 'boxes' were usually made of earthenware. Money was put into them which could only be retrieved by the breaking open of the containers. Boxing Day is observed as a holiday in the countries which acknowledge it, though the Christmas presents associated with it are now normally given before rather than after Christmas. The day itself tends to be a period of quiet recuperation after Christmas Day excesses.

Braggot Sunday

Another name for MID-LENT SUNDAY, formerly in Lancashire. It was the custom to drink braggot (or bragget, braggat, bracket, bragwort) on that day, a drink originally made of honey and ale fermented together. The honey was later replaced by sugar and spice. The various spellings are attempts to represent a Celtic word which described a kind of grain. Chaucer, in the *Miller's Tale*, has the line 'Her mouth was sweet as bragot'.

Bridal Day

An occasional synonym of WEDDING DAY. In early use 'bridal' meant 'wedding ale', and referred to the wedding feast. After 1600 the expression was associated more with the 'bride', the woman being married.

British Commonwealth Day

This was the name by which COMMONWEALTH DAY was known between 1958 and 1966.

Brose and Bannock Day

Another name for SHROVE TUESDAY in Scotland. For 'bannock' see BANNOCK DAY. 'Brose' is a food made by pouring boiling water or milk onto oatmeal or peasemeal, then adding a seasoning of salt and butter. In *Kidnapped*, by R. L. Stevenson, we find: 'Maclaren pressed them to taste 'the wife's brose', reminding them the wife was out of Athole'. There is some point to the reminder, since 'Athole brose' is a mixture of whisky and honey. Thomas Hood has a little poem on the subject:

Charm'd with a drink with Highlanders
compose,
A German traveller exclaim'd with glee,
Potztausend! sare, if dis be Athole Brose,
How goot dere Athole Boetry must be!

Brose and Bannock Day is sometimes referred to more simply as **Brose Day**.

Brotherhood Sunday

The Sunday nearest to Washington's Birthday (February 22nd), though in Malcolm Boyd's *Book of Days* there is a description of Brotherhood Night on January 26th. 'Brotherhood' here refers to a getting together of Anglicans, Roman Catholics and Jews. Boyd says that on Brotherhood Night, apart from a rabbi, priest and minister, a 'big name' needs to be present who will speak for not more than thirty minutes about a non-controversial subject. He must also be willing to do without a fee.

Budget Day

The day on which a state or local official presents an estimate of the probable revenue and expenditure for the following year, together with proposals for raising and spending such funds. 'Budget' originally meant a leather wallet or bag. In England, the Chancellor of the Exchequer carried the papers relating to the financial estimates in such a bag. When he revealed his proposals he was said to be 'opening the budget'. The modern meaning of the word dates from the mid-eighteenth century.

Bunker Hill Day

June 17th. Observed mainly in Boston, Massachusetts, and sometimes referred to as **Boston's Fourth of July**. The Battle of Bunker Hill was mainly fought on the neighbouring Breed's Hill on June 17th, 1775. Technically it was a victory for the British, who lost over a thousand men, over the American revolutionaries, who lost some 450 men, but it is remembered as a triumphant display of American heroism and patriotism. Since 1843 an impressive monument commemorating the battle has stood in Charlestown.

Burns Night

January 25th. The birthday of the Scottish poet Robert Burns (1759–96) has become an occasion for Scotsmen to gather together wherever they may be. In remote corners of the globe, bottles of Scotch whisky materialize and are used to wash down a Burns Night Supper which inevitably includes a haggis, or something vaguely resembling it. Its entry into the room is saluted with Burns's words: 'Hail Great Chieftain o' the Puddin-race!' The poet also provides the words of the grace:

> Some hae meat and canna eat,
> And some wad eat that want it;

> But we hae meat and we can eat
> Sae let the Lord be thankit.

The evening's celebrations include readings of Burns's poems, and ideally there will be a kilted bag-piper present. Burns's great contribution to international friendship, 'Auld Lang Syne', is sung to bring the evening to a close. It is perhaps curious that there is not an equivalent 'Shakespeare Night', when Englishmen gather together, especially since the English poet's birthday (probably) coincides with St George's Day.

busman's holiday

To have a busman's holiday is to use your holiday or leisure time to do what you normally do for a living. The *Oxford English Dictionary Supplement* cites a magazine writer in 1893; 'I shall indeed take a holiday soon . . . but it will be a "Busman's Holiday".' By the 1920s the London *Times* was referring to this 'proverbial' phrase, and it was in use on both sides of the Atlantic. 'Bus-man's holiday for the ladies, I should say,' writes Willa Cather in *The Professor's House* (1925). The phrase has been linked with the conscientiousness of London busmen, who would ride their own horse-drawn buses on their days off in order to see that the horses were not ill-treated. Perhaps a story of such a busman was circulating in the 1890s – if so, it has not yet been traced. Horse-drawn buses had been in regular use in London since the 1820s, and continued to be used until 1914. The busmen regularly worked a fifteen-hour day, and it would have required dedication indeed to put in an appearance on one's free day.

Bye Day

This is defined in *The Horseman's Dictionary*, by Bloodgood and Santini, as the day on which an irregular and informal meet of hounds, one not mentioned on the hunt fixture card, takes place.

bygone days

Days gone by. Sometimes used as the title of a local festival (e.g. at Delmont, Pennsylvania) where there is a historical theme. Shakespeare uses 'by-gone day' to refer to the day just ended in *The Winter's Tale* (I.ii):

Tell him you are sure
All in Bohemia's well – This satisfaction
The by-gone day proclaim'd.

C

Cake Day See HOGMANAY.

Calends

Also spelt as **Kalends**. The first day of any month in the Roman calendar. 'Calendar' itself derives from 'calends', which in turn comes from a verb meaning 'to proclaim' – the order of days in each month being publicly proclaimed on the first day. The Romans specified a particular day in the month by relating it to the next Calends, **Nones** or **Ides**. 'The sixth of the Calends of June' meant May 27th, for instance. 'The sixth of the Ides of June' meant June 8th, since in June the Ides fell on the thirteenth. The Roman system seems rather confusing to modern eyes, but basically Roman citizens were only required to remember that in March, May, July and October the Ides fell on the fifteenth of the month, while the Nones occurred on the ninth day before the Ides, i.e. the seventh. In all other months the Ides fell on the thirteenth and the Nones on the fifth.

English writers and poets sometimes imitated Roman usage, especially when dealing with Roman themes. Everyone is familiar with Shakespeare's 'Beware the Ides of March', the warning given to Julius Caesar. Sixteenth- and seventeenth-century literature is sprinkled with similar, if less well-known, references. The phrase 'on (or at) the Greek Calends' is sometimes found.

The Greeks did not make use of Calends, and the phrase therefore means 'never'. Oliver Wendell Holmes, in one of his Breakfast Table essays, remarks: 'His friends looked for it only on the Greek Calends, say on the 31st of April.' In rare instances, Calends was used to mean SETTLING or SETTLEMENT DAY, since debts were required to be settled on the first of each month.

Canada Day

July 1st. The modern name of what was previously DOMINION DAY.

Candlemas Day

February 2nd. A popular name for the feast of the PURIFICATION, now called the PRESENTATION OF OUR LORD. In early times the feast was celebrated with a great display of candles, and in Roman Catholic churches, this is the day on which all the candles which will be used throughout the year are consecrated. In Scotland it is one of the traditional quarter-days. Thomas Hardy refers to it (in *The Mayor of Casterbridge*) as the day on which agricultural workers were hired at the fair. The behaviour of certain animals on Candlemas Day is thought to be a good indication of weather to come. The Germans look closely at the badger that day; in the US it is GROUNDHOG DAY.

Canicular days

See DOG DAYS. 'Canicular' is from Latin *canicula* 'little dog', ultimately from *canis* 'dog'.

Cantate Sunday

Another name for ROGATION SUNDAY. The introit of the Latin mass for this day begins *Cantate Domino* 'Sing to the Lord'.

Care Sunday

The fifth Sunday in Lent. 'Care' in this expression has the meaning 'sorrow, trouble, grief'. The same day is also known as CARLING SUNDAY.

Carling Sunday

The fifth Sunday in Lent, when 'carlings' or 'carlines' were traditionally eaten. These were peas which had been soaked in water, then dried in an oven until they were parched. Since the peas were eaten on CARE SUNDAY, it is likely that 'carling' derives directly from 'care'. Another name for the day was **Carle Sunday**.

Carnation Day

January 29th. The birthday of William McKinley, twenty-fifth president of the United States, whose favourite flower was the carnation. The day was first celebrated in 1903, and was meant to arouse interest in political activities. It had some success for a few years. The carnation takes its name from Latin *caro, carnis* 'flesh', the original meaning of the word being 'flesh-coloured'.

Carnival Day

In modern times this would refer to a day of riotous celebration and revelry. Originally 'carnival' referred specifically to ASH WEDNESDAY EVE, when 'flesh (meat) is put away' for the Lenten period. 'Carnival' came to be associated with the festivities at Shrove-tide, which precede Lent, and later with any public celebration of a similar nature.

Carnival Thursday

An early term for the Thursday which preceded SHROVE TUESDAY. Pre-Lenten celebrations began on this day and ended on Shrove Tuesday night. According to an anonymous seventeenth-century writer the day was also known as MAD THURSDAY.

Cathern Day

November 25th. A corrupted form of ST CATHERINE'S DAY. In the eighteenth century, young women 'made merry' together on this day, referring to their revels as 'catherning'. At Worcester a rich brew of wine and spices was prepared in a Cathern bowl for the inhabitants of the College precincts.

Centenary Day

Also, especially in the US, **Centennial Day**. The day which occurs exactly one hundred years after a particular event. In Arnold Bennett's *Clayhanger*, much is made of the centenary of the establishment of Sunday Schools, a day which was celebrated in 1883. These schools were formerly of considerable importance and attracted large numbers of pupils. Bennett remarks in passing that the word 'centenary' itself was 'mispronounced in every manner conceivable.'

Chair days

According to the *Cornhill Magazine* (July 1865), the end period of one's life is known in Yorkshire as 'the chair day'. There is a better-known quotation in Shakespeare's *Henry VI, Part Two* (V.ii), where young Clifford finds the body of his father and exclaims:

Wast thou ordain'd, dear father,
To lose thy youth in peace and to achieve
The silvery livery of advised age,
And in thy reverence and thy chair-days
                                        thus
To die in ruffian battle.

The thought is that in old age a person spends a great deal of time sitting in a chair.

Charter Day

This is either a day appointed by a charter for some special purpose, or is the day upon which a borough, university, company or other corporation receives its royal or parliamentary charter.

Childermas Day

December 28th. Also known as HOLY INNO-CENTS' DAY. It commemorates the slaying by King Herod of all the male children in Bethlehem and the surrounding area (related in Matthew 2:16). The day of the week on which Holy Innocents' Day occurred was formerly considered to be unlucky throughout the year. Edward IV changed the date of his Coronation when he realized that it would fall on this day. This superstition led to the occasional use of 'Childermas Day' to refer not to the specific day itself, but to the same day of the week elsewhere in the year.

Christmas Day

December 25th. The feast day of Jesus Christ, celebrating his birth, otherwise known as the NATIVITY. The day was fixed by the Church (originally January 6th, Old Style) to coincide with an ancient period of celebration, linked with the winter solstice. Various customs have clustered around the day, some of them left-overs from pagan times, others – such as the Christmas tree, Christmas carols, the giving of presents, the sending of cards – more modern contributions. The Puritans were opposed to Christmas, and indeed the town-crier in Canterbury proclaimed on December 22nd, 1647, that by decree of the English parliament, Christmas would no longer be celebrated. It was by that time too well established, however.

An idealistic account of a Victorian Christmas Day is to be found in 'A Christmas Dinner', one of the *Sketches by Boz* of Charles Dickens. The day also figures strongly in Theodore Dreiser's *An American Tragedy*. Clyde Griffith is invited to share the Christmas day dinner with his rich relations. This introduction to society precipitates his eventual downfall. The '-mas' of 'Christmas' is the word 'mass' used in its Old English sense of 'feast day', though anyone could be forgiven for supposing that it refers to a mass of food and drink, consumed on the day. A comment on the drinking aspect was made by M.D., writing in *Punch Almanac* (1945). His poem begins:

> I'm dreaming of a tight Christmas,
> Just like the ones we used to know,
> When the port was flowing
> And faces showing
> That lovely alcoholic glow.

Christmas Eve

December 24th. In modern times this is a day of frantic last-minute shopping and preparation, coupled with an air of expectation. The children reluctantly go to bed, parents stay up late to wrap their presents, while those between parenthood and childhood disport themselves throughout the land. For many the day ends with a rare visit to church. There, as elsewhere, a general feeling of benevolent goodwill predominates. It is one of the good days of the year, to use Dickens's phrase, and it is Dickens, above all, who has made himself master of the Christmas literary scene. 'Once upon a time – of all the good days in the year, on Christmas Eve – old Scrooge sat busy in his counting-house.' There, in *A Christmas Carol*, Scrooge's nephew finds him, and hears him say that 'If I could work my will, every idiot who goes about with 'Merry Christmas' on his lips should be boiled with his own pudding, and buried with a stake of holly through his heart.' Fred, the nephew, defends the season:

> I have always thought of Christmas time, when it has come round – apart from the veneration due to its sacred name and origin, if anything belonging to it can be apart from that – as a good time; a kind, forgiving, charitable, pleasant time; the only time I know of, in the long calendar of the year, when men and women seem by one consent to open their shut-up hearts freely, and to think of people below them as if they really were fellow-passengers to the grave, and not another race of creatures bound on other journeys.

Scrooge, as we know, is eventually persuaded to his nephew's view. One of the miracles of Christmas is that, in spite of the blatant and sometimes ugly commercialism that now accompanies it, most people still are affected by the Christmas spirit.

Churchill Day

The Conservative MP Stefan Terlezki sponsored the Sir Winston Churchill National Day Bill in the British parliament in March 1987. Basically it sought to replace MAY DAY with a day honouring Sir Winston Churchill. In broader terms it would also have changed LABOUR DAY to a kind of Conservative Day, an idea which naturally appealed rather more to Conservative MPs than to their Labour counterparts. The Bill still exists, but is unlikely to become law. If it were to succeed, the idea would be to abolish May Day and replace it with Churchill Day on May 10th. It was on that date in 1940 that Sir Winston first became prime minister.

Churning Day

A day set aside for the making of butter by churning, or agitating, milk or cream. In Mrs Gaskell's *Cousin Phillis* we find: ' "We keep a house-servant," said cousin Holman, "but it is churning-day, and she is busy." '

Circumcision

January 1st. A church festival commemorating the Circumcision of Christ.

Citizenship Day

September 17th. Formerly called **Constitution Day**. The Constitution of the United States was signed on September 17th, 1787. The American Bar Association and other organizations make efforts to mark the anniversary of the occasion.

Civic Holiday

A term used in Canada for a public holiday not distinguished by another name. January 2nd, for instance, is usually a Civic Holiday in Quebec. The use of 'civic' is clearly influenced by the fondness among French-speakers for *civique*. The word simply means 'of citizens'.

Civil Day

The 'civil day' consists of twenty-four hours and begins at midnight. A day can be defined in other ways, for example as a natural day, an astronomical day, or a solar day (see DAY). 'Civil' in this case means 'legally recognized for the purposes of ordinary life'.

Class Day

This is a term used in the US but not in Britain. It is the day on which the senior class in a college celebrates the completion of the course. It is also used of the subsequent anniversaries, when reunions of former students are likely to take place.

Clean Shirt Day

According to James Boswell, in his *Life of Samuel Johnson*, Johnson was advised by an Irish painter how to live economically in London. Johnson much admired this 'sensible man' who, Boswell remarks, 'on clean shirt day went abroad, and paid visits'. On dirty shirt days he presumably kept his own company.

Close Sunday

Gillian Edwards, in *Hogmanay and Tiffany*, a book about the names of feasts and fasts, uses this term to translate Latin *Pascha clausum* 'the close of Easter', the end of Easter week. She suggests that it is the origin of LOW SUNDAY. The *Oxford English Dictionary* does not record the phrase, and there are other acceptable explanations for the term Low Sunday, but Miss Edwards tellingly cites the French *Pâques closes*, defined by Littré as QUASIMODO SUNDAY, which is another name for Low Sunday.

Cobbler's Monday

A Monday taken as a holiday, especially as a result of excessive drinking on Sunday. Brewer's *Dictionary of Phrase and Fable* links it with the much later expression 'to keep St Monday', which had the same meaning (see MONDAY). Brewer also accounts for the phrase by repeating a story first published in the *Journal of the Folk-Lore Society* (Vol. 1). There it is said that one of Oliver Cromwell's men, whose family name was Monday, died. Cromwell offered a reward for the best lines about his death, and received the following from a shoemaker-poet

> Blessed be the sabbath day,
> And cursed be worldly pelf,
> Tuesday will begin the week,
> Since Monday's hanged himself.

This is said to have pleased Cromwell so much that, in addition to giving the shoemaker his promised reward, he granted him and all his kind a holiday on every Monday thereafter. It is an amusing little tale in its way, but perhaps the most fitting comment one can make on it is to say 'Cobblers!' using the word in its slang sense of 'Rubbish!' The expression normally used in the seventeenth century was SHOEMAKER'S HOLIDAY, already well-known enough to be used as the title of a play by Thomas Dekker in 1599, the year of Cromwell's birth.

Collar Day

A day on which knights wear the collar of their order when taking part in a court or other ceremony. It is recorded that John Bastwick, an English Protestant who was pilloried for libel in 1637, remarked to those who had come to mock him that 'the Lords had collar days at court, but this was his collar day, and he rejoiced in it.' Jonathan Swift also used the term metaphorically in one of his letters to Stella (December 25th, 1710): 'I . . . went to court at two. It was a collar-day, that is, when the Knights of the Garter wear their collars . . . . This is likewise a collar-day all over England in every house, at least where there is brawn.' Swift obviously meant a 'day of celebration', but by the end of the eighteenth century 'collar day' had taken on a grimmer meaning in slang. It meant 'execution day, the day when a criminal was hanged'.

Collop Monday

The day before SHROVE TUESDAY. 'Collop' was used in the fourteenth century to describe a meal consisting of an egg fried on bacon. By the sixteenth century there was an expression 'collops and eggs', indicating that 'collop' was now thought to be the bacon itself. Collop Monday was certainly so-called because fried bacon and eggs were eaten that day, mainly in the northern counties. The origin of the word is unknown, though it has been suggested that the first element is 'coal'.

Colorado Day

The day on which Colorado commemorates its admission to the American Union on August 1st, 1876. The equivalent day is other states is generally known as ADMISSION DAY.

Columbus Day

The second Monday in October. It is a legal holiday in nearly all US states. It was originally observed on October 12th, the day when Columbus landed in the Bahamas in 1492, thus 'discovering' America. The day was designated a general holiday in 1892 by President Harrison, four hundred years after the event. Some people still refer to it as **Discovery Day** (it is officially known as **Discoverers' Day** in Hawaii).

Mark Twain, in *Pudd'nhead Wilson's Calendar*, writes 'October 12, the Discovery. It was wonderful to find America, but it would have been more wonderful to miss it.' In John Updike's *Rabbit Redux* there is a more down-to-earth comment on the 'municipal headache of the Columbus Day parade', with its 'Knights of Columbus floats, marching veterans, American flags'. Another potential headache was 'threatened protests from Scandinavian groups maintaining that Leif Ericson and not Columbus was the discoverer of America.'

Commencement

The day on which academic degrees are conferred. At Cambridge and Dublin universities the term normally refers to the taking of the full degree of Master or Doctor. In North America, Commencement is used far more frequently to refer to the conferring of Bachelor degrees. GRADUATION DAY would be the more usual British expression. Oliver Wendell Holmes, in one of his 'Breakfast table' essays, says: 'Commencement day reminds me of the start for the Derby.' 'Commence' in this context translates Latin *incipere*, which was used of someone entering formally upon the office of a Master or Doctor of the university. The word 'inception' is sometimes used as a synonym for Commencement.

Commemoration Day

Another name for ENCAENIA DAY at Oxford University, on which the founders and benefactors of the University are commemorated.

Commonwealth Day

The second Monday in March (since 1977). Between 1966 and 1976 it was observed on Queen Elizabeth II's official birthday, in June. Prior to that it was known as EMPIRE DAY and celebrated on May 24th, Queen Victoria's birthday.

Communion Sunday

A Sunday on which it was possible for parishioners to receive Holy Communion, the Christian sacrament which re-enacts the Last Supper. Most churches now make it possible for communion to be taken on any Sunday, but it was formerly restricted to certain Sundays in the year.

Company days

Days when guests are in the house. Becky Sharp writes to her friend Amelia, in Thackeray's *Vanity Fair*: 'I am to be treated as one of the family, except on company days, when the young ladies and I are to dine upstairs.'

Composition Day

The day when the children who attend the boarding school run by Jo and her husband, Friedrich Bhaer, present their literary compositions, in *Little Men* by Louisa M. Alcott.

Confederate Heroes Day

The name of CONFEDERATE MEMORIAL DAY in Texas, where the day is observed on January 19th, Robert E. Lee's birthday.

Confederate Memorial Day

A day which commemorates the servicemen of the Confederacy. The dates on which it is observed appear to vary considerably. In 1985, for instance, it was celebrated in Alabama on April 22nd, Florida on April 26th, Georgia on April 26th, Kentucky on June 3rd, Louisiana on June 3rd, Mississippi on April 29th, North Carolina on May 10th, Texas (called CONFEDERATE HEROES DAY) on January 19th. (Source: *World Holiday and Time Guide*, published by the Morgan Guaranty Trust Company.)

Congregation Day

At the older British universities this is the day on which there is a meeting of all the university members, usually for the purpose of granting or conferring academic degrees.

Constitution Day See CITIZENSHIP DAY.

Contango Day

A term used at the London Stock Exchange, and usually explained as a corrupt form of 'Continuation Day'. A buyer of stock pays to the seller a percentage of what is due on Contango Day. The actual transfer of stock from seller to buyer is postponed until the following SETTLING DAY. Professor Weekley, in his *Etymological Dictionary of Modern English*, wondered whether the word might not be derived from Spanish *contengo* 'I hold back', but the humorous change from 'continue' is more likely. A. A. Milne amused himself still further with the expression in 'More Cricket', one of the pieces subsequently published in *The Day's Play*. During a discussion about which day would be suitable for a cricket match to be held, one of the characters says: 'You won't get your stockbroker on Monday. It's

Contanger day or something with them every Monday.' 'Contanger', comes the reply, 'it sounds like a new kind of guano.'

Coronation Day

The day on which a king or queen, or the consort of a sovereign, is crowned. In Britain a day, as Shakespeare said, of 'general joy'. His remark in *Henry VIII* (IV.i) that the citizens 'are ever forward,/ In celebration of this day with shows,/ Pageants, and sights of honour' holds true in modern times. The last Coronation Day was on June 2nd, 1953, when Queen Elizabeth II was crowned. It was celebrated with street parties and all manner of amusements, having been declared a public holiday by royal proclamation.

Corpus Christi

The Thursday after TRINITY SUNDAY. The Latin words mean 'Christ's body', and the day is the commemoration of the Feast of the Blessed Sacrament or Body of Christ. It is a major festival of the Roman Catholic Church.

Court Day

This can mean either the day on which a legal or administrative court is held, or the day on which a royal personage holds court. Robert Burns was referring to the former in his *Twa Dogs*: 'I've notic'd, on our Laird's court-day.... Poor tenant bodies, scant o' cash.' The latter is referred to by Eileen and Rhoda Power, in *Boys and Girls of History*: 'There were irregular weeks when every red-letter day was a whole-holiday and its vigil a half-holiday. Added to these there were Founder's Days and Court Days, when the anniversaries of the Royal Family were celebrated.'

Crab Apple Night See DUCK APPLE NIGHT.

Crack-nut Night

A variant of NUT-CRACK NIGHT, or HALLOWE'EN. Nuts were baked in the fire until they cracked apart. In *The Vicar of Wakefield* by Oliver Goldsmith, there are two references to the cracking of nuts on MICHAELMAS EVE as an annual custom. In some instances 'Crack-nut Night' may have been applied to that day, September 28th.

Crime Day See PAY DAY.

Crispin's Day

October 25th. See ST CRISPIN'S DAY.

Cromwell's Day

September 3rd. Oliver Cromwell (1599–1658), Lord Protector of England, is remembered each year when a service takes place at his statue outside the Houses of Parliament. It is arranged annually by the Cromwell Association. September 3rd was of particular significance to Cromwell. It was on that day in 1650 that he won the battle of Dunbar. On the same day a year later he was the victor at the battle of Worcester. It was also the day on which he died in 1658.

Cross Days

Another name for the ROGATION DAYS, the three days (Monday, Tuesday and Wednesday) which precede ASCENSION DAY. In Shropshire, Cross Day was formerly a variant of CHILDERMAS, and was considered to be an unlucky day.

Crouchmas

Also known as **Crouchmas Day**. May 3rd. 'Crouch' here refers to the 'cross', and this long-obsolete festival celebrated the invention of the Cross. References to it occur until the early eighteenth century, for example in *The Paston Letters* (1463): 'Ye Fryday nexst after Crowchemesse Day.' It is just possible that the verb 'to crouch', which had the early sense of bowing in reverence, is connected with the 'cross' meaning.

Cup Final Day

In Britain a reference to Association football and the day on which the final match of the FA Cup knock-out competition is played at Wembley Stadium. A Saturday in May is the usual time for this event.

Cussing Day

A nickname for ASH WEDNESDAY. In church services on this day sinners are reminded of God's anger. Some people believe that Cussing Day was transposed into the KISSING DAY which occurs two days later in Yorkshire.

D

Daft Days

A Scottish term for the days of merry-making at the New Year. (The *Oxford English Dictionary* suggests 'at Christmas', but this is less likely.) A nineteenth-century Scottish song goes: 'At Yule, when the daft days are fairly set in, A ploy without him wadna be worth a pin.'

Dancing Days

The days of youth, as opposed to the CHAIR DAYS of age. In Shakespeare's *Romeo and Juliet*, Capulet tells his cousin to sit, 'For you and I are past our dancing days' (I.v). Jonathan Swift, in *Stella's Birthday*, writes:

As when a beauteous nymph decays,
We say, she's past her dancing days.

Danger Night

A local term in Lancashire for MISCHIEF NIGHT.

Darwin Show Day See HOBART REGATTA DAY.

day

This word is rather more complicated than it might seem. In normal usage it refers to the period of sunlight between successive periods of darkness. To be more precise, for there is quite literally a twilight area of meaning, it refers to the time when the sun is above the horizon. 'Day' also refers to a period of twenty-four hours. Normal usage once again would say that this period begins and ends at midnight, but that only applies to the CIVIL DAY. The **solar** or **astronomical day** is reckoned from noon to noon. There is also a **sidereal day** ('sidereal' means 'of the stars'). When the day is measured by reference to the stars it emerges as a period of twenty-three hours, fifty-six minutes, four point zero nine seconds. To put it another way, a year consists of 366 sidereal days, which are also sometimes known as **natural days**.

Apart from these highly technical applications, 'day' often takes on a special meaning in a particular context. Mary McCarthy, in *The Group*, writes: 'You had to know that the editors had 'days', like hostesses, when they were at home to reviewers'. Such days were in fact called AT-HOME DAYS or VISITING DAYS, but in ordinary speech the descriptive words were dropped. When someone says something like 'He was very good in his day', 'day' means a period of someone's life extending far beyond an individual day. We also speak of someone 'carrying the day', meaning 'to win'. 'Day' here refers loosely to the activities of the day itself or of a longer period. One final curiosity is that a 'day', as the entries in this book will reveal, can often be described by words one would not normally consider

26

to be synonyms, as in TWELFTH NIGHT or CHRISTMAS EVE.

Day

As a family name this has nothing to do with the period of time which is indicated by the word 'day'. It refers to an ancestor who worked in a dairy. A 'dairy', in its turn, was originally a place where a *dey* carried out her duties, 'dey' being derived from an Old Norse word for a maid, especially one who was a servant. Ultimately the dey was one who kneaded the dough and made the daily bread. The same sense lies at the root of the word 'lady', originally the loaf-kneader. The most famous bearer of this last name in modern times has surely been the American actress Doris Day, though she was born Doris Kappelhoff and adopted Day somewhat reluctantly. It was suggested to her by a band leader named Barney Rapp (born Rappaport), whose first idea was that she might become Doris Kapps, following his own lead. 'Day' eventually came to mind because of a song that Miss Kappelhoff had had a great deal of success with – 'Day after Day'. 'But I never did like it. Still don't. I think it's a phony name', wrote Doris Day in her book *Doris Day, Her Own Story*.

In Britain the name is also associated with the political commentator Sir Robin Day. The American writer Clarence Day was also well-known earlier this century. The latter published a book of autobiographical reminiscences under the title *These Were the Days*. Of the fictional characters who have been given this name, the best-known is Fancy Day, in Thomas Hardy's *Under the Greenwood Tree*. She is a beautiful and intelligent girl who is nevertheless rather vain. Halcyon Day is the central character in *Little Red Horses*, by G. B. Stern. The temptation to give such a punning name must be strong in real-life Day families.

Day, The

The name of a Conservative newspaper mentioned in *Pendennis* by William Thackeray.

Day name

In parts of West Africa it is the custom to give a child a name that indicates on which day of the week he or she was born. In western societies the day of birth sometimes influences the choice of name for the child, especially if that day happens to be a special one. Thus, a child born on Christmas Day might well become Noel or Noelle (French *Noël* 'Christmas') or perhaps be named Carol or Nicholas, Tiffany was once regularly given as a name to a girl born on the Epiphany, January 6th. An Easter birth can lead to Pascal or Pascale, Valentine's Day to Valentine, etc. The latter example reminds us that every day is a saint's day, and the name of the saint whose feast is being celebrated may suggest a name to the devout Catholic. On rare occasions a child receives a name of the Man Friday type, though the well-known example of the actress Tuesday Weld does not really apply, since Tuesday was not the name given to her at birth. In 1978 a British newspaper reported that a girl had been named Friday February Eleven because of her birth on that day.

Day of Accounts

Also **Day of Doom**, DAY OF JUDGEMENT, **Day of Retribution**, **Day of the Lord**, **Day of Wrath**. The day on which the dead are judged for their deeds while living. It was a day which haunted the medieval imagination.

Day of Atonement See YOM KIPPUR.

Day of Blowing the Shofar

The English translation of Hebrew **Yom Teruah**, which is how the Torah refers to ROSH HASHANAH, the Jewish New Year. The 'shofar' is the ram's-horn trumpet which was blown by the ancient Jews in battle, and which is used in synagogues on high holidays. In prayers the day is referred to as **Yom Hazikaron**, the **Day of Remembrance**.

Day of Good Will
December 26th. The name by which BOXING DAY is known in South Africa.

Day of Grace See GRACE DAY.

Day of Humiliation
A day when religious humility is practised, usually accompanied by fasting. The *Dictionary of National Biography*, for instance, in its article on Oliver Cromwell, says: 'The summer of 1658 was exceedingly unhealthy, and a malignant fever raged so generally in England that a day of public humiliation on account of it was ordered.'

Day of Immaculate Conception of Germaine Greer, Australia See DOTTY DAY.

Day of Judgement See JUDGEMENT DAY
A typical reference occurs in *Babbitt* by Sinclair Lewis:

> The pastor of the Pentecostal Communion Faith used to come to see me, and he showed me, right from the prophecies written in the Word of God, that the Day of Judgement is coming and all the members of the older churches are going straight to eternal damnation, because they only do lip-service and swallow the world, the flesh, and the devil.

See also ROSH HASHANAH.

Day of Peace
October 27th, 1986. An international and inter-denominational day of prayers for peace, presided over by Pope John Paul II in Assisi. The Pope appealed for a cease-fire on this day in the various arenas of war. Some of those who were fighting complied. As it happened, there were those within the Roman Catholic Church who were strongly opposed to the day. They maintained that the Pope was putting all religions on the same level. By chance the day coincided with BIG BANG DAY in Britain.

Day of Reckoning
A day when one will have to render an account of one's life and conduct to God. More generally, a day when an explanation will have to be given or retribution made to one's fellows, a day when a price will have to be paid for wrong-doings. Occasionally found as **Reckoning Day**.

Day of Remembrance See DAY OF BLOWING THE SHOFAR.

Day of Small Things, The
The title of a novel by O. Douglas (pen-name of Anna Buchan, the sister of John Buchan). The title is a quotation from Zechariah 4:10. In the King James version of the Bible it reads: 'For who hath despised the day of small things . . . they are the eyes of the Lord, which run to and fro through the whole earth.' The novel chronicles the lives of a few families living in a small Scottish town.

Day of the Covenant
December 16th. Originally known as DINGAAN'S DAY, then **Day of the Vow**. Day of the Covenant is the modern name for this South African holiday. It refers to the vow or covenant with God made by Pretorius and the Voortrekkers as they prepared for battle against Dingaan and the Zulus on December 16th, 1838. They vowed that if the Almighty granted them victory then the day would be observed as a Sabbath ever afterwards, and a church would be built in gratitude.

Day of the Dead
November 2nd. The *Dia de Muertos* of the Mexicans, normally called ALL SOULS' DAY in English-speaking countries. The action of Malcolm Lowry's superb novel *Under the Volcano* takes place on this day, a national holiday in Mexico. It is a day when cemeteries take on the appearance of picnic grounds, for it is thought that the spirits of the dead return to enjoy themselves with their relatives and friends. The children eat chocolate fashioned into tiny hearses, sugar

funeral wreaths and candy coffins. Lowry's novel can hardly be said to joke with death in that way; its preoccupation with death is very similar to that of the finest Elizabethan tragedies.

Day of the Fox, The
The title of a novel by Norman Lewis. The novel is set in Spain and the title refers to an ancient custom of burning foxes in midsummer fires. Foxes were thought to be under the spell of witches or to be witches in animal shape.

Day of the Jackal, The
The title of a novel by Frederick Forsyth about an attempt to assassinate President Charles de Gaulle. 'The Jackal' is the code-name chosen by the Englishman appointed to carry out the assassination. Fine novel though this is, the code-name does not really seem appropriate. The would-be killer makes it clear that he likes to operate alone, whereas jackals always hunt in packs. In figurative use, a jackal was someone who did subordinate preparatory work for someone else, rather like a researcher on a television programme. The allusion here was to the jackal's former reputation of going before the lion and hunting up his prey for him. Clearly this secondary sense of 'jackal' was not appropriate either. Nevertheless, the success of this novel caused a great many others to be written with similar titles.

Day of the Vow
December 16th. See DAY OF THE COVENANT.

Days of Awe See ROSH HASHANAH.

Days of Yore
A long time ago. **Yore-day** is found on rare occasions. The word 'yore' literally means 'of years', deriving from the genitive plural of 'year' in Old English. Washington Irving was especially fond of the expression 'of yore'. The following passage is from his description of Christmas in *The Sketch Book*:

It is a beautiful arrangement, also, derived from days of yore, that this festival, which commemorates the announcement of the religion of peace and love, has been made the season for gathering together of family connections, and drawing closer again those bands of kindred hearts, which the cares and pleasures and sorrows of the world are continually operating to cast loose.

Day's Play, The
A collection of humorous articles by A. A. Milne, first published in 1910.

D Day
Specifically associated with June 6th, 1944, when the Allies began the invasion of France during World War II, but in military use the term was a standard one for a day on which an operation would be launched. Most dictionaries explain the 'D' as simply representing the word 'day'. David Howarth, in his book *Dawn of D Day*, says that operations 'have to be planned and discussed before the date is decided on. It is convenient to refer to the date of the operation as D Day.' This glossing of 'D' as 'date' makes rather more sense. D Day is now used very generally, not just in military circles, to describe the day on which any particular action will occur.

Death Day
The day on which a person dies or the anniversary of that day. 'The death day of thy body is thy birth day to eternity', said one seventeenth-century writer. The feast days of most saints occur on their death days. **Dying Day** was a rare synonym in former times, but is usual in the modern phrase 'until my dying day'.

December the Fourteenth
The English title of a novel by Dmitri S. Merezhkovsky, translated by Nathalie A. Duddington. It concerns the plot to assassinate Czar Nicholas I on December 14th, 1825. The plot failed and the conspirators were hanged.

Decimal Day

February 15th, 1971. The day when Britain introduced a decimal currency system. In the former system there were twelve pennies in a shilling, and twenty shillings in a pound. There was a two-shilling piece called a 'florin' and a 'half-crown', worth two shillings and sixpence.

Decoration Day

Another name for MEMORIAL DAY. The last Monday in May; formerly May 30th. A legal holiday in most states of the US in honour of the war dead. It was called Decoration Day from the custom of decorating the graves of the war dead to mark the occasion. In *Dog Days*, by Ross Sankee, there is the following comment:

> Decoration Day was always a day apart when those who had died upholding the Union cause were honored. Names like Gettysburg, Cold Harbor, Chickmauga, Shiloh thrilled me to my toes. . . . On Decoration Day as well as Christmas Grandpa washed his begrimed, tobacco-stained beard and put on his uniform.

The day has also been described as a kind of lay All Souls' Day.

Dedication Day

The anniversary of the dedication of a church, observed as a festival.

Defenders' Day

September 12th. An optional bank holiday in the state of Maryland. It commemorates the defer.e of Fort McHenry against the British in 1814, an event which inspired Francis Scott Key, when he saw the flag still flying next morning, to write 'The Star Spangled Banner'.

Degrees Day

A day on which university degrees are conferred. Other names include GRADUATION DAY, COMMENCEMENT, PRESENTATION DAY. However, 'degree-day' has a quite different technical meaning, defined (rather unhelpfully) by *Webster's Dictionary* as 'a unit that represents one degree of declination from a given point (as 65°) in the mean daily outdoor temperature and that is used to measure heat requirements.'

Delivery Day

Used of the day on which a mother delivers, or gives birth to, her child.

Derby Day

The day on which the annual horse-race, named for the Earl of Derby in 1780, is run. This is on the second day of the summer meeting at Epsom in late May or early June. Until 1891 the British parliament adjourned on Derby Day; in modern times many companies unofficially adjourn for the day, transferring to open-decked buses parked near the course and indulging in splendid picnics. The eating and drinking certainly lasts rather longer than the five-minute race, which is over 1½ miles. The Derby can never be won by the same horse twice, since it is for three-year-old colts and fillies only. Derby Day features strongly in the opening chapters of *Sybil* by Benjamin Disraeli. It is also of importance in D. H. Lawrence's short story, *The Rocking-Horse Winner*. A. P. Herbert has a poem on the subject, and it has attracted the attention of many painters. 'Derby' is also applied to important horse races in other countries, such as the Kentucky Derby, run since 1875 on Churchill Downs, Louisville.

Devil's Night

October 30th. This term is well-established in Michigan, where Detroit newspapers report each year on the number of fires which were started as a result of Devil's Night activities. It does not seem to be used elsewhere.

Diamond Day

For racing fans this is the day in July when the main race at Ascot is the King George VI and Queen Elizabeth Diamond Stakes, a flat race over one and a half miles.

Diamond Jubilee
The sixtieth anniversary of a monarch's reign or similar important event. See JUBILEE.

Dies Irae
A Latin phrase which means 'day of wrath', used to refer to DOOMSDAY, JUDGEMENT DAY, etc. They are the opening words, used as a title, of a Latin hymn about the Last Judgement. Ruskin pointed out in *Praeterita*: 'Men have been curiously judging themselves by always calling the day they expected *'Dies Irae'*, instead of *'Dies Amoris'* ['day of love'].' The best-known English version of the Latin hymn is perhaps that of Sir Walter Scott, in 'The Lay of the Last Minstrel'. It begins: 'O day of wrath, O dreadful day.' The hymn has also appealed to many composers, such as Berlioz, Bruckner, Dvorak, Mozart, Schumann and Verdi.

dies non
Part of a Latin phrase, *dies non juridicus*, referring to a day on which no legal business is transacted. Used mainly in legal contexts, but occasionally elsewhere: 'Sunday was always a *dies non* with the Greshambury Mercury [a coach] and, consequently, Frank's letter was not delivered at the house till Monday morning' (*Dr Thorne*, Anthony Trollope).

diet
Formerly in Scotland a day fixed for a particular meeting or assembly, and more specifically, the day on which someone was cited to appear in court. The word then came to mean the court session itself, especially one occupying a single day or part of one. This general sense of 'meeting' also underlies 'diet' when used to describe a parliamentary assembly. Ultimately the word is connected with Latin *dies* 'day'. A similar sense development occurred in German, as in *Reichstag*, *Bundestag*. The 'diets' of those who are slimming derive from a Greek word meaning 'mode of life'.

Dingaan's Day
December 16th. The early name of what became the **Day of the Vow** and is now DAY OF THE COVENANT in South Africa. Daphne Rooke, in her novel *Mittee*, writes: 'The Coester boys were at the end of the yard, getting into practice for the sports on Dingaan's Day.' Dingaan was the name of the Zulu leader who was defeated by Pretorius on this day.

Dipping Day
May 1st. Also known as **Dippy Day**. A name used in Cornwall, referring to the custom of sprinkling people with dew water in order to bring them luck. This is said to have been the origin of the custom which later degenerated into the throwing of water over anyone not wearing a sprig of hawthorn, more for the amusement of the thrower than the welfare of the recipient.

Discoverers' Day
The second Monday in October. The term used in Hawaii for COLUMBUS DAY.

Discovery Day
A former name of COLUMBUS DAY in the US, but now the name of a holiday celebrated in Newfoundland in June, and in the Yukon in August.

Dismal Days
Evil or unlucky days; in later use days of disaster, gloom or depression, the days of old age. 'Days' in this phrase is a tautology from an etymological point of view, since the word 'dismal' was originally the English form of Latin *dies mali* 'evil days'. 'Dismal' was at first used as a noun; later it became an adjective which was applied only to days. By Shakespeare's time it was used more generally. In the medieval calendar the dismal days were also known as **Egyptian Days**, either because they had been computed by Egyptian astrologers or because they were connected with the Egyptian plagues. The days concerned were: January 1st and 25th, February 4th and 26th, March 1st and 28th, April 10th and

20th, May 3rd and 25th, June 10th and 16th, July 13th and 22nd, August 1st and 30th, September 3rd and 21st, October 3rd and 22nd, November 5th and 28th, December 7th and 22nd.

Distaff's Day

Also **St Distaff's Day** or **Rock Day**. January 7th. On a hand spinning-wheel, the flax to be spun was placed on the 'distaff' or 'rock'. Since spinning was so typical of the work done by women, 'distaff' came to be used symbolically of the female sex – hence the distaff side of the family, the female branch. January 7th was traditionally the day on which women resumed their labours after the Christmas holidays, which ended on TWELFTH NIGHT. The ploughmen on that day would amuse themselves by setting fire to the flax, and would have a bucket of water thrown over them for their pains. Hence the poem by Robert Herrick:

> Partly work and partly play
> You must on St Distaff's Day:
> From the plough soon free your team;
> Then come home and fother them;
> If the maids a-spinning go,
> Burn the flax and fire the tow.
> Bring in pails of water then,
> Let the maids bewash the men.
> Give St Distaff all the right;
> Then bid Christmas sport goodnight,
> And next morrow every one
> To his own vocation.

Dog days

The hottest and most unhealthy days of the year, also known as **canicular days**. The expression originally referred to the days when the 'dog star', Sirius, the brightest of the fixed stars, was thought to add its heat to that of the sun. Many different methods have been used to calculate which days in any given year are the dog days, and how many of them there are. It is impossible to be precise, but they fall generally in July and early August. They also occur slightly later in modern times than they would have occurred when the ancients wrote about

them. By the sixteenth century their name was being associated with the behaviour of dogs, who were said to run mad during the dog star season. Shakespeare has one passing reference to dog days, in *Henry VIII*, V.iv.: 'There is a fellow somewhat near the door, he should be a brazier by his face, for, o' my conscience, twenty of the dog-days now reign in's nose.' Perhaps a more typical literary reference is that in Thomas Hardy's *The Mayor of Casterbridge*: 'I am sometimes that dry in the dog days that I could drink a quarter barrel.' *Dog Days* by Ross Santee is a book about the author's youth in Iowa, using the dogs he owned at the time as focal points.

Doleing Day

A variant of GOODING DAY in parts of Sussex, thought the term is now obsolete. 'Dole' here refers to a distribution of food or money for charitable purposes. On this day (December 21st, ST THOMAS'S DAY) women who were not normally allowed to beg went from house to house in the parish begging for something to make Christmas a little brighter.

Dominion Day

July 1st. Now known as **Canada Day**. The Dominion of Canada came into being on July 1st, 1867. The original suggestion had been for it to be called the Kingdom of Canada. Lord Derby, the Colonial Secretary at the time, suggested the change to Dominion, 'for fear the name would wound the sensibilities of the Yankees.' Four provinces formed the Dominion at first; others followed later.

Dookie Apple Night See DUCK APPLE NIGHT.

Doomsday

The final day of judgement. In the phrase 'till doomsday' the meaning is 'for ever'. The usual spelling in earlier times was 'Domesday', as in the Domesday Book, which records the survey of England carried out by order of William the Conqueror.

After the assassination of Julius Caesar, Shakespeare has Trebonius report on the reaction of the Roman people: 'Men, wives and children stare, cry out, and run/ As it were doomsday' (*Julius Caesar*, III.i). Cleopatra is also thinking of death when she tells Charmian 'I'll give thee leave/ To play till doomsday' (*Antony and Cleopatra*, V.ii).

Dotty Day

A number of 'dotty' days were suggested by the British humorous writer Miles Kington in *The Times* (January 9th, 1985). Mr Kington pointed out that diaries contained rather boring entries against certain days, such as 'Early Closing Day in Lagos'. He suggested that one's own diary could be brightened up considerably by adding such days as **First Sunday after Placido Domingo**; **Stepfather's Day**; **Bash-a-Pom Day, Melbourne**; **Day of Miraculous Conception of Germaine Greer, Australia.**

Double Decker Day See *Introduction* p. x.

Doughnut Day

A local name for SHROVE TUESDAY in the nineteenth century. The essayist William Hazlitt refers to the eating of doughnuts fried in hogs' lard at Baldock, Hertfordshire.

Drawing-room Day

A day on which a royal person holds a formal reception, especially one at which ladies are 'presented'. The reception itself was referred to as 'the drawing-room', because it was held in the withdrawing-room. This was the room to which the ladies withdrew after dinner so that the gentlemen could enjoy their brandy, cigars and manly conversation in peace.

'I hope this will be a lesson to you, Spavin,' she said, 'and that on the next Drawing-room day my brother, Sir Pitt, will not be inconvenienced by being obliged to take four of us in his carriage to wait upon His Majesty, because my *own* carriage is not forth-coming.' It appears there had been a difference on the last Drawing-room day. Hence the degradation which the Colonel had almost suffered, of being obliged to enter the presence of his Sovereign in a hack cab. (*Vanity Fair*, William Thackeray)

Dream Days

The title of a book by Kenneth Grahame, author of *The Wind in the Willows*. Grahame first became known for his book *The Golden Age*, studies of childhood. His *Dream Days* was a sequel of a similar kind, published in 1898, the title pleasantly reversing the more usual 'day-dreams'.

Drink Day See PAY DAY.

Duck Apple Night

Also **Dookie Apple Night**. Local names for HALLOWE'EN in Liverpool and Newcastle, where children traditionally duck for apples. The apples are floated in a bowl or tub of water and have to be picked out with the teeth. The Opies (*The Lore and Language of Schoolchildren*) explain that nuts or coins are sometimes used instead of apples, causing the player to immerse his head. **Crab Apple Night** is another variant on this theme.

Durin's Day

In the mythological works of J. R. R. Tolkien, the first day of the Dwarvish year, but so-called only if the moon and sun shone in the sky at the same time. Durin I, who gave his name to the day, was the oldest and most renowned of the Seven Fathers of the Dwarves.

Dying Day See DEATH DAY.

Dyzemas Day

This is said by Brewer to be a 'tithe day', there being a Portuguese word *dizimas*, linked with Latin *decima* 'a tenth part' or 'tithe'. Other commentators have linked it with CHILDERMAS. It is certainly tempting to see it as a variant of **Dysmas** or **Dismas**

Day. Dismas is the name traditionally associated with the good or penitent thief who was crucified at the same time as Jesus. His 'day' is March 25th, from an old belief that this was the date of the Crucifixion, and therefore of Dismas's confession.

E

Earls Court Day

May 9th, 1987. Recognized by Kansas, Virginia, Wyoming, Iowa and Minnesota and referring to the London hall where William 'Buffalo Bill' Cody opened his wild-west show in 1887. A plaque was unveiled at the Earls Court Exhibition Centre on the same day.

Early May Bank Holiday

A term used by British officialdom to refer to the first Monday in May, when the MAY DAY or LABOUR DAY holiday is observed.

Earth Day

March 21st. This day is now observed in North America and Western Europe by those who wish to draw attention to the natural environment, and the importance of protecting it from pollution and other destructive forces.

Easter Day

Also known as **Easter Sunday**. The great festival of the Christian Church, commemorating the resurrection of Christ. Easter Day occurs between March 22nd and April 25th each year, its precise date being adjusted according to the time of the full moon that occurs on or after the vernal equinox. For some time civic authorities have expressed a wish to fix the date of Easter Day and this may one day happen.

The day is popularly associated with eggs, formerly decorated and in some cases rolled down slopes as part of the Easter celebrations. This custom led to local names for Easter Day, such as PACE-EGG DAY (see PASCH DAY). In modern times the eggs are usually chocolate ones, as are the 'bunnies' presented to children. The eggs were explained by the Church as symbols of the resurrection (new life), though in pagan times they were symbols of fertility. Other Easter associations include parades and the wearing of finery, such as new bonnets. O. Henry deals with the subject of Easter in his own very special way in *The Day Resurgent*. Danny McGree, after several abortive attempts, discovers the meaning of Easter.

Easter Eve

Also known as **Easter Saturday**, this is the day before EASTER DAY. *Easter Eve* is the title of a short story by Chekhov. A traveller on his way to visit a monastery watches fireworks as he crosses a river by ferry. The ferryman laments the death of a friend.

Easter Monday

A day of celebration following EASTER DAY. In London a great Easter parade takes place in Hyde Park. Various traditional games, such as egg-rolling, are carried on in local areas. The day is observed as a public holiday in most parts of Britain, part of a long weekend which includes Good Friday. This is also the case in Commonwealth countries such as Canada and Australia. In the US Easter Monday is a holiday only in North Carolina.

Easter Sunday See EASTER DAY.

Egg Saturday
The Saturday before SHROVE TUESDAY. Brewer's *Dictionary of Phrase and Fable* says that it was also called **Egg Feast**, especially in Oxfordshire. The following day was also known as **Egg Sunday**. The weekend offered a final chance to eat plenty of eggs, since they were formerly forbidden during Lent.

Egyptian Days
In medieval times, a variant of DISMAL DAYS, the two days in each month considered to be unlucky.

Eighth Day, The
The title of a novel by Thornton Wilder. One of the characters, Dr Gillies, makes a speech on New Year's Day, 1900, which explains the title:

'The Bible says that God created man on the sixth day and rested, but each of those days was many millions of years long. That day of rest must have been a short one. Man is not an end but a beginning. We are at the beginning of the second week. We are children of the eighth day.'

Eight Hour Day
An alternative name for LABOUR DAY in Tasmania, Australia. There is a monument in Melbourne which commemorates the introduction of the eight-hour working day in 1856, after much industrial strife.

Election Day
A day legally appointed for the election of public officials. Used in Britain especially when a General Election takes place, one in which every constituency elects a representative. In the US it applies especially to the first Tuesday after the first Monday in November in an even year, when national elections take place. Many states observe the day as a legal holiday. There is a fine description of an early Election Day in Nathaniel Hawthorne's *The Scarlet Letter*. It is 'the day on which the political year of the colony commenced'. There is a procession of statesmen, priests and soldiers before the people, and various sporting activities. An Election Sermon is also given.

Emancipation Day
June 19th. President Lincoln's proclamation freeing the slaves was issued on January 1st, 1863. The day was formerly observed as the anniversary of the Emancipation Proclamation, though some states preferred to observe the day on which they adopted the Thirteenth Amendment. Texas now seems to be the only state which formally recognizes this day.

Ember Days See GOLDEN FRIDAY.

Empire Day
May 24th. This was the name by which COMMONWEALTH DAY was formerly known (1903–57). In Canada and elsewhere it is known as VICTORIA DAY, since the birthday of Queen Victoria was chosen as the day on which schoolchildren should be made aware of the extent of the British Empire.

Encaenia Day
The anniversary of the dedication of a church, or at Oxford University, the annual commemoration of founders and benefactors, held in June. The latter observance features strongly in Jeffrey Archer's novel, *Not a Penny More, Not a Penny Less*. 'Encaenia' is the Latin form of a Greek word for 'dedication festival (of a temple)'. It is pronounced 'enseenia'.

Endday See TAP DAY.

Ender Day
The obsolete phrase 'this ender day' meant a day in the recent past. In the works of

J. R. R. Tolkien the **Enderi** are days added to the calendar in the middle of the year to make it the proper length without spoiling the equal lengths of the months.

Epiphany

January 6th. Also known as **Twelfth Day**. 'Epiphany' is from a Greek word which means 'to manifest, to show'. The word is used of the Christian festival which commemorates the showing of the Christ child to the Gentiles – the Magi. The name Tiffany, a form of the Greek name Theophania 'manifestation of God', was once bestowed on girls who were born on this day.

Equinox

About March 21st (**Vernal equinox**) or September 23rd (**Autumnal equinox**). 'Equinox' is from Latin words meaning 'equal night', and refers to the times when the sun crosses the equator. At such times day and night are everywhere of equal length. Shakespeare uses the word figuratively in *Othello*, II.iii. Iago says of Cassio:

> And do but see his vice;
> 'Tis to his virtue a just equinox,
> The one as long as th' other.

Evacuation Day

March 17th. Celebrated in the Boston area, in modern times on the Monday nearest March 17th. On that day in 1776 Boston was evacuated by the British forces as General Howe conceded defeat to Washington. 'Evacuation Day' has also been used to describe the similar evacuation by the British army of New York. This occurred on November 25th, 1783. In a British context the expression is likely to refer to September 1st, 1939, or similar days that year when children were evacuated from cities and other likely targets for bombing attacks to safer areas. By the evening of September 3rd, 1939, nearly a million and a half people – mainly children but including adult escorts – had gone to the rural reception areas. Thirty years later some of those who had been war-time evacuees published accounts of their experiences in *The Evacuees*, edited by B. S. Johnson.

Eve of St Agnes See ST AGNES' EVE.

Evil Days See DISMAL DAYS.

Evil May Day

Also known as **Ill May Day**. May 1st, 1517. The day on which there was an insurrection by London apprentices and other young people. They were protesting against 'privileged foreigners, whose advantages in trade had occasioned great jealousy' (Nares, quoted in the *Oxford English Dictionary*). The incident was made the basis of an anonymous play of the time, *Sir Thomas More*. It was also turned into fictional form by E. Everett Green in his novel *Evil May Day*.

Exaltation of the (Holy) Cross

September 14th. Another name for HOLY CROSS DAY.

Exhibition Day See HOBART REGATTA DAY.

F

Fair Day

The day on which a fair is held, the normal reference in literature being to a fair held for purposes of trade rather than purely for pleasure. Hugh Walpole remarks in *Rogue Herries*:

> In the past Keswick had had few Fairs but its own. It was too small a place. The chartered Fair on the 2nd of August for the sale of leather, and the Cattle Fairs on the first Thursday in May and on each Thursday fortnight for six weeks after; on the Saturday nearest Whitsuntide and Martinmas for hiring servants, and on the first Saturday after the 29th of October for the sale of cheese and rams. Saturday the year through was market-day for provisions and corn.

The fairs were an important part of rural life, and were referred to in speech as focal points. 'Come fair-day we shall have to light up before we start for home-along.' That remark occurs in *Fellow Townsmen* by Thomas Hardy, and probably reflects normal usage. *Fair Day* by Patrick Logan (Appletree Press, 1986), is an interesting study of Irish fairs and markets. There was formerly a proverbial saying, 'a day after the fair', which meant 'too late'. 'You came a day after the fair', says a character in *The Man of Mode* by Sir George Etherege (1676). Occasionally 'fair' in the phrase 'fair day' is used adjectivally. The phrase than means 'broad daylight'. Fair Days is also another name for the Goosegrass, formerly used as food for geese.

Fall Harvest Day

The second Saturday in October in Westminster, Maryland. Celebrated by a demonstration of nineteenth-century farming methods, a pumpkin contest, horse-and-wagon rides, etc. This kind of fall festival, held from mid-September to mid-October, is a common local event in many different states. It takes other names, such as **Fall Fun Day** in Waterloo, Iowa, and activities vary according to the locality.

Family Day

The name by which EASTER MONDAY is known in South Africa.

Farmer's Day

In Florida this is linked with COLUMBUS DAY. It is meant to stimulate interest in agriculture.

Fasching

The equivalent in Munich, and formerly in Venice, of the MARDI GRAS. German *Fasching* is a form of *Fast Nacht* 'Eve of the Fast'.

Fast Day

In New Hampshire a day in spring proclaimed by the state governor as a public holiday. The day was originally intended to be set aside for prayer, as well as abstinence from food, but as one American commentator says: 'the manner of observance has changed through the years'. In recent years Fast Day has been in late April. In *Lolita* Nabokov writes at one point: 'May 30 is a Fast Day by Proclamation in New Hampshire but not in the Carolinas.' The unusualness of the day makes it stick in the mind of the book's hero, Humbert Humbert. Generally a fast day is any day observed as a fast, when little or no food is eaten. In Scotland, COMMUNION SUNDAY was formerly preceded by a fast day, work being suspended for that day.

Fastens-een

Also **Fastens-eve**, **Fastens-Even**. A name for the eve or day before the fast of Lent, i.e. SHROVE TUESDAY, used in Scotland and in Northern English dialects. **Fasten Day** was the Old English form of FAST DAY.

Fasten Tuesday

Also **Fastens Tuesday**. Variants of FASTENS-EEN, etc., or SHROVE TUESDAY.

Fasting Day

An alternative form of FAST DAY. As one religious writer of the seventeenth century expressed it: 'Fasting days are soul-fatting days.' See also FISH DAY.

Fastingong

An early English expression for SHROVE TUESDAY. It was sometimes expanded to **Fastingong Eve** or **Fastingong Tuesday** in the same sense. In the *Paston Letters* of the fifteenth century there is also a reference to **Fastingong Sunday**, or SHROVE SUNDAY. In certain dialects (e.g. Norfolk), the word emerged as **Fastgong**. Literally the word means 'fast-going', presumably in the sense 'approaching a time of fast'.

Father's Day

The third Sunday in June. The day 'appointed', as *Webster's Dictionary* expresses it, 'for the honoring of fathers'. Cynics might ask: 'who so appointed it?' In an article in the London *Times* (June 13th, 1986), Joseph Kelly explained at length why he, as a father, had forbidden his children to offer him cards or presents on Father's Day. They would be spending their pocket money (which he had supplied) on cards which 'contain sticky and sickly sentiments that if voiced in public by child to father would have father leaping in direction of child with either a thermometer or a straitjacket.' As for the presents, they slot fathers into pigeon-holes – 'Dad the slightly absurd figure of fun.' The cartoon accompanying the article shows a card being handed over to father which bears the words 'Happy Rip-off Day'. Mr Kelly admits that his reaction to the day might be a little extreme, but his humorous remarks provide serious food for thought about what he calls 'a feast of consumerism'.

Fat Tuesday

A translation of French MARDI GRAS, or SHROVE TUESDAY. The previous day is also occasionally referred to as **Fat Monday**.

Favorable Day

A term used by Arthur Miller in his play *All My Sons*:

Keller: What is that, favorable day?
Frank: Well, a favorable day for a person is a fortunate day according to his stars. In other words it would be practically impossible for him to have died on his favorable day.

Feast Day

The day on which a particular saint is commemorated, usually the day of the saint's death, though ST JOHN'S DAY, for instance, celebrates the birthday of John the Baptist on June 24th. Feast Day also applies to the annual celebration in a village, originally celebrated on the feast day of the saint to whom the local church is dedicated. See more at FEAST SUNDAY and WAKES SUNDAY, the latter being an alternative name. Laurie Lee tells us in *Cider with Rosie* that the village feast day of his youth was The Parochial Church Tea and Annual Entertainment. A 'feast' can correctly be used to describe the general sporting activities which we would now tend to describe as a 'fete'. Both English 'feast' and French 'fête' derive from a Latin word *festus* 'holiday' (also giving Spanish *fiesta*). 'Feast' in the sense of a banquet was a slightly later development, though the Church certainly meant to emphasize the distinction between feast and fast days.

Feast Monday

The day following **Feast Sunday**. It was 'kept by women and children only, the men being at work', Flora Thompson tells us in *Lark Rise to Candleford*. 'The women made their houses very clean and neat for Feast Monday, and, with hollyhocks nodding in at the open windows and a sight of the clean, yellow stubble of the cleared fields beyond, and the hum of friendly talk and laughter within, the tea parties were very pleasant.' Miss Thompson records that by the 1880s Feast Monday was dying out, just as Feast Sunday was doing. In Lark Rise 'early in that century the scene of the Feast had shifted from the site of the church to that of the only inn in the parish.' The villagers 'enjoyed the extra food and drink and the excitement of seeing so many people about, never dreaming that they were celebrating the dedication five hundred years before of the little old church in the mother village which so few of them attended.'

Feast of Crispian See ST CRISPIN'S DAY.

Feast of St Grouse See GLORIOUS TWELFTH, THE.

Feast of Stephen December 26th. See ST STEPHEN'S DAY.

Feast Sunday

Another name for WAKES SUNDAY, when an English parish church holds its annual celebration. In *The Feast of July*, by H. E. Bates, Feast Sunday occurs on the first Sunday in July. 'We might starve all winter long, but the Feast is different. Everybody eats till they bust on Feast Sunday.' Another character remarks: 'I'll buy you a hat for Big Feast Sunday.' Another village feast day is lovingly described in *Tom Brown's Schooldays* by Thomas Hughes:

> They are literally, so far as one can ascertain, feasts of the dedication, i.e. they were first established in the churchyard, on the day on which the village church was opened for public worship, which was on the wake or festival of the patron saint, and have been held on the same day in every year since that time. There was no longer any remembrance of why the 'veast' had been instituted, but nevertheless it had a pleasant and almost sacred character of its own. For it was then that all the children of the village, wherever they were scattered, tried to get home for a holiday to visit their fathers and mothers and friends, bringing with them their wages or some little gift from up the country for the folks.

Hughes goes on to lament the passing of the village feast as he knew it (in the vale of Berkshire in the 1830s). He blames the local gentry and farmers, who no longer contributed prizes for the various sports, or attended the celebrations.

Fete Day

This expression has two distinct meanings. One is the day on which a fete (pronounced 'fate') is held, a public festival. The second may be found in occasional references to fête-day, where 'fête' would be pronounced French-style as 'fett'. Here the expression refers to the day on which a person celebrates his name-day, i.e. the feast of the saint whose name he shares. Thus in Charlotte Brontë's novel *Villette*, Monsieur Emanuel says: 'It was my fête-day; everybody wished me happiness but you.' Monsieur Emanuel had the right to expect greetings such as would normally be given on a person's birthday in England or the USA. For the origin of *fête* (English 'fete' is from the same word) see FEAST DAY.

Field Day

The day of a military review. In Dickens's *The Pickwick Papers*, Mr Pickwick and his friends attend such a review at Rochester, where 'the manoeuvres of half a dozen regiments were to be inspected by the eagle eye of the commander-in-chief. Temporary fortifications had been erected, the citadel was to be attacked and taken, and a mine was to be sprung.' Mr Pickwick and his friends unfortunately choose a place to stand which proves to be rather dangerous; 'the whole of the half-dozen regiments, with fixed bayonets, charged at double-quick time down upon the very spot on which Mr Pickwick and his friends were stationed.' Charles Dickens is at his most comic in his description of this particular field day. For Pickwick it is certainly an exciting time, a day of unusual excitement and action, which is the frequent figurative meaning of 'field day'. Newspapers, for example, are frequently said – to the point of its being a cliché – to be having a field day with a particular story. In the US a field day is often what British speakers of English would call a school SPORTS DAY. For huntsmen it is also a day on which the hunt meets, a day which will be spent 'in the field'.

Fifth Day

Thursday. Mainly used by the Society of Friends (Quakers). It avoids the reference to the pagan god Thor.

Fifth of July

The name of a play by Lanford Wilson. It was a considerable hit on Broadway in the late 1970s. A production at the Theatre Royal, Bristol, with Garrick Hagon in the leading role, was also a great success in 1987. Irving Wardle, reviewing the latter production in *The Times*, described the play

as 'an Independence Day reunion for a group of 1960s veterans, survivors of civil riots, anti-war demonstrations and campaigns for instant paradise.' The point of the title is that it is the day when the celebrations are over, and it is time to get back to normal life.

Fifth of November

Also known as GUY FAWKES DAY, BONFIRE NIGHT, **Fireworks Day**. The date itself, however, is also given name status. See, for instance, the quotation at SATURDAY. It is also equated with other named days in the following passage from Washington Irving's *The Sketch Book*, where he is discussing the inhabitants of Little Britain, an area of London:

> The inhabitants most religiously eat pancakes on Shrove Tuesday, hot cross buns on Good Friday, and roast goose at Michaelmas; they send love-letters on Valentine's Day, burn the Pope on the fifth of November, and kiss all the girls under the mistletoe at Christmas.

Fig Sunday

Also known as **Fig Pudding Day**. A dialectical name for PALM SUNDAY. The custom of eating figs on this day (still observed in 1939 according to Joyce Conyngham Green in *Salmagundi*) appears to derive from Christ's cursing of the barren fig tree, related at Mark 12. This actually occurred, however, on the day after Palm Sunday. In *Lark Rise to Candleford*, Flora Thompson writes:

> Palm Sunday, known locally as Fig Sunday, was a minor hamlet festival. The children loved the old custom of eating figs on Palm Sunday. The week before, the innkeeper's wife would get in a stock to be sold in pennyworths in her small grocery store. Some of the more expert cooks among the women would use them to make fig puddings for dinner and the children bought pennyworths and ate them out of sssssssscrews of blue sugar paper on their way to Sunday school.

Fireworks Day

Another name for GUY FAWKES DAY, November 5th.

First, The

September 1st. Used in sporting circles to refer to the day on which partridge shooting begins.

First Day

Sunday. A term mainly used by the Society of Friends (Quakers). It avoids the reference to sun-worship inherent in the work 'Sunday' itself.

First Night

The night on which a play or other theatrical entertainment is presented for the first time in a new production. The very first production of a new play would be called a **premiere**.

First Sunday after Placido Domingo See

DOTTY DAY.

First Sunday after the Derby

Described as such by David Niven in *The Moon's a Balloon*:

> Every summer on the First Sunday After the Derby (it is not thus described in the Book of Common Prayer but so many boys of noble birth had racehorse owner fathers that at Heatherdown, it far outranked Rogation Sunday, the Sunday after Advent, and the Twenty-first Sunday after Trinity) a prize was given to the boy with the most beautiful garden.

Fish Day

A day on which fish is eaten, usually because of a Church edict. Also known as a FASTING DAY. 'Come, thou shalt go home, and we'll have flesh for holidays, fish for fasting days, and moreo'er puddings and flapjacks; and thou shalt be welcomed' (Shakespeare's *Pericles*, II.i).

Fishin' Day

The first Monday in May in Seymour, Texas. The city closes down while everyone 'goes fishin'' on Lake Kemp. There are boat races and other water sports as well as fishing tournaments. Also called **Fish Day**.

Flag Day

June 14th (USA). The official US flag was adopted on June 14th, 1777. The anniversary of the day is observed in several US states, especially in schools. In Pennsylvania the day is a legal holiday. There is a fine description of its local celebration in *Lake Wobegon Days* by Garrison Keillor. The first flag is said to have been made by a lady called Betsy Ross, and presented by her to General George Washington. In Britain a 'flag day' is one on which money is collected for a charitable purpose by the selling of little paper flags. The equivalent day in the US is called a TAG DAY.

Flitting Day

May 25th. A term used formerly in Scotland to describe the day on which families changed from one rented house to another. Houses were normally rented by the year, and a decision had to be made around Candelmas as to whether a tenant intended to 'sit or flit'. According to R. Chambers, in *The Book of Days*, 'for some unexplained reason the Scotch "remove" oftener than their southern neighbours.'

Football Day

A local name for SHROVE TUESDAY, which was formerly 'the great football day in England' according to a nineteenth-century commentator. In *The Every-Day Book*, by William Hone, there is a letter which describes the game of football which was played in the Kingston-upon-Thames area on this day in 1815. The players would first of all go from door to door asking for money, then at midday the football was 'turned loose'. Anyone who could get near it kicked it, not worrying too much about where it went. Patient shop-keepers in the areas where a game was to be played boarded up their windows, rather as they might do today in a town where visiting football supporters were due to arrive. The games continued for about four hours, after which the players retired to public houses and spent the money they had earlier collected. Another correspondent in the same book reports on the playing of the game in various parts of Scotland. In Inverness there was also a game between the married and unmarried women, one which the married women inevitably won.

Ford's Day

A day of celebration in Aldous Huxley's *Brave New World* (1932). The novel is set in a future when his Fordship Mustapha Mond is the Resident Controller for Western Europe and is able to tell his people: 'You all remember, I suppose, that beautiful and inspired saying of Our Ford's: History is bunk.' The reference is to the motor-manufacturer Henry Ford, who uttered those words in a court room in 1919, during his libel suit against the *Chicago Tribune*. Ford is ironically given God-like status in the novel, characters using expressions like 'Thank Ford!' and 'By Ford!'

Forefathers' Day

December 21st. The anniversary of the day on which the first settlers landed at Plymouth, Mass., in 1620. Observed in Protestant churches, but not a legal holiday.

Foundation Day

An early name in some states for AUSTRALIA DAY. In Western Australia this term is still used (more correctly STATE FOUNDATION DAY) and the day is observed on or near June 1st.

Founder's Day

The day on which members of an institution, school, etc., commemorate the founder. In London, for instance, the Chelsea Pensioners parade on Founder's Day at the Royal Hospital on May 29th, the birthday of Charles II, the hospital's founder. In *The Newcomes*, by William Thackeray, there is a description of Founder's Day at Grey Friars, when the boys

and old-boys of the school observe 'the death-day of the founder of the place' by means of a formal dinner, a Latin oration, service and speeches. Thackeray himself was a pupil at Charterhouse, upon which 'Grey Friars' was clearly modelled. A rather similar literary description of Founder's Day is found in *Martin Arrowsmith* by Sinclair Lewis:

> January 30th, the birthday of the late Dr. Warburton Stonedge, founder of the medical department of Winnemac, was annually celebrated by a banquet rich in fraternalism and speeches and large lack of wine. All the faculty reserved their soundest observations for the event, and all the students were expected to be present.

Founder's Day has a special meaning in South Africa, where it is observed on April 6th. It commemorates the landing of Jan van Riebeeck at the Cape in 1652.

Four an' Twenty Day

January 18th. This was TWELFTH DAY before the Gregorian calendar was adopted in 1752. Some Scots continued to celebrate it, referring to it by this name or as Old Twelfth Day.

Fourteenth of October, The

This is the title of a novel by Bryher, first published in 1954. It is set in the year 1066 and tells the story of the Battle of Hastings from the point of view of a young Saxon. Dame Edith Sitwell was moved to comment that the book had made her believe in reincarnation, 'for I believe this book to be the record, not of an acute imagination – though this, also, is present – but of a memory, not obliterated by the centuries that have passed.'

Fourth Day

Wednesday. An expression favoured by the Society of Friends (Quakers). It avoids the reference to the pagan god Woden in the word 'Wednesday'.

Fourth of July

The patriotic American holiday, commemorating the adoption of the Declaration of Independence, 1776, by delegates of the Thirteen Colonies. Also known as **Independence Day**. Alfred Lord Tennyson once made the best of it from an English point of view:

> What wonder if in noble heat
> Those men thine arms withstood,
> Retaught the lesson thou had'st taught,
> And in thy spirit with thee fought, –
> Who sprang from English blood.

Margaret Walker's novel *Jubilee* contains a chapter called 'Fourth of July Celebration'. It opens: 'Lee County was planning a hanging on the Fourth of July.' There is a full description of 'barbecue day' and the festive celebrations which accompany the hanging of two black slave women. Mark Twain has a rather less horrific comment on the day:

> July 4. Statistics show that we lose more fools on this day than in all the other days of the year put together. This proves, by the number left in stock, that one Fourth of July per year is now inadequate, the country has grown so.
> (*Pudd'nhead Wilson's Calendar*)

Fourth of June

The date of George III's birth in 1738. Mrs Gaskell refers to it in *My Lady Ludlow*: 'They are as loyally disposed as any children can be. They come up here every fourth of June, and drink his Majesty's health'. In 1762 George III visited Eton College and the day has been commemorated ever since by a major celebration on or near June 4th. It is fully described in the novel *The Fourth of June* by David Benedictus.

frabjous day

A wonderful day, an outrageously fabulous day. The word is one of Lewis Carroll's distinctive inventions in *Through the Looking Glass*:

> 'And hast thou slain the Jabberwock?

> Come to my arms, my beamish boy!
> O frabjous day! Callooh! Callay!'
> He chortled in his joy.'

John Steinbeck used 'O frabjous day!' as a chapter title in *Sweet Thursday*.

Franklin D. Roosevelt Day

January 30th. An optional bank holiday in Kentucky. Franklin Delano Roosevelt (1882–1945) was President of the United States during four administrations. He was stricken with polio in 1921 but recovered partial use of his legs. He aligned the US with Britain during World War II. He afterwards did much work in the cause of international peace through the United Nations.

Franklin's Birthday

January 17th. Benjamin Franklin was born on this day in 1706. It is celebrated each year by different societies and institutions, such as the Poor Richard Club, the Franklin Society, the Printers and Publishers Association, etc. Franklin is remembered as a writer, printer, scientist and statesman, a man of great common sense and wit. He helped to draft, and signed, the Declaration of Independence. He also helped to establish the University of Pennsylvania, where his birthday is also commemorated each year.

Fraternal Day

The second Tuesday in October. It was established as a legal holiday in Alabama in 1915 as a day when 'all religions, creeds and beliefs unite in good will'. Later the holiday was linked with COLUMBUS DAY.

Friday

The sixth day of the week. The name associates the day with the goddess Frigg, or Freya, the Northern European equivalent of Venus, to whom the Romans dedicated this day. For Muslims it is the Sabbath day, for Christians it was for a long time the day on which fish was eaten instead of meat. The street in London where the fishmongers had their market is still known as Friday Street.

In literature the most famous reference to the day occurs in Defoe's *Robinson Crusoe*. The castaway adopts as servant a native: 'I let him know his name should be Friday, which was the day I saved his life: I called him so for the memory of the time.' With equal modesty Robinson Crusoe tells Friday his own name: 'I likewise taught him to say Master, and let him know that was to be my name.' This character, Man Friday, has led to the modern secretarial 'girl Friday', sought by various employers, 'no doubt because they wish to have a totally dependent slave who will call them, or at least think of them, as Master. Girls applying for such posts might do well to remember that Man Friday eventually disappeared overboard and was rather quickly forgotten by Crusoe. Special Fridays are sometimes known by individual names, especially GOOD FRIDAY. See also AMAMI NIGHT, BLACK FRIDAY, FRIDAY IN LIDE, FRIDAY THE THIR-TEENTH, GOLDEN FRIDAY, RED FRIDAY, WINTER FRIDAY.

Friday in Lide

The first Friday in March, celebrated as a holiday by Cornish tin-miners in former times. 'Lide' was an Old English word for 'March', possibly connected with the word 'loud'. It was replaced in general usage by 'March' but continued to be used in dialect, especially in Cornwall.

Friday the Thirteenth

When the thirteenth of any month falls on a Friday it is considered by many superstitious people to be an especially unlucky day. Friday is unlucky in itself because Christ was crucified on that day. Thirteen is supposed to be an unlucky number because of the thirteen who sat down at the Last Supper. In the eighteenth century it was popularly believed that the hangman's wages comprised thirteen half-pence. At the end of the nineteenth century a Thirteen Club was formed in the US in an attempt to show that the number was no more unlucky than any other number. Most people would agree with this view, but still feel rather uneasy when another Friday the Thirteenth comes along. Those who have a very real fear of such a day are said to be triskaidekaphobic.

Fritter Thursday

The Thursday following SHROVE TUESDAY, when it was formerly the custom to eat apple fritters. 'Fritter' in this sense has to do with 'frying'. When one fritters away one's time, whether by eating apple fritters or not, the verb ultimately derives from a word meaning 'fracture'.

Frontier Day

Local celebrations under this name are held each year in several states, especially in July and August. The idea is to remind everyone of the sports and customs of early days.

Fuirsday

A Scottish dialect form of THURSDAY.

Funday See *Introduction*, p. x.

Furry Day

May 8th. The day when the traditional Furry Dance is performed at Helston, Cornwall. 'Furry' has been explained as deriving from a Gaelic word *fer* 'a fair' or from Latin *feriae* 'festival'. In the eighteenth century it was thought that the word was a corruption of 'Floral', hence the song 'The Floral Dance'.

G

gala day

A day of festivity, finery and show. A **gala night** at a theatre is likewise a special celebratory evening when those participating dress up for the occasion. 'Gala' was borrowed in the early seventeenth century from both French and Italian, and originally referred to the dress itself. Those wearing fine clothes or uniform were said to be 'in gala'. 'Days of gala' was a phrase in use by the eighteenth century, leading on naturally to the modern sense of 'gala day'. There is a fine description of a local gala day in Mrs Gaskell's *Wives and Daughters*, where its importance to the community is shown, even though the visitors to the big house are obliged 'to talk on stilts' for many hours. In the film *Duck Soup*, Groucho Marx (as Rufus T. Firefly) is told that it is a gala day. He replies: 'A gal a day is enough for me. I don't think I can handle any more.'

Gang Days

Another term for the ROGATION DAYS. Sometimes specified as **Gang Monday**, **Gang Tuesday**, **Gang Wednesday**. 'Gang' is used here in its obsolete sense of 'going', or more specifically, 'walking'. The gang days were so-called because processions occurred on them.

Gardeners' Sunday

The name of a variety of rose.

Garland Day

An obsolete name for MAY DAY, because the May Queen was traditionally crowned with a garland, and was sometimes referred to as 'the garland'. The term has a local significance in Abbotsbury, Dorset. Children carry a large garland mounted on a pole on May 13th. They are recalling the former custom of carrying wreaths out to sea on this day. The wreaths or garlands were cast onto the waves in order to bring luck to the mackerel fishing.

gaudy day

Also **gaudy night**. A day of rejoicing, a festival day. Specifically, the day on which a college 'gaudy' is held. 'Gaudy' in this sense is an annual dinner in commemoration of someone or some event in the history of a college. Shakespeare uses the term in its more general sense, when Antony says to Cleopatra:

Come,
Let's have one other gaudy night. Call to
me
All my sad captains: fill our bowls once
more;
Let's mock the midnight bell.
(*Antony and Cleopatra*, III.xii)

'Gaudy' derives from Latin *gaudium* 'joy' in the sense quoted above. Shakespeare also uses the word in its normal modern sense, referring to something that is too brightly coloured for good taste:

Costly thy habit as thy purse can buy,
But not express'd in fancy; rich, not gaudy;
For the apparel oft proclaims the man.
(*Hamlet*, I.iii)

The derivation of the word in this meaning is somewhat obscure.

Georgemas

April 23rd. An occasional variant of ST GEORGE'S DAY.

Geranium Day

Held early in April, this is a flag day organized by the Greater London Fund for the Blind. Various charities concerned with helping the blind combine their efforts to collect money. Geranium Day began in the 1920s, and in modern times a sticker which shows a scarlet geranium is given to those who contribute. A spokesman for the Royal National Institute for the Blind was unable to explain why the geranium had been chosen for the occasion. In some ways the scarlet geranium is an unsuitable flower for those who cannot see it, since it has very little scent. Some of the books which deal with 'the language of flowers' say that its symbolic meaning is 'consolation', which possibly explains its use. The rose and poppy were already being used for flag days when the first Geranium Day was observed, so another flower no doubt seemed suitable.

German Day

Also known as **German Pioneer Day**, **German Settlement Day**. October 6th. This is said to be the date of the first German settlement in America at Germantown, Pennsylvania. Descendants of those settlers celebrated the occasion from 1908, though there were problems during World War I. In areas where there are a large number of Americans of German stock, local celebrations take place annually, a reminder that it was not only the English Puritans who founded the US.

Gesuffa Day See TOAST 'N JELLY DAY.

Girl Scout Day

March 12th. Mrs Juliette Gordon Low founded the American Girl Scout movement on March 12th, 1912. For the first three years the girls were known, like their British counterparts, as Girl Guides. The movement promotes good citizenship, sociability and the outdoor life amongst girls aged seven to seventeen.

'Gloomy Sunday'

The English title of a Hungarian song which was first heard in the USA in 1936. It received much publicity when it was banned from radio broadcasts, not because of explicit sexual references but because it was said to be causing listeners to commit suicide. 'Gloomy' aptly describes its overall mood. There have been several popular songs which have reflected Sunday in a more cheerful light. They include: 'One Sunday Afternoon', from the 1948 film of the same name; 'Put on Your Sunday Clothes' from the show *Hello, Dolly*; 'Sunday Monday or Always', from the 1943 film *Dixie*, with Bing Crosby and Dorothy Lamour. There was also the haunting music from the film *Never on Sunday*, 1960.

Glorious Fourth, The

Normally a reference to the FOURTH OF JULY. Mark Twain says: 'Even the Glorious Fourth was in some sense a failure, for it rained hard; there was no procession in consequence.' In *Dog Days* by Ross Santee, the author says: 'There was the "Glorious Fourth of July", and as often the inglorious fifth when over-zealous pooches retrieving firecrackers were blasted and burned and were gun-shy the rest of their lives.' The expression is applied to the fourth of June in the novel by David Benedictus about Speech Day at Eton. 'A visit to Eton on Saturday, the Glorious Fourth,' he writes, 'was no small matter for a fairly unspoilt girl in her teens' (*The Fourth of June*).

Glorious Twelfth, The

A reference to August 12th in a sporting context, or to July 12th in the context of Irish politics. Grouse-shooting legally begins on August 12th, or on the following day if the twelfth is a Sunday. In *The Twelfth*, by J. K. Stanford, where the day is mentioned as 'one of the main social events of a gentleman's year', occurs the passage: 'The morning papers, especially *The Times*, would all be carrying special articles on the Twelfth, and the cheaper ones would invariably prefix the word "glorious" or refer somehow to the "Feast of St Grouse".' In *Willie*, by Heather Robertson, the reference is clearly to ORANGE DAY: 'One summer he called down the wrath of God on the Orange Lodge the night before the Glorious Twelfth.'

God's Sunday

A term used until the fifteenth century for EASTER DAY.

Gold Cup Day

The last day of the four-day Royal Ascot race meeting. The Ascot Gold Cup was instituted in 1807, as a race over 2½ miles. The original cup was stolen in 1907.

Golden Friday

The Friday in each of the Ember weeks had this name. There are four Ember weeks in the year, appointed for fasting and prayer. These weeks begin on the first Sunday of Lent, on WHIT SUNDAY, on the Sundays following HOLY CROSS DAY (September 14th) and ST LUCY'S DAY (December 13th). In each of these weeks three days are fast days – the Wednesdays, Fridays and Saturdays. These are known as the **Ember Days**. In the Roman Catholic Church, priests are usually ordained on an Ember Saturday; in the Church of England ordinations usually occur on the following day. The word 'ember' here is not the same as the embers of a dying fire, but is thought to derive from

an Old English word which refers to the revolution of time.

Golden Jubilee

A celebration of the fiftieth anniversary of a particular event. The Golden Jubilee of Queen Victoria, for instance, was celebrated on June 20th, 1887. There is a very full description of how it was celebrated in rural England in *Lark Rise to Candleford* by Flora Thompson:

> The mingled scents of hot tea, dough cake, tobacco smoke and trampled grass lent a holiday savour to a simple menu. But if the provisions were simple in quality, the quantity was prodigious. Clothes baskets of bread and butter and jam cut in thick slices and watering cans of tea, already milked and sugared, were handed round and disappeared in a twinkling. 'God bless my soul,' one old clergyman exclaimed. 'Where on earth do they put it all!' They put three-fourths of it in the same handy receptacle he himself used for his four-course dinners; but the fourth part went into their pockets. That was their little weakness – not to be satisfied with a bellyful, but to manage somehow to secure a portion to take home for next day.

Good Day

A salutation used when meeting someone or when going away. It is a direct translation of, but not parallel in usage to, French *Bonjour* and German *Guten Tag*! The original English expression would have been 'God give you (a) good day' or 'Have (a) good day'. The latter expression, now associated with Californians, would have been considered normal usage by medieval Englishmen.

Good Friday

The Friday before EASTER DAY. 'Good' in this context means 'observed as holy by the Church'. In former times Christmas and Shrove-tide were also described as good-tides. Good Friday is particularly holy because it is considered to be the anniversary of the death of Christ. On this day in 1664 Samuel Pepys went 'home to the only Lenten supper I have had of wiggs and ale'. 'Wiggs' are yeast buns, plain or spiced with nutmeg and ginger. They are traditionally wedge-shaped, hence their name. Later versions of the bun, now round, may have become our modern cross buns, or rather, the buns we call hot cross buns even when they are cold.

Peter de Vries, in *Let Me Count the Ways*, remarks: 'I think they should call it *Pretty Good Friday*, what with all the doubts they have to work out a compromise with.' In most parts of Britain and in the Commonwealth countries, Good Friday is a public holiday, part of the Easter weekend celebrations. In the US it is observed as a holiday only in California, Connecticut, Delaware, Florida, Hawaii, Indiana, Kentucky, Lousiana, Maryland, New Jersey, North Dakota, Pennsylvania, Tennessee and Wisconsin.

Gooding Day

December 21st. A term in English dialectal use. It was explained by an early nineteenth-century writer as follows: 'To go a gooding is a custom observed in several parts of England on St Thomas's Day by women only, who ask alms, and in return for them wish all that is good to their benefactors.'

Good Old Days

Celebrated as a single day of festivities at Manning, Iowa, in early August. Horseshoe pitching, a wood-sawing contest, egg-throwing and similar delights precede an open-air dance in the evening. In general usage, the 'good old days' are the days of one's youth, or days safely enough in the past to be comfortably blurred by a selective memory which refuses to recall what was bad about them.

Good Road Days See PROCLAMATION DAYS.

Good Thief Sunday

The second Sunday in October. The Good Thief, traditionally called Dismas or Dysmas, was crucified with Jesus Christ, but repented before his death. Christ promised him that he would enter Paradise. The Good Thief's feast day is March 25th, the traditional date of the Crucifixion, but in the US the National Catholic Prison Chaplains Association observes the second Sunday in October as Good Thief Sunday, with masses in honour of St Dismas. The saint is the patron of persons condemned to death, and more widely, of prisoners in general.

Gowkie Day

Also **Gowkin' Day**. April 1st. These are Scottish terms for APRIL FOOLS' DAY, based on the word 'gowk' or 'gouk' which in turn derives from an Old Norse word *gauker* meaning 'cuckoo', later 'fool'. 'Hunting the gowk' is going on a fool's errand, and thus becoming an April fool. The phrase leads to the alternative name **Huntigowk Day**.

Grace Day

In commercial practice three grace days are allowed by law for the payment of a bill of exchange. A bill drawn on a particular day and payable sixty days after sight would in fact become due after sixty-three days. A grace day in a theological context is a day allowed for repentance, more commonly called a DAY OF GRACE.

Graduation Day

In Britain the day on which one graduates from a university, i.e. obtains a first degree. In the US the term can be used of the completion of any educational course.

Grand Days

The *Oxford English Dictionary* cites an early eighteenth-century book of law terms:

Grand Days are those which are solemnly kept in every term in the Inns of Court and Chancery, viz., in Easter term, Ascension Day; in Trinity term, St John

49

Baptist; in Michaelmas term, All Saints; in Hilary term, the Feast of the Purification of the Blessed Virgin. And these are no days in court.

A seventeenth-century citation equates Grand Days with GAUDY DAYS.

Grand National Day

The day on which the Grand National steeplechase is run, in March or April. This famous horse race has been staged since 1839 at Aintree, Liverpool. The course is 4½ miles long and has thirty fences, including Becher's Brook, named for Captain Becher, winner of the first Grand National, who fell at it. For a literary description of the scene at Aintree on Grand National Day see *Objection Sustained* by Enid Bagnold. The race also figures strongly in J. C. Squire's short story *The Dead Cert*.

Grandparents' Day

A day observed locally and at various times. In Vermont, for instance, schoolchildren invite their real or 'adopted' grandparents to school. There is an assembly in the afternoon for cookies and drinks.

Graveyard Cleaning Day

'The paper prints his picture helping the Boy Scouts last year on Graveyard Cleaning Day' (Ken Kesey, *One Flew Over the Cuckoo's Nest*).

Greek Independence Day

March 25th. North Carolina observed this in 1985 as an optional bank holiday. Greek communities in many parts of the US organize parades and other celebrations to mark the occasion.

Green Ribbon Day

March 17th. Another name for ST PATRICK'S DAY, when green ribbons and shamrocks are worn in Ireland.

Green Thursday

An occasional synonym for MAUNDY THURSDAY, according to the *Oxford English Dictionary*, which does not, however, explain the significance of 'green' in this case.

Grey Cup Day

Mid-November, Canada. The day on which the Canadian football final between teams from the Eastern and Western Conferences of the Canadian Football League is played. The trophy is a cup donated by Earl Grey, who was Governor-General of Canada, in 1909. Parties are held throughout Canada on this day. In many sports and social clubs two television sets are arranged so that supporters of the eastern team can watch one, while the western supporters watch the other.

> The streets of Ottawa were icy, bitterly cold, but, for all that, a parade was in progress. Desperately high-spirited westerners came to town to see their American imports, NFL rejects to the man, do battle with the East's imports for Canada's national football trophy, the Grey Cup. . . . Back at the Château Laurier, the grizzled, middle-aged bellhops had broken out in rakish Grey Cup boaters. More westerners in high heels and Stetsons milled about, many of them reeling. All the unanchored lobby furniture had been removed.

As this passage from Mordecai Richler's *Joshua Then and Now* indicates, Grey Cup Day is an occasion for drinking on the grand scale.

Grotto Day

August 5th. The *Oxford English Dictionary* rightly gives this date, ST JAMES'S DAY, Old Style (many sources say July 25th), as the day on which children constructed little grottoes in the streets made from oyster shells (see also OYSTER DAY). The emblem of St James the Great (or 'the Elder') was a scallop shell. This seems to have given rise to a popular saying that 'he who eats oysters on St James's Day will not want money'. This was at a time – late eighteenth and early nineteenth centuries – when oysters were far more commonly eaten than they are today. The eating of the oysters meant that large numbers of shells became available for the children. The grottoes they built may merely have been decorative, making use of materials that happened to be at hand (rather like the necklaces, etc., of horse chestnuts made later in the year). Some commentators think that the grottoes were meant to represent the shrine of St James himself, traditionally said to be in Spain, a great centre of pilgrimage. This seems too sophisticated an explanation, unless the grottoes were built only by Catholic children. It is more likely that children begged for pennies as reward for their efforts at decoration, not because they were offering pilgrims a cheap alternative, as Brewer, for instance, suggests. The Opies (*Lore and Language of Schoolchildren*) report that grotto-building was mainly a London activity, and that it was still being practised in the 1950s. Londoners are used to being asked for a 'Penny for the guy', but one suspects that 'Penny for the grotter', which was common in the nineteenth century, would now cause them some puzzlement.

Groundhog Day

February 2nd. A popular name in the US for CANDLEMAS, because of the legend associated with the behaviour of the groundhog. The groundhog, or woodchuck, is a thickset burrowing rodent, with grizzled fur and small ears, which lives in the northeastern US and Canada. It hibernates in winter, but is said to emerge from its winter quarters on this day. If it sees its own shadow because it is sunny, it knows that winter will last for a further six weeks and it therefore goes back to sleep. If it is cloudy the groundhog knows that winter will soon be over and it is all right to stay awake. The legend was subjected to scientific scrutiny by weathermen some years ago. They discovered that the groundhog, if indeed it did make decisions on such a basis, would have been right only 28% of the time. The day is best celebrated by the members of a club in Pennsylvania. They dress suitably for the occasion and play tunes like 'Me and My Shadow' and 'Baby, It's Cold Outside'.

Grouse Day

August 12th, when grouse-shooting begins. See GLORIOUS TWELFTH. It is jokingly said that the game-bird has much to grouse, or grumble, about but this secondary meaning of the word does not seem to be connected with the bird in any way. It was being used by British soldiers in India at the end of the nineteenth century.

Gule of August

August 1st. Another term for LAMMAS DAY. The expression Gule of August has been in use since the fourteenth century, but is of unknown origin. There have, of course, been many ingenious suggestions made as to how the phrase came about. This day in the Roman calendar would be *dies Sancti Petri ad vincula* 'the day of St Peter in chains'. Some have linked 'gule' with the end of *vincula*. Latin *gula* is 'throat', which has led to some far-fetched explanations not worth repeating here. Welsh *gwyl* 'festival' may simply be a transliteration of 'gule', though some say it is from Latin *vigilia* 'vigil'. The link with Welsh seems to offer the most promising solution to the mystery.

Gunpowder Plot Day

Also **Gunpowder Treason Day**. Variant names for GUY FAWKES DAY. The plot in which Guy Fawkes was involved, which was intended to blow up the Houses of Parliament on November 5th, 1605, while the king, lords and commoners were assembled there, was known almost immediately as the Gunpowder Plot.

Guy Fawkes Day

November 5th. Also known as BONFIRE NIGHT, FIREWORKS DAY. Guy Fawkes (1570–1606) was one of the principal conspirators in the Gunpowder Plot, which was intended to kill James I and the members of parliament on November 5th, 1605. Barrels of gunpowder had been placed in the cellars of the Houses of Parliament. After the plot had been discovered at the last minute, Fawkes and his accomplices were tried and executed. Children still make effigies of Guy Fawkes, which they call guys, and display them in the streets. They even use the traditional formula of 'Penny for the guy' when they ask passers-by for money (which will be spent on fireworks), although they would probably be offended if a penny was actually given to them. This begging, to which the police normally turn a blind eye, goes on for several days. The guys then become the centre-piece of bonfires on the night of November 5th, when fireworks fill the sky over most of Britain. Enthusiasm for the day remains high amongst children, and some go to great lengths to ensure that they collect enough money for a good firework display. A correspondent to *The Times* in 1951 reported that on September 18th he had just been asked to spare a penny for the guy.

H

halcyon days

Days of peace; specifically a period of about fourteen days of calm weather in mid-winter. 'Halcyon' refers to a type of king-fisher which the ancients believed to breed about the time of the winter solstice in a nest whcih floated on the sea. It was believed that the bird could charm the waves so that they remained specially calm. As William Shenstone put it, in the eighteenth century:

There came the halcyon, whom the sea
obeys,
When she her nest upon the water lays.

Shakespeare refers to halcyon days in *Henry VI, Part One*, I.ii. He has a still more imaginative reference in *King Lear*, II.ii. Kent is talking about 'smiling rogues' who 'in the nature of their lords rebel',

Bring oil to fire, snow to their colder
moods;
Renege, affirm and turn their halcyon
breaks
With every gale and vary of their masters.

A young lady named Halcyon Day is the central character in G. B. Stern's *Little Red Horses*.

half-day

Normally a reference to a morning or an afternoon. In Jamaica this expression is used of noon, or mid-day.

Half-holiday

This is usually an afternoon granted as a holiday to schoolchildren for a special reason. In *The Old Curiosity Shop* by Charles Dickens, the schoolmaster grants such a holiday to his charges, but asks them to be quiet, because there is a young boy in the village who is dying:

> But there was the sun shining and there were the birds singing, as the sun only shines and the birds only sing on holidays and half-holidays; there were the trees waving to all free boys to climb and nestle among their leafy branches; the hay, entreating them to come and scatter it to the pure air. . . . It was more than boy could bear, and with a joyous whoop the whole cluster took to their heels and spread themselves about, shouting and laughing as they went.

Dickens reports on the normal reasons for granting half-holidays as the village parents come to complain to the schoolmaster:

> A few confined themselves to hints, such as politely enquiring what red-letter day or saint's day the almanack said it was; a few argued that it was a slight to the Throne and an affront to the Church and State, and savoured of revolutionary principles, to grant a half-holiday upon any

lighter occasion than the birthday of the Monarch.

Halifax Day

Also known as **Halifax Resolutions Day**, **Halifax Independence Day**, **Halifax Resolutions of Independence Day**. Observed on or about April 12th in North Carolina. The Resolutions adopted by North Carolina on April 12th, 1776, played their part in the acceptance of the Declaration of Independence.

Halliday

This family name is a Northern English form of Holiday, a personal name given in the Middle Ages to a child born or baptized on a holy day. Christmas, Easter, Midwinter, etc., are other names bestowed for similar reasons which have survived as family names.

Hallowe'en

October 31st. The eve of ALL HALLOWS' DAY (or in its more usual modern form, ALL SAINTS' DAY). For the ancient Celts it was Old Year's Night, and the night of all the witches. The Church officially 'converted' the following day to All Saints' Day, but the witching tradition lives on in the world of children. In North America it is TRICK OR TREAT NIGHT, when householders do well to stock up with candy bars and the like. Since 1973 it has been marked in New York by a light-hearted parade which begins in Greenwich Village at 6.00 p.m. Anyone who feels like it joins in as it wends its way to Washington Square Park. *Hallowe'en Party* is the title of one of Agatha Christie's Hercule Poirot stories. The night is also of dramatic importance in Harper Lee's *To Kill a Mockingbird*, when the children get attacked on their way home. *Hallowe'en Hauntings* is a typical collection of ghost stories suitable for the occasion, edited by Peter Haining. In poetry, Robert Burns has celebrated the day in both *Hallowe'en* and *Tam O'Shanter*.

Hallowmas See ALL HALLOWS' DAY.

Handsel Monday

The first Monday of the year in Scotland, when it was the custom to give servants and children a small present. The present itself was less important than the good luck that was supposed to accompany it. 'Handsel' was basically something given into the hands of someone else as a token of good luck. It was especially a gift made to someone at the beginning of something, not only the beginning of a new year but when any new situation arose. The modern housewarming present could be described as a handsel. As a New Year's gift, however, the handsel was traditional from the fourteenth century until the nineteenth century. 'Handsel' acquired another meaning from an early date, namely a first instalment or payment. The word was also used to describe the first money taken by a trader on a particular day. The latter was subject to various superstitions – there were those, for instance, who spat upon the first coins they received for good luck. Both Brewer (*Dictionary of Phrase and Fable*) and Jahn (*Concise Dictionary of Holidays*) say that Handsel Monday was replaced by Boxing Day. On Boxing Day, however, it was the presents themselves which were important – they were not looked upon as tokens of good luck.

Happy days

This seems to have been a salutation in the seventeenth century. The Lord Mayor in Shakespeare's *Richard III* greets the king: 'God bless your Grace with health and happy days' (III.i). In *Pericles*, Lord Helicanus greets the noble men who visit him with 'Happy day, my lords' (II.iv). As a toast when drinking, the expression 'Happy days' is far more modern, though it may have led to the bestowing of Happy as a nickname on men who bore the family name Day in the British armed services. *Happy Days* was the title of a book by the American writer H. L. Mencken, published in 1940. (He later wrote books called *Newspaper Days* and *Heathen Days*.) One of Samuel Beckett's plays has this title. It was also the title of an American television series, set in the 1950s, about a family and a group of young friends.

Harry S Truman's Birthday

May 8th. Celebrated in Missouri, where President Truman was born on May 8th, 1884. He died in 1972. Mr Truman was thirty-eight before he took up a political appointment as a county judge. He was a successful president, described in his obituary in the London *Times* as a 'man of integrity and simplicity'. One minor curiosity is that the president's middle *name* was S. His parents did not wish to offend the paternal grandfather, whose first name was Shippe, or the maternal grandfather, a Solomon, by choosing one of those names rather than the other. The 'S' pleased them both.

Heathen's Feasting Day

A name used by the Puritans of the early seventeenth century to describe CHRISTMAS DAY.

Heaving Day

A name applied to EASTER MONDAY (**Heaving Monday**) and the following day (**Heaving Tuesday**). On the Monday in certain parts of England, e.g. Shropshire, Cheshire, Lancashire, men would lift women aloft, either in their joined hands or in a chair which might be specially decorated for the occasion. They would then demand payment of a kiss before releasing them. On the Tuesday the women treated the men in a similar fashion. 'The women's heaving day was the most amusing,' says William Hone in his *Every-Day Book*. Heaving occurred at all levels of society; Edward I was raised by the ladies of his court. Originally the custom is said to have represented the Resurrection.

Hensday See STERRENDEI.

Heritage Day

Local celebrations in many American states are given this name, with the aim of telling the young something about the past. Such a day is also observed in Kingston, Ontario, on the third Monday of February, according to a letter from Mrs Rita Carey of that city.

Hevenesdei Also **Hevensday**. See STERRENDEI.

hey-day

Originally an exclamation of surprise or wonder. It is recorded as such in the early sixteenth century and was still being used by nineteenth-century writers such as Dickens. 'Hey' was simply a meaningless sound, meant to attract attention. The second element '-day' was probably also meaningless at first, though it later came to be identified with the word 'day'. Since the original exclamation was often used when the speaker was especially excited, 'hey-day' came to be associated with the state of excitement or exaltation. At this time the expression clearly became linked with some senses of 'high day' to give rise to a new meaning: a period when excited feelings are at their height, a time of fullest vigour, youth, enjoyment and prosperity. This is the normal modern meaning, with perhaps an emphasis on youthfulness.

One of John Galsworthy's lesser-known works is a little satirical essay called *Hey-Day*. The writer considers the nature of human civlization at its height, and sees many bad things about it. He nevertheless concludes that humanity is worth more than religious judgement. Perhaps the most intense use of 'heyday' occurs in Shakespeare. The playwright refers in *The Tempest* to sexual excitement as 'the fire i' the blood'. In *Hamlet*, III.iv, the Prince tells his mother:

You cannot call it love; for at your age
The heyday in the blood is tame, it's humble
And waits upon the judgement.

High Day

A day of special celebration, especially of a religious nature. Matthew Arnold writes in one of his essays 'Here, the summer has, even on its high days and holidays, something mournful'. A secondary meaning refers to the time of day when the sun is high in the sky. 'High-day noon' was a seventeenth-century expression. 'High day' was also commonly confused with 'heyday', as in Smollett's *Humphrey Clinker*: 'in the high-day of youth and exultation'. For Shakespeare, high days seem to have been associated with the use of high-flown, poetic language. In *The Merchant of Venice*, II.viii, a servant describes the young Venetian who is at the door:

I have not seen
So likely an ambassador of love:
A day in April never came so sweet
To show how costly summer was at hand

Portia replies:

Thou wilt say anon he is some kin to thee
Thou spend'st such high-day wit in praising
him.

Highdei See STERRENDEI.

High Holiday

The Jewish holidays ROSH HASHANAH and YOM KIPPUR are both High Holidays. Joseph Heller, in *Good as Gold*, jokes: 'The annual autumnal heat wave known among Jews as the High Holidays, and elsewhere as Indian summer, had already come and gone.' In a non-Jewish context the phrase is equivalent to HIGH DAY. Flora Thompson writes in *Lark Rise to Candleford* (of Queen Victoria's Golden Jubilee): 'He did not care for "do's", and had gone to work at his bench at the shop alone while his workmates held high holiday.'

Hiroshima Day

August 6th. A day when many people throughout the world remember the dropping of the first atomic bomb on the Japanese city of Hiroshima on August 6th, 1945.

Hobart Cup Day See MELBOURNE CUP DAY.

Hobart Regatta Day

A local holiday in Southern Tasmania, Australia, celebrated in February. The similar local holiday in Northern Tasmania is observed on the first Monday in November and is called RECREATION DAY. Other local holidays in Australia are traditionally held on the occasion of agricultural shows or trade picnics. They include **Alice Springs Show Day**, **Tennant Creek Show Day**, **Katherine Show Day**, **Darwin Show Day** (all in July), **Exhibition Day** (Brisbane), **Melbourne Show Day** (both in August).

Hock Tuesday

Also known as **Hock Day**. The second Tuesday after EASTER DAY. The previous day was also known as **Hock Monday**. Hock Tuesday was once an important day in the English rural calendar, being a term day, when rents became due, and also marking the beginning of the summer season. It was the custom to collect money for parish purposes on this day by light-hearted methods, especially by binding passers-by with ropes and demanding a forfeit for their release. Another name for the day was therefore BINDING TUESDAY. A later development was for ropes to be stretched across roads and a forfeit demanded before vehicles or persons were allowed to continue. The Opies report (*The Lore and Language of Schoolchildren*) that a Yorkshireman recalling his childhood in 1955 spoke of Hock Tuesday as KISSING DAY. His contemporaries had stretched ropes across the roads leading to school and had demanded a kiss or forfeit from the girls. The origin of the word 'hock', applied to this particular day and to hock-tide, the Monday and Tuesday, is an etymological mystery. It is clear, however, that Hock Day was once as well-established as APRIL FOOL'S DAY, and it seems a pity that the customs associated with it have mostly died out.

Hogmanay

The Scottish and Northern English name for December 31st. In earliest use it was the word used by children when they visited houses on this day and asked for their traditional present of an oatmeal cake (hence the name **Cake Day**). It is clear that 'Hogmanay' derives from a French expression *aguillanneuf*, which corresponds exactly to early Scottish usage. There appears to be some reference here to the 'New Year', but the exact sense of the French expression is obscure. Many suggestions have of course been made, ranging from Cotgrave's apparently plausible link with mistletoe (French *gui*) to the anonymously ridiculous *'homme est né'*, 'man is born'. The word is only found in Scotland from the seventeenth century, which has not prevented speculation about Gaelic, Old Norse, Greek and other possible origins for the word. All are discussed at length in Gillian Edwards's *Hogmanay and Tiffany*, an erudite discussion of the names of various feasts, fasts and holidays.

Hoke Day A variant of **Hock Day**. See HOCK TUESDAY.

holiday

Originally the same as HOLY DAY, but since holy days were those when no work was done, the secondary meaning of 'day of recreation' quickly developed. In Britain the word can now be applied to a period lasting several weeks – 'Did you have a good holiday?' refers to the complete vacation, as American speakers would express it. Shakespeare often uses 'holiday' in its modern sense:

> If all the year were playing holidays
> To sport would be as tedious as to work
> But when they seldom come, they wish'd
> for come.
> *(Henry IV, Part One, I.ii)*

Shakespeare also refers to 'speaking holiday', which is using rather flowery language, not the language that one would normally use. A nineteenth-century phrase in London was 'to have a holiday at Peckham'. It meant 'to go without dinner', being both a holiday from 'pecking' and a reference to being 'peckish'. See also BLIND MAN'S HOLIDAY, BUSMAN'S HOLIDAY.

Hollow Sunday, The

The title of a novel by Robert Harling, published in 1967. It concerns the launch of a newspaper, *New Sunday*, its success and failure.

Holy Cross Day

September 14th. Also known as the festival of the **Exaltation of the (Holy) Cross**. It commemorates the miraculous appearance of the Cross to Constantine. Robert Browning's poem 'Holy Cross Day' recalls the fact that the Jews in Rome were formerly compelled to attend a Christian sermon on this day. Shakespeare refers to this day by an older name, HOLY ROOD DAY. It was also known as ROOD DAY.

Holy Day

A day set apart for religious observance, usually for a special church festival. 'Holy day' is the original form of 'holiday', but the two forms now have a different meaning, exemplified by the comment in the *Daily News* (April 7th, 1871): 'Good Friday has become a general holiday rather than a holy day.'

Holy Firecracker Day

July 4th. In John Updike's *Couples*, this phrase is used in place of the date in a letter which Foxy writes to Piet. In the letter there is a reference to 'coining funny phrases for her lover'.

Holy Innocents' Day

December 28th. See CHILDERMAS DAY, of which this is a more modern version. It is also called **Innocents' Day**.

Holy Rood Day

September 14th. An early name for HOLY CROSS DAY. The origin of 'rood' is discussed under ROOD DAY, by which name this day was also known. In Shakespeare's *Henry IV, Part One*, I.i, the Earl of Westmoreland reports to the king about a battle that has taken place:

On Holy-rood day, the gallant Hotspur
                                    there,
Young Harry Percy, and brave Archibald,
That ever-valiant and approved Scot,
At Holmedon met,
Where they did spend a sad and bloody
                                    hour.

Holy Thursday

A name variously applied to ASCENSION DAY, CORPUS CHRISTI and MAUNDY THURSDAY. For traditionalists it applies only to Ascension Day.

Hooray Days

The Canadian authors Fra Newman and Claudette Boulanger use this expressive term in their book for children, *Hooray for Today*. It captures immediately a child's reaction to a holiday or special day in the calendar. 'Hooray' has been used in English as a cheer since the beginning of the eighteenth century, when it began to replace 'Huzza!'. While 'Hooray' is used for popular acclamation, the more dignified form is 'Hurrah!'

Hospital Day

May 12th. The birthday of Florence Nightingale (1820–1910), the English hospital administrator and reformer of nurses' training, has been celebrated as Hospital Day in the US since 1921. In *The Plague and I* Betty Macdonald writes:

On Hospital Day, May twelfth, we could have as many visitors as we liked from nine to twelve-thirty and from two to four in the afternoon. Even former patients, not usually allowed in the grounds of the hospital within a year of their discharge, could come in and visit.

In England, in the nineteenth century, it was usual to have a **Hospital Saturday** and a **Hospital Sunday**. On the Saturday, money for local hospitals was collected in the streets and factories. On the Sunday, similar collections were made in the churches. No particular days in the year were set aside for these collections, so each area decided when they should be. Hospital Saturday later became ALEXANDRA ROSE DAY.

Huey P. Long Day

August 30th. Celebrated in Louisiana only, on or near this day, as an optional bank holiday. Huey Pierce Long (1893–1935) was Governor of Louisiana and a US senator. He promoted a 'Share-the-Wealth' programme by fairly ruthless means, and was assassinated at Baton Rouge in 1935.

Huntigowk Day

April 1st. A variant in Scotland of GOWKIE DAY, or APRIL FOOLS' DAY.

I

Ides See CALENDS.

Ignite
The evening of the annual Ig festival, according to *Wiley's Dictionary* in Johnny Hart's *B.C.* cartoon strip.

Ilkaday
A Scottish term referring to 'every day (but Sunday)'. 'Ilka' derives from Old English *aelc*, which in its southern English form led to 'each'.

Ill May Day See EVIL MAY DAY.

Inauguration Day
January 20th following a presidential election in the US. It was formerly held on March 4th, but the date was changed from 1933. It has been said with some truth that the ceremonies associated with the inauguration of the American President are more elaborate than those of any other head of state. One of the highlights of those ceremonies is the address by the President. There is a curious reference to this in *My Autobiography* by Charlie Chaplin. Chaplin met a certain Judge Henshaw of Augusta, who said to him:

'You know that the most undignified part of a man's anatomy is his arse, and your comedies prove it. When you kick a portly gentleman there, you strip him of all his dignity. Even the impressiveness of a presidential inauguration would collapse if you came up behind the President and kicked him in the rear.'

Another literary source combines this idea of ridicule with the pomp and circumstance of a formal inauguration, though in this case not that of an American president. In *Clochemerle* by Gabriel Chevallier, the public urinal in the village is inaugurated in an appropriate way on April 7th, 1923.

Independence Day
July 4th. An official name for the day which commemorates the adoption of the Declaration of Independence in 1776 by the Thirteen American Colonies. More usually referred to as the FOURTH OF JULY. Texas celebrates its own Independence Day as well – see TEXAS INDEPENDENCE DAY.

Indiana Day
A celebration commemorating Indiana's admission into the American Union on December 11th, 1816. In other states the equivalent anniversary is usually known as ADMISSION DAY.

Innocents' Day
December 28th. A shortened form of **Holy Innocents' Day**, itself a more modern form of CHILDERMAS DAY.

insipid day
The word 'insipid' is normally applied only to the sense of taste, describing something that has little flavour. Jonathan Swift is one of several writers who used the word metaphorically, to mean 'lacking excitement or interest'. In Swift's case he often applied the word to uneventful days. Thus he says of February 27th, 1712, in his *Journal to Stella*: 'I passed a very insipid day, and dined privately with a friend in the neighbourhood.' A year earlier he wrote: 'This was an insipid snowy day, no walking day.'

Intake Day
'All new intakes of National Servicemen,' writes David Lodge, in his novel *Ginger, You're Barmy*, 'were required to report to their training regiments on Thursdays, at fortnightly intervals. . . . Intake day was also, officially, release day.'

International Women's Day
Early March, usually on a Sunday. It has been celebrated since 1911 and is marked, in Britain, by a series of exhibitions, entertainments, films, etc.

Ivy Day
October 6th. The anniversary of the death of Charles Stewart Parnell (1846–91), the Irish statesman. He was leader of the Home Rule Party and a member of parliament. His involvement in a divorce case led to his partial downfall in 1890, though he remained leader of a minority who became known as the Parnellites. Ivy, an evergreen and symbolic, therefore, of Ireland, was chosen by Parnell as an emblem, a foil to Disraeli's primrose. In literature the day figures strongly in the short story by James Joyce, *Ivy Day in the Committee Room*:

> Mr Hynes took off his hat, shook it and then turned down the collar of his coat, displaying, as he did so, an ivy leaf in the lapel. 'If this man was alive,' he said, pointing to the leaf, 'we'd have no talk of an address of welcome.'

The reference is to a visit to Ireland by King Edward VII.

J

Jackson Day

January 8th. Also known as BATTLE OF NEW ORLEANS DAY, **Old Hickory's Day**. Andrew Jackson (1767–1845) was the seventh President of the United States. He became a military hero when he commanded troops in the important Battle of New Orleans, 1812. The nickname Old Hickory, a reference to the American hardwood of the walnut family, an especially tough wood, was a compliment to his strength of character.

Jefferson Davis' Birthday

June 3rd. Jefferson Davis (1808–89) was president of the Confederacy from 1861 to 1865. In 1985 his birthday was still being commemorated in Alabama, Florida, Georgia and Mississippi – the last-named being the state he represented as senator. In Kentucky his name is linked to CONFEDERATE MEMORIAL DAY.

Jewish New Year See ROSH HASHANAH.

Jubilate Sunday

The third Sunday after Easter in the Roman Catholic Church. The introit of the Latin mass for the day begins with the word *Jubilate* 'Cry aloud!'

Jubilee

In modern usage a day on which the anniversary of an important event is celebrated.

It is now usually qualified as a SILVER JUBILEE, GOLDEN JUBILEE, or DIAMOND JUBILEE. In Jewish history the year of Jubilee was to be kept every fifty years. During the year, fields were to be left uncultivated, Hebrew slaves set free and lands or houses that had been sold were to be returned to their former owners or their heirs. This year of Jubilee was to be proclaimed by the blowing throughout the land of ram's-horn trumpets. The word 'jubilee' derived from the Hebrew word for 'ram', used by extension to refer to the ram's horn. At a very early date, however, the word became confused with Latin *jubilare* 'to shout with exultation'. A jubilee has therefore been seen for centuries as 'a period of jubilation'.

In the Roman Catholic Church, 'jubilee' acquired a special sense when Boniface VIII instituted it as a year when remission from sin might be obtained by making a pilgrimage to Rome. At first this year of jubilee was to occur every hundred years. Later it was shortened to fifty years, then twenty-five. The modern use of 'jubilee' in a non-religious context mainly came about in the nineteenth century. At first 'the Jubilee' meant the fiftieth anniversary only. The term was applied to the celebrations marking George III's fiftieth anniversary as monarch, on October 25th, 1809. Later the terms 'silver', 'golden' and 'diamond' were borrowed from the 'silver feast' or 'silver wedding', etc., of Germany.

There is a short story called *Jubilee* by Grahame Greene. It concerns an old prostitute who opens a brothel during the week of the 'King's jubilee'. The novel of the same name by Margaret Walker is meant to be a *Gone With the Wind* from the black person's point of view. It follows the adventures of a slave girl before and after emancipation. The title is derived from a traditional negro spiritual which begins: 'We are climbing Jacob's ladder, for the year of Jubilee!'

Judgement Day

Another form of DOOMSDAY, DAY OF ACCOUNTS, DAY OF JUDGEMENT, etc. A reference to God's final judgement. 'We won't let on a word about it till the Judgement Day', says Mary, in *The Tinker's Wedding*, by J. M. Synge. In Shakespeare's *Richard III*,

I.iv, there is a discussion between the two murderers:

2nd Murd. What, shall I stab him as he sleeps?

1st Murd. No; he'll say 'twas done cowardly, when he wakes.

2nd Murd. Why, he shall never wake until the great judgement-day.

1st Murd. Why, then he'll say we stabb'd him sleeping.

2nd Murd. The urging of that word judgement hath bred a kind of remorse in me.

1st Murd. What, art thou afraid?

2nd Murd. Not to kill him, having a warrant; but to be damn'd for killing him, from the which no warrant can defend me.

Judica Sunday See PASSION SUNDAY.

Jumbo Day See *Introduction* p. x.

K

Kalends See CALENDS.

Katherine Show Day See HOBART REGATTA DAY.

K-Day

A military term for the day on which a convoy system or any particular convoy lane will be introduced.

Kids' Day

The fourth Saturday in September. A day sponsored by Kiwanis International, the organisation of business and professional men. In 1958, 2,537 Kiwanis Clubs participated, entertaining over a million boys and girls. The day also raises funds for local youth services.

King Kamehameha Day

June 11th. The birthday of King Kamehameha I (known as 'the Great') is celebrated as a holiday in Hawaii. Kamehameha (1758–1819) was the monarch who united the islands and established law and order. Celebrations include canoe, surfboard and swimming races. There is a native feast and a torchlight procession.

King's Birthday or Queen's Birthday

Now observed in most states of Australia on a Monday in early June. This holiday was first observed in 1788, the first year of settle-ment. Governor Phillip declared that the birthday of George III, June 4th, was to be a holiday for convicts and settlers. Subsequently the actual birthday of the reigning British monarch was observed as a holiday, but in 1936, after the death of George V, it was decided to continue to observe the date of that king's birthday, June 3rd.

Kissing Day

In parts of Yorkshire this was a late survival of HOCK TUESDAY. In the Yorkshire Dales children were also still celebrating **Kissing Friday** in the 1950s. This was probably a watered-down hock-tide custom, but it had been transferred to a slightly earlier time, the Friday following SHROVE TUESDAY. It completed a full week which began with COLLOP MONDAY, then continued with SHROVE TUESDAY, ASH WEDNESDAY and FRITTER THURSDAY. On the Friday a girl could be kissed by any boy she met. It was considered bad form to resist.

Knickerbocker Holiday

The title of a Broadway musical produced in 1938. The words were by Maxwell Anderson, the music by Kurt Weill. 'Knickerbocker' was the supposed last name of the author of *History of New York* (1809), in fact written by Washington Irving. The name was applied to descendants of the early

Dutch settlers of New York, and later to any resident of the city or state of New York. It is familiar to children because of the Knickerbocker Glory, an ice-cream, and was formerly associated with knickerbockers, the loose-fitting trousers gathered at the knee. These were the knee-breeches worn by Dutchmen in former times, shown in George Cruikshank's illustrations to Washington Irving's book. 'Knickerbockers' was obviously a rather lengthy description of short trousers, and the word was reduced to 'knickers' in ordinary speech. This word in turn was applied to the undergarment for ladies which bore some resemblance to knickerbockers. The latter garment is now considered to be amusing, so that mere mention of the word 'knickers' is enough to earn British comedians a laugh. Washington Irving, who began all this with his use of the name, seems to have adapted slightly a real Dutch family name, found in New York from the beginning of the eighteenth century as Knickerbacker. This would have meant a baker of knickers or nickers, small marbles of baked clay used by schoolboys.

Krazy Daze See TOAST 'N JELLY DAY.

Kruger Day
October 10th. A holiday in South Africa commemorating the birthday of Stephanus Johannes Paulus Kruger (1825–1904), president of the South African Republic from 1883 to 1900.

L

Labor Day

The first Monday in September. The day which recognizes the contribution to society of the working man – a legal holiday throughout the US and Canada. It is mentioned in American literature fairly frequently, and is made much of in *Consenting Adults* by Peter de Vries:

> She went into labor on Labor Day, making that Ambrose's birthday, a fitting enough irony for someone who was never to do an honest day's work in his life.

Labour Day

May 1st. The British equivalent of the American LABOR DAY, though in Britain the term MAY DAY is more common than Labour Day. In Australia Labour Day is commonly used, and is observed at different times in the different states – March in Western Australia and Victoria, May in Queensland, and October in Australian Capital Territory, New South Wales and South Australia.

The idea of an international working-class holiday was proposed in Paris in 1889 and first celebrated in 1890. May 1st was chosen as the date because the labour movement in the USA had tried to impose the eight-hour day by direct action from May 1st, 1886. It is therefore strange that the Americans themselves choose to celebrate the day in September.

lack-a-day See ALACK-A-DAY.

Ladies' Day

The title of the English version (by Dudley Fitts) of Aristophanes' comedy, *Thesmophoriazusae*, literally 'the women celebrating the Thesmophoria'. This was a festival attended by women only. The play concerns the introduction of a man in disguise into the proceedings. The Thesmophoria was usually held in October, and was in honour of Demeter.

Lady Day

March 25th. Otherwise known as the feast of the ANNUNCIATION. It was originally called **Our Lady Day** and could be used of three other days in the year, all connected with the Virgin Mary. These were December 8th, the Conception of the Virgin; September 8th, the Nativity; August 15th, the Assumption. **Old Lady Day** (now April 6th), was important in the rural calendar. New agricultural appointments were taken up – see Thomas Hardy's essay on *The Dorsetshire Labourer*. It was therefore commonly referred to in speech as a reference point. 'It is nearly two months till Lady Day,' says a character in George Eliot's *Amos Barton*. There was an old prophecy that 'when my Lord falls in my Lady's lap, England beware of some mishap.' It meant that there would be trouble in the realm if Easter Sunday fell on Lady Day. The Dead Letter Office of the British Post Office is said to have delivered correctly a letter that was addressed simply to 'March 25th'. It was passed on to a certain Lady Day, the wife of a judge, Lord Day.

Laetare Sunday

Another name for MOTHERING SUNDAY or MID-LENT SUNDAY. The Latin Introit for the day begins with the word *Laetare* 'Rejoice'.

Lammas Day

August 1st. The same day was known as the GULE OF AUGUST. 'Lammas' was originally 'loaf-mass', a reference to the fact that it was a harvest festival in the early English church. Loaves of bread, made from the first corn to ripen, were consecrated at the mass. The pronunciation and spelling of 'lammas' has naturally led to the assumption that it is a 'lamb-mass', but the true etymology is not in doubt. In Scotland Lammas Day is one of the traditional Quarter Days. There is a famous reference to the day, or more accurately, to the previous day, in Shakespeare's *Romeo and Juliet*. The Nurse is discussing Juliet:

Nurse   How long is it now to Lammas-tide?
Lady Capulet A fortnight and odd days.
Nurse   Even or odd, of all days in the year,
              Come Lammas Eve at night shall she be fourteen.

From the sixteenth to the nineteenth century the phrase 'at **Latter Lammas (Day)**' was used to indicate a time that would never come. It was equated with the Greek Calends (see CALENDS). Susan Howatch's novel, *The Devil on Lammas Night*, makes a great deal of the fact that Lammas, along with Candlemas, Walpurgis Night and Hallowe'en, is an important day in the occult calendar.

Lampshade Saturday

The invention of Pearson Phillips, and described by him in an article in *The Times* in May 1987. He was commenting on the gentle art of pulling the legs of innocent American tourists, one of whom happened to find him sitting outside his cottage repairing a lampshade. He couldn't help responding to her enquiry about what he was doing by explaining that it was Lampshade Saturday, 'a day in spring when people take off all their lampshades to repair and clean them after their long winter usage'. The tourist was apparently perfectly satisfied with this explanation, and compared it with cleaning the drapes on Washington's Birthday back in Idaho.

Landing Day

An alternative name (e.g. in Wisconsin) for COLUMBUS DAY.

Lanimer Day

Earlier **Landimere's Day**. A day on which the boundary marks of the burgh are inspected in Lanarkshire and Aberdeen. 'Lanimer' or 'landimere' means 'boundary of land'. In Lanark itself on Lanimer Day (traditionally the Thursday which falls between June 6th and 12th) there is a colourful procession. The Lanimer Queen is crowned and receives the homage of her lieges, both queen and subjects having been supplied by a local school.

Last Day

The day of judgement; the end of the world. 'Last days' normally refers to the period immediately preceding someone's death. There is a chapter called 'The Last Day' in Trollope's *The Small House at Allington*. It begins: 'Last days are wretched days'. In this case the reference is to the parting that will soon take place.

Last Night

A phrase which mainly recalls the Last Night of the Proms, the eight-week season of Promenade concerts which are held in the Albert Hall, London. The Last Night occurs on a Saturday in mid-September and includes the *Fantasia of Sea Songs* composed by Sir Henry Wood, who founded the Proms. A setting of Blake's 'Jerusalem' and Elgar's *Pomp and Circumstance* have become other essential ingredients of the evening's entertainment.

Late May Bank Holiday
A modern term used by the British Civil Service to refer to WHIT MONDAY.

Latter-day
This expression simply means 'of recent times', but it has become strongly associated with the Church of Jesus Christ of Latter-day Saints, a sect founded in 1830 by Joseph Smith. Members of the church are popularly known as Mormons.

Latter Lammas Day See LAMMAS DAY.

Launceston Cup Day See MELBOURNE CUP DAY.

Law Day
May 1st. An attempt was made in the US to establish this name for May 1st. Another suggestion was **Loyalty Day**. The American Communist Party normally disseminated its doctrines on this day – MAY DAY or LABOUR DAY – and these suggested names were meant to remind American citizens that they could live freely under the laws of the land, and that they owed loyalty to their country. Neither term came into general use.

Lay Day
A day allowed for the loading or unloading of cargo, or a day when a vessel remains in port. 'Lay' in this case is possibly a shortened form of 'delay'.

League of Nations Day
January 10th. The League of Nations was founded on this day in 1920 with the main object of preventing war. At one time there were sixty member nations, but since the USA and the USSR were not among them, the League was fatally flawed. It was disbanded in 1946 and replaced by the United Nations.

Leap Day
February 29th. The so-called 'intercalary' day, one inserted between others in the normal calendar, which occurs in a leap year. There was formerly a tradition that women could propose to men during a leap year, the men paying a forfeit if they refused the offer. In some areas this privilege of proposing was restricted to Leap Day, which was sometimes known as **Bachelor's Day**.

Leave Day
The poet Coleridge refers to his 'friendless wanderings on our leave-days' in his *Biographical Sketches*. He adds an explanatory note: 'The Christ Hospital phrase, not for holidays altogether, but for those on which the boys are permitted to go beyond the precincts of the school'. At certain other schools such days were known as **Leave Out Days**.

Lei Day
May 1st. This is the name of MAY DAY in Hawaii. As part of the celebrations, prizes are offered to those wearing the most beautiful or distinctive leis. A lei is a Hawaiian wreath or necklace made of flowers or leaves.

Levee Day
'I called at the Lord Treasurer's; it was his levee day.' The 'levee' referred to in that remark by Jonathan Swift, in one of his letters to Stella (1711), was an assembly for men only held in the early afternoon by the sovereign or his representative. Originally the levee was a morning reception of visitors, the word deriving from the French verb *se lever* 'to get up (out of bed)'. This original meaning was completely forgotten when the word reached the US. The levees, or receptions, of the President were usually held in the late evenings. In modern usage, a levee

is often held in honour of a particular person.

Lexington Day
Another name for PATRIOT'S DAY.

Liberation Day
May 9th. Commemorated in Jersey, in the Channel Islands, which were occupied by the German army during World War II.

Lifeboat Day
In modern times this is a day, usually in March, when members of the public are asked to buy flags in the shape of lifeboats as a contribution to the funds of the Royal National Lifeboat Institution. It is said to have been the tragic accident in 1886, which led to the loss of 2 lifeboats and 27 men who had gone to the rescue of the barque *The Mexico*, which eventually led to the establishment of charity flag days. A disaster fund of £50,000 was raised in that instance, but in 1891 the first **Lifeboat Saturday** was observed. It had been arranged by Sir Charles Macara, a Manchester cotton magnate, who had realized that many people would be willing to contribute regularly to the voluntary service. On the first Saturday, 30,000 people watched a parade of bands and boats through Manchester, contributing money as they did so. The parades continued until World War I, when voluntary subscriptions fell badly. The financial crisis that resulted led to the printing and sale of flags. As a writer in the London *Times* expressed it (March 15th, 1986), the loose change that members of the public give on Lifeboat Day 'is a small price for the bravery of the volunteers who risk their lives for those in peril on the sea.'

Lincoln's Birthday
February 12th. Observed on the first Monday in February as a legal holiday by some American states. It is known as **Lincoln Day** in Arizona and Connecticut. South Dakota has a **Lincoln-Washington Day**, Ohio a **Washington-Lincoln Day**. Other states have PRESIDENTS DAY in honour

of these two presidents. Abraham Lincoln (1809–65) was born in a log cabin in Kentucky and was mostly self-taught. He later practised law, and became sixteenth president of the USA in 1860. After his assassination in 1865 by John Wilkes Booth he became a symbol of American democracy. The following passage occurs in Mary McCarthy's *The Group*:

> 'It was Lincoln's Birthday, which was why Grace had the afternoon off.'
> 'And Kay?' said Helena.
> 'Kay was working,' said Norine. 'The stores don't observe Lincoln's Birthday. They cash in on the fact that the other wage slaves get the day off. It's a big white-collar shopping spree. When do you think a forty-eight-hour-week stenographer gets a chance to buy herself a dress?'

Lincoln-Washington Day
The third Monday in February, South Dakota. See LINCOLN'S BIRTHDAY and WASHINGTON'S BIRTHDAY.

Little Easter Sunday
An obsolete term which is thought to have referred to LOW SUNDAY.

livelong day, the
All day, the entire length of the day. This expression occurs mostly in poetry or rhetorical speech, and is not quite what it seems to be. It originally had nothing to do with a period of time one lived through, but was a 'lief long day', where 'lief' means 'dear'. The word was used as an emotional intensifier of 'long'. By the end of the sixteenth century, 'lief' had faded from general usage, and the verb 'live' was substituted by folk-etymology. Shakespeare uses 'livelong' to describe both 'day' and 'night'. When Lennox talks of the bad omens that precede the discovery of the king's murder in *Macbeth*, he says that 'the obscure bird Clamour'd the livelong night'. Dickens uses the word in fairly ordinary speech: 'From the time when my daughter and himself

were children together, and walking about, arm in arm, the livelong day' (*David Copperfield*).

Loaf day

A day when no regular work is done, when workers loaf about. 'To loaf' in this sense appeared in US slang in the early nineteenth century. It has nothing to do with 'loaf of bread', but may have been adapted by German immigrants from *Landläufer*, literally someone who runs around the country, a vagabond. 'Loaf day' itself may well have been influenced by Swedish *lofdag* or Dutch *verlofdag*, both meaning a holiday, a day when 'leave' is taken. LEAVE DAY in English has a different sense.

Loëndë See STERRENDEI.

Long Barnaby

June 11th. By Old Style reckoning this was the longest day of the year. Also known as BARNABY DAY, ST BARNABAS' DAY, **Barnaby Bright**.

Longest Day

June 21st. The day of the SUMMER SOLSTICE. It is often confused with MIDSUMMER DAY, but the 21st, not the 24th of June is the 'Methuselah of the year', as Matthew Prior called it. The Darryl F. Zanuck film *The Longest Day* was about D DAY.

Long Friday

An Old English variant of GOOD FRIDAY.

Long Rope Day

A local name in England, especially in parts of Sussex, for GOOD FRIDAY, which was used until recent times. It was the practice for adults as well as children to skip in ropes that stretched across a road, although the beach was a favourite place for it to take place.

Lord Mayor's Day

November 9th. The day on which the Lord Mayor of London is admitted to office, now usually observed on the second Friday in November. It is followed by the Lord Mayor's Show on the second Saturday in November. In *The Country Church*, by Washington Irving, there is a remark about a woman who rides about in a carriage: 'Life to her was a perpetual revel; it was one long Lord Mayor's day'. According to Thomas Hood, however, Lord Mayor's Day was not particularly pleasant. In his 'Ode for the Ninth of November' he suggested that the ceremonies should be shifted to June:

Was there no better day
To fix on, than November Ninth so shivery
And dull for showing off the Livery's
livery?

In a later verse he says:

O Lud! I say
Do change your day
To some time when your Show can really
show;
When silk can seem like silk, and gold can
glow

The weather on Lord Mayor's Day seems to have obsessed him, for he has another poem beginning:

How well I remember the ninth of
November,
The sky was very foggy, the sun looking
groggy,
In fact, altogether pea-soup colour'd
weather.

Irving's impression of the day was coloured by the time he spent living in Little Britain, a part of London once owned by the Dukes of Brittany.

The Lord Mayor's day is the great anniversary. The Lord Mayor is looked up to by the inhabitants of Little Britain as the greatest potentate upon earth; his gilt coach with six horses as the summit of human splendour; and his procession, with all the Sheriffs and Aldermen in his train, as the grandest of earthly pageants. How they exult in the idea that the King himself dare not enter the city without first knocking at the gate of Temple Bar, and asking permission of the Lord Mayor.

Lord's Day
Properly **The Lord's Day**, but the shorter form is usual. A Christian description of SUNDAY, parallel to French *dimanche*, Spanish *Domingo*, Italian *Domenica*, each of which refers to 'day of the Lord' in the original expressions. In the seventeenth and eighteenth centuries, Lord's Day was commonly used in ordinary speech and writing, and not just by the Puritans, who would have wanted to avoid the pagan reference to sun-worship in Sunday. In modern times, Lord's Day is used when a speaker or writer wishes to draw attention to the sacred nature of the day, as in the Lord's Day Observance Society.

Lost Day
According to a nineteenth-century *Sailor's Word Book*, this was the day that was lost when travelling around the world in a westerly direction. In a different context, 'lost days' would refer to the eleven days that were dropped when England finally adopted the Gregorian Calendar in 1752. See OLD CHRISTMAS DAY.

Lost Sunday
The third Sunday before Lent, said to be called this because it was not significant enough to have a special name. In fact it is also known as SEPTUAGESIMA SUNDAY. *Lost Friday*, by Ernest Jason Fredericks, is a novel about a man who is unconscious for twenty-four hours and therefore loses a day.

Lou Bunch Day
Late August, in Central City, Colorado. The day of celebration is described as a 'salute to the madams and girls of Colorado's first century'. Events include a bed race, a Madams and Miners Ball, and the election of a Madam of the Year and Sporting House Girl of the Year.

Lousy Wednesday See SWEET THURSDAY.

Love Day
In the Middle Ages, this was a day appointed for a meeting between those who were in dispute. The meeting was meant to lead to an amicable agreement. Girls born on such a day were sometimes given Loveday as a first name. There is some evidence to suggest that by the sixteenth century the term was being re-interpreted as 'a day devoted to love-making'. By the late seventeenth century it had become obsolete. Shakespeare has one reference to a love day, in *Titus Andronicus*, I.i: 'This day shall be a love-day, Tamora.'

Low Sunday
Also known as **Low Easterday**. The Sunday following the 'high' feast of Easter, when church services are once again normal after the special celebrations. This same day is also QUASIMODO SUNDAY.

Loyalty Day
May 1st. See LAW DAY.

Lucky Day
''Tis a lucky day, boy, and we'll do good deeds on it', says the Shepherd in *The Winter's Tale* (III.iii). A well-known song repeats the theme: 'This is my lucky day'. Fortunately, most people experience particular days when everything seems to go right, contrasting with DISMAL DAYS when everything goes wrong. The superstitious sometimes notice a pattern about their lucky days. Henry VII was convinced that Saturday was his lucky day, while for Napoleon it was the second day of every month.

Lukesmas
October 18th. An expression formerly used in Scotland for ST LUKE'S DAY. It was a day on which accounts normally had to be paid.

Lupercalia
February 15th. An ancient Roman festival, mentioned from time to time in English literature, especially in Shakespeare's *Julius Caesar* (III.ii). On this day worshippers gathered at a cave called the Lupercal, where Romulus and Remus were supposed to have been suckled by a wolf. Goats and

a dog were sacrificed, and two young men were then smeared with the sacrificial blood. They donned the goat skins and ran around the Palatine with strips of goat's hide in their hands. Women placed themselves so that they could be struck by these thongs, which they believed would make them fertile. The thongs had a special name, *februa* 'means of purification'. The month in which they were used received the name February. The Lupercalia was in honour of a god known as Lupercus, who was prob-ably Faunus, or Pan. The origin of his name is unclear, though it is traditionally associated with Latin *lupus* 'wolf'.

Lyndon B. Johnson's Birthday

August 27th. An optional public holiday in Texas. Lyndon Baines Johnson assumed the presidency of the United States on the assassination of President Kennedy in November 1963. He had previously been a Congressman from Texas and a US Senator.

M

Mad Sunday

The name on the Isle of Man for the Sunday before the TT (Tourist Trophy) motorcycle races, a rest day for the professional riders but something of a field day for the amateurs, thousands of whom follow the 38 mile circuit. In 1987 Mad Sunday occurred on May 31st. It resulted in the death of a woman pillion passenger and serious injuries to two other motorcyclists, after a crash at the notorious Ballaugh bridge.

Mad Thursday

'Otherwise called CARNIVAL THURSDAY', according to an early seventeenth-century writer. It was the day when riotous celebrations began, ending several days later on the night of SHROVE TUESDAY, a final fling before the Lenten period.

Majuba Day

February 27th. This was formerly celebrated by the Boers in South Africa. It commemorated a victory by Piet Joubert and his men over the British at Majuba Hill in the first South African war. 'Majuba' means 'hill of doves' in the Zulu language.

'Make my Day'

An expression made famous by a cold-eyed Clint Eastwood in many a spaghetti western, challenging an opponent to draw on him. There is a law in Colorado which makes it legal for anyone to shoot an intruder in their home if they have the slightest fear that they might be in danger. It is known to the locals as the 'Make My Day law'.

Mallard, The

January 14th at All Souls College, Oxford. In 1722 Hearne recorded in his diary:

> Last Monday, the 14th inst, was All Souls College Mallard, at which time 'tis usual with the fellows and their friends to have a supper, and to sit up all night drinking and singing. Their song is the mallard, and formerly they used to ramble about the college with sticks and poles, etc., in quest of the mallard. They tell you the custom arose from a swinging old mallard, that had been lost at the foundation of the college, and found many years after in the sink.

In 1899 the song of the mallard was still being sung at college gaudies. A mallard is a male wild duck.

March Day

A day on which a court met to make judgements about infractions of border laws. 'March' here is used in its sense of boundary or border, indicated by some kind of 'mark'.

March the Ninth

A novel by R. C. Hutchinson, published in 1957. It concerns a German officer who is being taken to Nuremberg for trial after World War II. He is wounded while escaping, and the central figure of the book becomes involved with him as a doctor.

Mardi Gras

Another name for SHROVE TUESDAY, used especially in Louisiana. The French words *mardi gras* literally mean 'fat Tuesday', and refer to the final feasting that takes place before Lent begins. The expression is sometimes extended to mean a period of carnival which comes to an end on Shrove Tuesday. This is from *The Eighth Day* by Thornton Wilder:

> Once a year – sturdy Protestants though they were – the brewers of Hoboken gave a great pre-Lenten ball (their *Fasching*, their *Mardi Gras*) in honour of King Gambrinus, the inventor of beer.

Market Day

The fixed day on which a market is held, and a day when farmers and farm-workers flooded into the market towns in former times. 'I am able to endure much,' says the rebel Jack Cade, in Shakespeare's *Henry VI, Part Two*, IV.ii. 'No question of that,' remarks Dick the Butcher in an aside, 'for I have seen him whipt three market days together.' Someone else who endured much on market days was the wife of Burns's Tam o' Shanter. As she says to her husband, 'frae November till October/ Ae market day thou was na sober.'

Martin Luther King's Birthday

January 15th. The birthday of Dr Martin Luther King Jr, the black American clergyman and civil rights leader, dedicated to passive resistance, was commemorated by twenty-four US states in 1985, under various names and on different days. The most popular way of referring to the day was Martin Luther King's Birthday. As such it was observed in Florida, Illinois, Indiana, Louisiana, Maryland, Massachusetts, Michigan, New Jersey, North Carolina, West Virginia and Wisconsin. In most cases, January 15th, a Tuesday, was the day of commemoration. In Indiana it was put back to the following Monday, January 21st. In Michigan it was put forward by one day and celebrated on January 14th. In other states the day became **Martin Luther King Jr Day** (California, Connecticut, New York, Pennsylvania, Tennessee), **Martin Luther King Jr's Birthday** (Georgia, Kansas), **Martin Luther King Jr Birthday** (District of Columbia), **Martin Luther King Day** (Ohio), **Birthday of Martin Luther King Jr** (Kentucky). In Alabama it became **Martin Luther King and Robert E. Lee's Birthday**, observed on January 21st. Virginia on the same day celebrated **Lee-Jackson-King Day**, allowing different sections of the community to observe it in very different ways.

Martinmas

November 11th. The feast day of St Martin. It was traditionally an important day in the calendar, being the usual time for hiring servants, often at a Martinmas fair. It was also the day on which cattle were slaughtered and salted for use during the winter. In Scotland it was a legal term-day. **Martlemas** is an obsolete variant of Martinmas. The word occurs in that form in Shakespeare's *Henry IV, Part Two*, II.ii. Poins asks Bardolph: 'How doth the martlemas, your master?' The reference is to Falstaff, and the allusion is to Martinmas beef, fatted and ready for slaughter. There is probably also a pun on 'mass'. The phrase 'a Martinmas summer' is a variant of 'a St Martin's summer', or as we would now tend to say, 'an Indian summer'.

Martinmas Sunday

The Sunday nearest to MARTINMAS.

Martlemas See MARTINMAS.

Maryland Day

March 25th. An optional bank holiday in the state of Maryland. It commemorates the arrival of the colonists in 1634.

Maundy Thursday

The Thursday before EASTER DAY. 'Maundy' is from a French word, ultimately from Latin *mandatum* 'commandment'. This refers to Christ's words after he had washed the feet of his disciples: 'A new commandment I give to you, that you love one another.' The ceremonial washing of the feet is still observed in the Roman Catholic Church. It was formerly carried out by English monarchs, James II having been the last to do it personally, according to tradition, though Samuel Pepys noted in his diary on April 4th, 1667, that 'the King [Charles II] did not wash the poor people's feet himself, but the Bishop of London did it for him.' Queen Elizabeth II usually distributes Maundy money on this day to a number of aged and poor people, the number corresponding to her age. The money takes the form of specially struck silver coins.

Maybe Tuesday

A possibility envisaged by Peter de Vries, in his novel *The Tunnel of Love*.

> Another possible folk custom that occurred to me was something that would fall on a day known as Maybe Tuesday, a day nationally observed by building on the already emerging folklore of the quiz show. The quiz show would be reversed. Television crews in every city and town in the country would enter homes and instead of giving away money or gifts for questions answered correctly would take away some article of furniture or other possession for everyone that was not.

Mr de Vries saw this as a day-long ceremony which would continue until a family was completely stripped of their belongings. He explained the name as being inspired by the thought, 'maybe next time it would happen to you'.

May Day

May 1st. This is still an important day in the children's calendar, especially in rural areas. A blushing young girl is elected May Queen and presides over the day's festivities. These mostly imitate to a greater or lesser extent the celebrations of former times, when a great maypole stood on the village green, decorated with flowers, and everyone danced round it. In *Lark Rise to Candleford*, Flora Thompson says that this was still 'the greatest day of the year from the children's point of view', but she adds that 'the maypole and the May games and May dances in which whole parishes had joined had long been forgotten.' The children in Flora Thompson's time marked the day by preparing a huge May garland in the shape of a bell. A procession then carried the garland around the village.

Dickens has an essay on May Day in his *Sketches by Boz*. His general theme is summed up in his last line – 'How has May day decayed!' – but he also reminds us that the London chimney-sweeps, at the beginning of the nineteenth century, had made the day their own. Popular legend had it that a young sweep who had been stolen from his parents at an early age had been rediscovered by his mother on this day, and that she had instigated celebrations to mark the event. By the time Dickens came to write of the day, in 1836, these city revels had also sadly degenerated. It is possible that the Church quietly helped them on their way, since they were rather uncomfortable reminders of pagan festivals in honour of Spring. Certainly the minister in Mrs Gaskell's *Cousin Phillis*, perhaps based partly on her own father, dislikes the expression 'May-day'. His wife hastily revises the statement that her daughter was 'seventeen last May-day' to 'seventeen on the first day of May last'.

In the adult world May Day is associated with Socialism, not to say Communism. The May Day parade in Red Square, Moscow, is an awesome event, and there are those who celebrate LABOUR DAY on May 1st in Britain. For this reason there has been a movement recently among British Conservative members of parliament to abolish May Day, grafting an extra day's holiday instead onto the Late May Bank Holiday. *The Times* (May 19th, 1986) reported that three Tories had said the day should be retained, since 'its unfailingly foul weather is a poignant warning of socialism's grim austerities.' A Labour MP replied that the wet, miserable and cold weather is 'a true reflection of the miseries suffered by so many as a result of the policies of this Tory administration.' Neither side seems to have made anything of the fact that 'May-day' is an international distress call. This has nothing to do with any inherent qualities of the day itself, but is based on the loosely similar pronunciation of French *M'aidez!* 'Help me!' The American equivalent of BIG BANG DAY was also called May Day.

Mayoring Day

Often in May in Britain. The day on which the new mayor of a borough parades through the streets. Sometimes the day becomes **Mayor's Sunday** and includes a church service. Local customs, such as the distribution by the new mayor of pennies, also survive in some areas.

M-Day

The day on which the War Department orders active mobilization for war, according to *Webster's Dictionary*.

Meal Monday

The second Monday in February. This was formerly a holiday granted to students at St Andrews and Edinburgh universities. They were meant to go home and return with enough meal to last them to the end of the session. 'Meal' here means 'oatmeal'.

Mecklenburg Declaration of Independence Day

May 20th. An optional bank holiday in North Carolina. The declaration referred to was adopted on May 20th, 1775, and stated that the residents of Mecklenburg County were to be free of British rule. This preceded

the general Declaration of Independence by over a year.

Melancholy Day See BELAGCHOLLY DAY.

Melbourne Cup Day

The first Tuesday in November. Observed as a holiday in the Metropolitan area of Victoria in honour of the famous horse-race. In South Australia, in May, **Adelaide Cup Day** is celebrated. Southern Tasmania has the **Hobart Cup Day** on or near January 23rd, while Northern Tasmania has its **Launceston Cup Day** a month later.

Melbourne Show Day See HOBART REGATTA DAY.

Memorial Day

The last Monday in May; formerly May 30th and still observed by some American states on that date. This is the official name of the day that is more generally known as DECORATION DAY, when the graves of the war-dead are decorated. There is a poem by Cy Warman called 'Memorial Day'. A less reverent reference is made by Bernard Malamud, in *The Natural*: 'What a butchering we took from the Pirates in the first game and here we are six runs behind in this. It's Memorial Day, all right, but not for the soldiers.'

Meresdei See STERRENDEI.

Mettarë See STERRENDEI.

Michaelmas

September 29th. The feast day of St Michael, and of secular importance in being one of the QUARTER DAYS. Michaelmas was commonly used as a point of reference in the year. Shakespeare has two instances of such usage, one in *Henry IV, Part One*, II.iv, where Francis replies to a question about his age by saying: 'Let me see, about Michaelmas next I shall be—.' In *The Merry Wives of Windsor*, the servant Simple is asked for the Book of Riddles. He replies: 'Why, did you not lend it to Alice Shortcake upon

Allhallowmas last, a fortnight afore Michaelmas.' Oliver Goldsmith indicates in *The Vicar of Wakefield* that **Michaelmas Eve**, September 28th, was also considered to be special: 'Michaelmas Eve happening on the next day, we were invited to burn nuts and play tricks at neighbour Flamborough's.' Goldsmith describes an evening of family games, such as Hunt the Slipper, and refers to his 'honest neighbour's goose and dumplings'. It was traditional to eat goose at this time, an old saying insisting that 'if you eat goose on Michaelmas Day, you never want money all the year round'. Charles Churchill's poem 'The Months' contains the lines

September, when by custom (right divine), Geese are ordained to bleed at Michael's shrine.

Attempts have been made to link Queen Elizabeth I with goose-eating on this day, but the tradition probably arose because the geese happened to be ready for eating at this time of year.

Middleday See TAP DAY.

Mid-Lent Carnival
The middle Thursday of Lent, which was formerly celebrated as a day of relaxation from fasting.

Mid-Lent Sunday
The fourth Sunday in Lent, also known as MOTHERING SUNDAY, REFECTION SUNDAY, REFRESHMENT SUNDAY. An older form of the name was **Mid-Lenten Sunday**. It was the custom for servants to return home on this day and give presents to their parents, especially their mothers. This was known as 'mid-lenting', or 'mothering'.

Midsummer Day
June 24th. Frequently found as **Midsummer's Day**. It is also the feast day of St John the Baptist. In a different context it is one of the official QUARTER DAYS in England. Traces of the pagan festivals which occurred on the eve of this day are still found, bonfires being lit in certain areas. Perhaps for some

it is still the time 'when it is well known all kinds of ghosts, goblins and fairies become visible and walk abroad', as Washington Irving said. Shakespeare's audiences certainly believed this, and no doubt found his *A Midsummer Night's Dream* quite suitable. O. Henry followed this with a sentimental but enjoyable story *A Midsummer Knight's Dream*. In George Orwell's *Animal Farm* it is the anniversary of the Rebellion, to be observed by the firing of Mr Jones's gun.

Midsummer Eve is the day when girls can discover whether their sweethearts are true to them. They need only hang up in the house an orpine plant, otherwise known as Midsummer Men. If the leaves bend to the right, their lovers are faithful; if they bend to the left, they are not. Others say that two plants should be used, one nominated to be the girl's and the other her lover's. The plant that dies first will show which of them will be unfaithful. Some might think that such doings account for the phrase 'midsummer madness', alluded to by Shakespeare in *Twelfth Night*, III.iv. In fact it was previously thought that madness in dogs was brought on by midsummer heat.

Mid-week
An occasional synonym for WEDNESDAY or FOURTH DAY, in Quaker use. It parallels German *Mittwoch* 'Wednesday'.

Mind Day
An archaic term for the anniversary of a person's death, or for the day on which a person's death is commemorated by a requiem service. John Stow, in his *Survey of London*, writes:

Robert Chicheley, grocer, mayor of London 1422, appointed by his testament that on his mind day a competent dinner should be ordained for two thousand four hundred poor men, householders of this city, and every man to have twopence in money.

This day is also known as **Year Day**.

Mischief Night

November 4th. This is now the usual date for Mischief Night in the North of England. Children play pranks of a mostly good-humoured kind, though inevitably more serious hooliganism also occurs. The Opies comment that Mischief Night in the nineteenth century was always on April 30th. They are unable to account for the change in date. It seems likely that it was Mischief Night customs, exported to the US, which gave rise to DEVIL'S NIGHT in Michigan. Local English variations of the name include **Mischievous Night** and **Danger Night**.

Monday

The second day of the week. The word means 'day of the Moon', and in this sense is parallel to French *lundi* German *Montag*, etc. As the day when work is normally resumed after a day of rest, Monday does not have a good reputation. We speak of a Monday morning feeling, rather as ministers of the church in the nineteenth century spoke of feeling Mondayish, or said that they were suffering from Mondayishness. In the case of the clergymen, of course, it was the after-effects of the work done on Sunday that caused the illness, rather than the resumption of work. In the eighteenth and nineteenth centuries, when workmen often became intoxicated on Sunday, an enforced holiday on Monday was sometimes necessary. This was humorously referred to as 'keeping St Monday'. Maria Edgeworth associated this custom especially with Irish shoemakers, but she may have had in mind the expression SHOEMAKER'S HOLIDAY.

One of the most remarkable achievements of Eleanor H. Porter's Pollyanna, who was glad no matter what, was to find a reason to be glad that it was Monday. As Nancy, the kitchen maid, explained:

'I know it does sound nutty, ma'am. But let me tell ye. That blessed lamb found out I hated Monday mornin's somethin' awful; an' what does she up an' tell me one day but this: 'Well, anyhow, Nancy,

I should think you could be gladder on Monday mornin' than on any other day in the week, because 'twould be a whole *week* before you'd have another one'. An' I'm blest if I hain't thought of it ev'ry Monday mornin' since – an' it *has* helped, ma'am.'

In a letter to *The Times* (March 20th, 1987) Dr Magnus Pyke proposed 'that Monday, never a particularly popular day, be abolished.' He pointed out that the resulting six-day weeks would provide nine more Saturdays for sports activities each year, and nine more Sundays for worship. The idea does not seem to have been taken very seriously. See also BLACK MONDAY, BLOODY MONDAY, COBBLERS' MONDAY, COLLOP MONDAY, EASTER MONDAY, HANDSEL MONDAY, MEAL MONDAY, PARSON'S HOLIDAY, PLOUGH MONDAY.

Monday First

In Northern English dialects, 'next Monday', 'Monday following'. Similarly **Tuesday First**, **Wednesday First**, **Sabbath First**, etc.

Monendei See STERRENDEI.

Money Day

A term in Liverpool for the day on which the unemployment benefit cheque arrives, according to Robert Chesshyre in an *Observer* article, May 31st, 1987.

Moratorium Day

A day of peaceful protest against the American military involvement in Vietnam that was staged in mid-October, 1969. 'Moratorium' is from a Latin word that means 'to delay' and is used here in its sense of 'a suspension of activity'. John Updike recorded the day for posterity in his novel *Rabbit Redux*:

They have passed a church, the big gray Presbyterian at Weiser and Park; on its steps cluster some women in overcoats, two young men with backwards collars, nuns and schoolchildren carrying signs and unlit candles protesting the war. This is Moratorium Day.

Updike records also the views of those who did not support the peace movement:

'I don't have much use for Tricky Dick and never have,' Pop is explaining, 'but the poor devil, he's trying to do the decent thing over there, get us out so the roof doesn't fall in until after we leave, and these queer preachers so shortsighted they can't see across the pulpit go organizing these parades that all they do is convince the little yellow Reds over there they're winning.'

Mothering Sunday

Mid-Lent Sunday. This is not the same as MOTHER'S DAY. Mothering Sunday was originally a day on which the Church laid emphasis on Mother Church. People were encouraged to return to the Church at which they had been baptized. This usually meant returning to the place where one's parents lived, and it was natural for those returning to take presents for their parents, especially their mothers. The traditional present was the simnel cake, a rich currant cake. Mrs Gaskell, in *My Lady Ludlow*, refers to another traditional dish:

We had plum porridge and mince-pies at Christmas, fritters and pancakes on Shrove Tuesday, furmenty on Mothering Sunday, violet cakes in Passion Week, tansy-pudding on Easter Sunday, three-cornered cakes on Trinity Sunday, and so on through the year.

'Furmenty' is a form of 'frumenty', from Latin *frumentum* 'corn'. The dish was made of wheat boiled in milk and seasoned with cinnamon, sugar, etc.

Mother-in-law Day

March 5th. An attempt to launch this day was made in Amarillo, Texas, in 1934. It was initiated by the editor of the local newspaper, who later reported that it had been observed by 'several families'. For some reason the idea of Mother-in-law

Day did not seem to catch the public's imagination.

Mother's Day

The second Sunday in May in the US; observed on the same day as MOTHERING SUNDAY in Britain. The Opies, in *The Lore and Language of Schoolchildren*, tell us that a Miss Anna Jarvis of Philadelphia, whose own mother died on May 9th, 1906, 'determined that a day should be set aside in the American calendar to honour motherhood.' By the use of what the Opies call 'emotional blackmail' Miss Jarvis had her way, and Mother's Day has been observed since 1913. It has also spawned FATHER'S DAY, and in some areas, GRANDPARENTS' DAY. Miss Jarvis was clearly unaware that MOTHERING SUNDAY already existed, and no-one seems to have pointed it out to her. Some commentators try to say that Mother's Day is American, while Mothering Sunday is British; however the former day is now regularly observed in Britain and the old customs associated with Mothering Sunday have unfortunately fallen into disuse.

Moving Day

May 1st. In the nineteenth century this was the usual day for changing one's place of residence in New York and Boston, since leases normally expired then.

Multitude's Idle Day

One of the alternative names for CHRISTMAS DAY used by the seventeenth-century Puritans, who did not approve of the celebrations.

Mumping Day

December 21st. The day on which the poor people in a parish would go mumping, i.e. calling at the houses of those who were better off, begging for corn and other provisions. The verb 'to mump' meant both 'to beg from a householder' and 'to cheat'. Those who went begging were colloquially said to be 'on the mump', and there were several other slang expressions of a similar kind. 'Mumper's brass' was money, a 'mumper's hall' was an ale-house. It is not clear whether the verb 'to mump' derived from a Dutch verb meaning 'to cheat', or whether it was ultimately imitative of the mumbling sound made by an inarticulate or toothless person. The *Oxford English Dictionary* identifies Mumping Day with ST THOMAS'S DAY, December 21st, on the authority of an early eighteenth-century writer who refers to the practice in Herefordshire. Eric Partridge, in his *Dictionary of Historical Slang*, equates it with BOXING DAY, December 26th.

Muster Day
The day on which troops are assembled in order to be inspected, introduced into service and counted. 'Muster' is ultimately derived from Latin *monstrare* 'to show'. Muster Days are held in New Hampshire in June each year. Sham battles take place between colonial regiments, and there are parades.

N

name day

The feast day of the saint whose name a person bears. In Roman Catholic countries this is often a day which is at least as important as a person's birthday. Royal name days in such countries may be celebrated as public holidays. 'We are straightforward people here,' says a character in Ivan Turgenev's *A Quiet Backwater*. 'Even on namedays we don't put on dress-coats to visit each other.'

Napoleon's Day See LUCKY DAY.

natal day

Used occasionally for 'birthday', especially in literary contexts: 'O, youth on whom the kindest ray/Has shed an influence from your natal day' (T. Cooke, 'Tales'). The expression is also used of a town's 'birthday'. At Dartmouth and Halifax, in Nova Scotia, such days have been celebrated with parades, fireworks and other attractions.

National Anti-Drugs Day

March 11th, 1987. A worthy day sponsored by students at King's College, London. It was meant to encourage students to offer help to friends who were drug abusers.

National Day

A day on which a country reminds itself of its national identity. Celebrated in many countries by this name, for example in Nigeria on October 1st and in Switzerland on August 1st.

National No Smoking Day

Such a day is now regularly observed in English-speaking countries, or is proclaimed, at least, by societies of non-smokers. It provides a yearly occasion for reminding everyone of the evils of smoking. In Britain National No Smoking Day was observed in 1987 on March 11th. ASH (Action on Smoking and Health) later claimed that 50,000 smokers gave up the habit permanently on that day. There was presumably a good reason for not observing the day a week earlier, on ASH WEDNESDAY, when it is traditional to give something up for Lent. Such timing would have appealed to punsters, but would perhaps have trivialized the serious intentions of the anti-smoking campaigners.

Nativity, The

Normally a reference to December 25th, and the birth of Jesus Christ. The term is also used of the Church festivals which commemorate the births of the Virgin Mary, on September 8th, and St John the Baptist, on June 24th. 'Nativity', like 'natural', 'native', 'nation', etc., derives from a Latin verb *nascor* 'to be born'.

Natural day See DAY.

Ne'erday
A Scottish form of NEW YEAR'S DAY.

Negro Day
Saturday. This now obsolete term was used in Jamaica in the nineteenth century. On Saturdays slaves were allowed to work their own provision grounds.

Nelson Day
It was Sir Arthur Conan Doyle who proposed that this day should be celebrated annually, but nothing came of the idea. Conan Doyle said in a letter to *The Times* that it would be more fitting to observe Lord Nelson's birthday, September 29th, as a day of commemoration rather than the anniversary of the Battle of Trafalgar, which was also the day of Nelson's death. In any case, Conan Doyle said, the name TRAFALGAR DAY 'must be offensive to our neighbours'.

Nettle Day
May 29th. A regional name for ROYAL OAK DAY, taking its name from the custom of stinging children with nettles, or pushing them into a nettle patch, if they failed to wear a sprig of oak on this day.

Nevada Day
October 31st. The anniversary of Nevada's admission to the American Union in 1864. See also ADMISSION DAY.

New Year's Day
January 1st. This has been the date of the New Year since 1600 in Scotland, 1752 in England. It was previously March 25th, LADY DAY. The year also began in March for the early Romans, which is why September, October, November and December are based on the Latin words *septem* 'seven', *octo* 'eight', *novem* 'nine' and *decem* 'ten'. In many countries, including Scotland, the New Year is celebrated with greater enthusiasm than is Christmas. The Scots appear to take the advice of Robert Burns, expressed in a poem written for New Year's Day, 1790: 'Let us

th' important *now* employ, And live as those who never die.' Nevertheless, Burns admitted in the same poem that the New Year was a time to be philosophical. Charles Lamb, in one of his *Essays of Elia*, says that 'no one ever regarded the First of January with indifference'. He describes the day as 'the nativity of our common Adam', everyone's second birthday, and goes on rather sadly to reflect upon time's passing. Lamb was writing his thoughts on New Year's Eve, 1820.

Sixteen years later Charles Dickens offered his thoughts on the season in one of his *Sketches by Boz*. He maintains an optimistic note for most of his essay, urging his readers to celebrate, but as the church bells announce the first moments of 1837, he also thinks of the passing of time:

> We measure man's life by years, and it is a solemn knell that warns us we have passed another of the landmarks which stand between us and the grave. Disguise it as we may, the reflection will force itself on our minds, that when the next bell announces the arrival of a new year, we may be insensible alike of the timely warning we have so often neglected, and of all the warm feelings that glow within us now.

New Year's Eve
December 31st. Known also in Scotland as HOGMANAY. A day which normally ends in festive gatherings, in public places such as Times Square or Trafalgar Square, in dance-halls and the like, or in the home, with everyone waiting to greet the New Year with a cheerful rendering of 'Auld Lang Syne'. The transition from one year to the next is traditionally marked by the ringing of church bells. Lord Tennyson, in his poem 'New Year's Eve', told them to

> Ring out the grief that saps the mind,
> For those that here we see no more;
> Ring out the feud of rich and poor,
> Ring in redress of all mankind.
> Ring out a slowly dying cause,
> And ancient forms of party strife;

Ring in the nobler modes of life,
With sweeter manners, purer laws.

Nickanan Night

A former name in Cornwall for the night of SHROVE TUESDAY. It was a time of licensed misbehaviour, such as rubbing sooty hands into someone's face, splashing them with water, etc. The origin of 'nickanan' is obscure.

Nine-Day

A Jamaican expression referring to the nine days of mourning after someone's death, ending with **Nine-Night**, a celebration which lays the ghost of the deceased. The practice presumably derives from the *novena* of the Roman Catholic Church, when special prayers are said for nine successive days. From the same source may come the expression 'a nine days' wonder', in common use since the end of the sixteenth century. Shakespeare alludes to it curiously in *Henry VI, Part Three*, III.ii:

King Edward	You'd think it strange if I should marry her.
Clarence	Why, Clarence, to myself.
Gloucester	That would be a ten days' wonder at the least
Clarence	That's a day longer than a wonder lasts.

Ninth of November, Ode for the

See LORD MAYOR'S DAY.

Nippy Lug Day

The Friday following SHROVE TUESDAY. A name used in Westmorland, where the children traditionally pinched each other's ears on this day. 'Nip' is used in its normal sense of 'pinch'. 'Lug' was originally the flap of a cap which covered the ear, but came to be used in Scotland and the North of England for the ear itself. Scottish teachers were sometimes known to their pupils in the nineteenth century as 'nip-lugs', because they pulled the ears of pupils who annoyed them.

Nones See CALENDS.

nowadays

At the present time. This expression was used by Chaucer in the late fourteenth century and has survived as a linguistic fossil. It reflects a time when 'a' was regularly used as a preposition meaning 'on' in an expression like 'He comes here a-Mondays'. 'A-days' was also used to contrast day-time with night-time. 'Nowadays' is written either as one word or with hyphens, as formerly: 'Lacqueys were never so saucy and pragmatical, as they are now-a-days' (Addison, *The Spectator* (1712)). The *Oxford English Dictionary* quotes a rare use of 'now-a-nights', but this did not come into general usage.

Nuptial Day

An occasional synonym for WEDDING DAY. The word ultimately links with Latin *nubere* 'to marry' and with 'nubile', which means 'marriageable'. In Shakespeare's *A Midsummer Night's Dream*, Puck reports to Oberon abut the 'rude mechanicals' who 'were met together to rehearse a play/ Intended for great Theseus' nuptial day' (III.ii).

Nut-crack Night

Also called CRACK-NUT NIGHT. A colloquial name for HALLOWE'EN, derived from the habit of baking nuts in the fire until they cracked apart.

Nut Monday

The first Monday in August, according to the *Oxford English Dictionary*. William Hone, in his *Every-Day Book*, mentions **Nutting Day** as September 14th. It seems likely that in different rural areas a day was granted to schoolchildren for the gathering of nuts whenever the nuts happened to be ripe. Hone has more to say about nut-gathering in the context of PLAY-DAY.

O

Oak Apple Day
May 29th. Another name for ROYAL OAK DAY or RESTORATION DAY. It takes its name from the sprig of oak-apples worn in commemoration of Charles II, who escaped his pursuers by hiding in an oak tree in September 1651. A dialectal variant of this name is **Oak Ball Day**.

Oatmeal Monday
A variant of MEAL MONDAY.

October the Twelfth
The anniversary of the Battle of the Cowshed in George Orwell's *Animal Farm*. Mr Jones's gun was to be fired on this day to mark the occasion.

off day
A day when usual standards are not maintained. To say that someone is having an off day implies that he could usually be expected to do a lot better, or be in a better mood. This modern meaning contrasts with the older meaning, which roughly corresponded with what we would now call a 'day off', a day away from one's usual work. 'Such horses as Queen's Crawley possessed went to plough, or ran in the Trafalgar Coach: and it was with a team of these very horses, on an off-day, that Miss Sharp was brought to the Hall' (William Thackeray, *Vanity Fair*). The *Manchester Guardian*

reported in 1897 that 'in future all such meetings be held on "off days" in preference to "market days".' The modern sense is presumably elliptical for 'off-form day'.

Offering Day
A day appointed by the Church for the payment of money to a curate by the parishioners. It is mentioned in the *Book of Common Prayer* (1548). 'Offerings' were not only given in religious homage. They were also defined in 1440 as 'presaunts to a lorde at Crystemasse, or other tymys'. Offering Day in the fifteenth century was therefore a kind of BOXING DAY in reverse.

Old Christmas Day
January 6th. In *Desperate Remedies*, by Thomas Hardy, a couple are discussing when they are to marry:

> 'Christmas Day, then,' he said. . . . 'I meant Old Christmas Day,' she said evasively. 'H'm, people do not usually attach that meaning to the words. . . . 'Tis a fortnight longer still, but never mind.'

References are sometimes found in literature to **Old Candlemas**, **Old Midsummer Day**, etc. All such names reflect the fact that England and Scotland changed in 1752 from the Julian calendar, introduced by Pope Gregory XIII in 1582. The Julian calendar was based on a year which was about eleven and a quarter minutes too long. By the sixteenth century the vernal equinox which had fallen on March 21st in the time of Julius Caesar was now occurring on March 11th. When England finally adopted the Gregorian calendar it was necessary to 'drop' eleven days. Accordingly, in 1752, September 2nd was followed by September 14th. That year, and in all subsequent years, Christmas Day arrived eleven days early. There were many ordinary people who found it very hard to accept that eleven days had disappeared, and in rural areas especially they continued to refer to the days by the Julian calendar, adding the word 'Old'. It is usual to indicate dates before 1752 as O.S. (Old Style) and dates after 1752 as N.S. (New Style). For those who tend to do things belatedly, or who wish to delay matters, as in Hardy's novel, a sudden return to the Julian calendar offers a wonderful excuse.

Old Hickory's Day
January 8th. See JACKSON DAY and BATTLE OF NEW ORLEANS DAY.

Old Home Day
A popular name in Pennsylvania for a day, usually in late August or early September, of civil celebration. There is usually a parade, an ox roasted in a public place, a talent contest, etc.

Old Man's Day
October 2nd at Braughing, Hertfordshire. The villagers who walk in procession to the churchyard on this day are commemorating a curious incident which occurred in the sixteenth century. A coffin which was being carried to the churchyard was dropped by its bearers, who slipped on dead leaves. The jolt revived the old man who was inside the coffin, who thus escaped being buried alive. He subsequently lived long enough to marry, and to leave bequests in his will to the parish in gratitude for his escape.

Old Midsummer Eve
July 4th. For the 'Old' reference, see OLD CHRISTMAS DAY. Thomas Hardy again comments on rural usage in *The Superstitious Man's Fancy*:

> Last night, being Old Midsummer Eve, some of us went to the Church porch, and didn't get home till near one. (On Midsummer Night it is believed hereabout that the faint shapes of all the folk in the parish who are going to be at death's door within the year can be seen entering the church. Those who get over their illness come out again after a while; those that are doomed to die do not return.)

Old Year's Day
December 31st. NEW YEAR'S EVE is also sometimes refered to as **Old Year's Night**.

One Day of the Year, The
The title of a play by Alan Seymour, published in 1960, about ANZAC DAY. The phrase is sometimes used as a synonym for that day.

Open Day
A day when an institution such as a school, college or hospital allows visitors into its premises to observe what takes place during a normal working day.

Orange Day
July 12th. Also known as **Orangemen's Day**, **The Twelfth**, **The Glorious Twelfth**. An annual commemoration of William III's victory over James II at the Battle of the Boyne in 1760. William, a Protestant, was William of Orange, the name of a French principality. James II was a Roman Catholic. The Orange Order was founded in 1795 with the aim of maintaining the Protestant Constitution. Orange Day sees parades of Orangemen throughout Northern Ireland, and elsewhere where there are communities of Irish Protestants.

Orange Wednesday
A novel by Leslie Thomas. It was described by the *Sunday Express* as having 'plenty of sex, violence and mystery, and the topicality

of a secret Great Power treaty to reunify Germany.'

Orientation Day

A day when newcomers to an organization, country, etc., have its ways of going about things explained to them. The London *Times*, for instance, reported on October 27th, 1986 on Orientation Day at the American Church in London. Bewildered Americans, temporarily working in England, were told about the English dislike of touching one another, or even standing too close to one another in order to speak. Mothers were given advice about how their children could mingle with locals, in spite of the fences which separate the houses. The general theme was that a shared language did not mean that there would be no problems in adjusting to life in another country.

Our Lady Day

The earlier name for LADY DAY.

Oyster Day

August 5th. This was ST JAMES'S DAY, Old Style. See also GROTTO DAY. There is an anonymous, and not very good, poem in William Hone's *Every-Day Book*, which begins:

> Green-grocers rise at dawn of sun –
> August the fifth – come haste away!
> To Billingsgate the thousands run –
> 'Tis Oyster Day! 'Tis Oyster Day!

The custom of making grottoes from the oyster shells is referred to later in the poem:

Poor creatures of the ocean's wave!
Born, fed, and fatted for our prey;
E'en boys, your shells when parted, crave,
Perspective for the 'Grotto Day'.
With watchful eye in many a band
The urchin weights at eve appear;
They raise their 'lights' with voice and hand
'A grotto comes but once a year'.

P

Pace Day

A Scottish form of PASCH DAY, or EASTER DAY. **Pace Monday** also occurs instead of EASTER MONDAY.

Pack Rag Day

May 1st, according to some sources, though others say it was September 29th, or MICHAELMAS. It was the day when hired labourers or servants changed farms or moved from one employer to another. They would have carried their clothes in a pack.

Palm Sunday

The Sunday before Easter Day. It commemorates the triumphant entry that Christ made into Jerusalem, when people 'took branches of palm trees and went out to meet him' (John 12:12). For the significance of the palms, see PALMY DAYS. The day has sometimes acquired a particular local meaning. In her *Life of Charlotte Brontë*, for instance, Mrs Gaskell remarks that 'the factory people from Birstall and Batley woollen mills' go to Lady Anne's Well on Palm Sunday. Lady Anne was supposedly eaten by wolves as she sat at the well, and its waters thereafter had a remarkable medicinal quality. As for Palm Sunday, 'it is still believed that the waters assume a strange variety of colours at six o'clock in the morning on that day'.

In her novel *The Red and the Green*, Iris Murdoch makes some interesting remarks about Irish Catholics, on their way home after mass on this day,

> now parading about, more slowly, more confidently, carrying palms in their hands. For them it seemed, and for their sins, Christ was even now entering Jerusalem, and their demeanour exhibited already a satisfaction, even a possessiveness, which made the congregation of the Mariners' Church, trotting more soberly homeward with averted eyes, feel unreal and perfunctory, unconnected with the great events to honour which these arrogant strollers were almost casually decked.

In early dialect use, Palm Sunday was known as **Palmsun**, much as WHIT SUNDAY gave rise to Whitsun. This led to **Palmsun Even**, for the eve of Palm Sunday. From the custom of eating figs on Palm Sunday comes its alternative name, FIG SUNDAY.

palmy days

Days of triumph or success. The allusion is to the leaf or branch of the palm tree which was carried or worn in ancient times as a symbol of victory. 'To bear the palm' therefore meant 'to triumph'. In a more general sense, palmy days are associated with the days of one's youth, when one was most active, strong and good-looking.

Pan-American Day

April 14th. This is the anniversary of the founding of the Pan-American Union in 1890.

Pancake Day

A popular name for SHROVE TUESDAY. The custom of eating pancakes on this day dates from at least the sixteenth century. The bell that was rung at about eleven in the morning, calling people to confession, was also the signal for work to stop and festivities to begin. In many areas the bell was known as the Pancake Bell. It is still known by that name in Scarborough, where it is now rung at noon on Shrove Tuesday. It signals not only the time to fry pancakes, but to begin skipping on the foreshore – a curious custom kept up by thousands of local people. Another local custom that has survived is the Pancake Race at Olney, in Buckinghamshire. It is said that a housewife who was making pancakes suddenly heard the bells summoning her to church and dashed along the road with frying pan still in hand. That was in the fifteenth century. The race now takes place just before midday and lasts only about a minute, though it attracts great media attention. The housewives taking part in the race must wear an apron and headscarf, and must toss their pancakes three times during the sprint of just over four hundred yards. Since 1949 a similar race has been run in the town of Liberal, Kansas.

Papist's Massing Day

One of the insulting terms used for CHRISTMAS DAY by the Puritans of the seventeenth century.

Parson's Holiday

Monday, according to Jonathan Swift in his *Journal to Stella*. (A 'journal' was originally a day-book, from French *jour* 'day'. Similarly, the word 'diary' ultimately comes from Latin *dies* 'day'.) There was formerly an expression 'parson's week', which referred to thirteen days. It was the holiday taken by a parson who was excused duty on a given Sunday, beginning on the preceding Monday and ending on a Saturday.

Partridge Day

September 1st. A colloquial way of referring to the day on which it becomes legally permissible in England to shoot partridges. Occasionally, on the analogy of GROUSE DAY and ST GROUSE'S DAY, it becomes **St Partridge's Day**: 'What on earth brings you here, old fellow? Why aren't you in the stubbles celebrating St Partridge?' (Mrs Humphry Ward, *Robert Elsmere*).

Pasch Day

A Scottish and Northern English dialectal variant of EASTER DAY. Also applied sometimes to GOOD FRIDAY. 'Pasch' ultimately derives from a Hebrew word meaning 'the 'Passover'. 'Easter eggs' are similarly known as 'pasch eggs', 'pace eggs' or 'paste eggs'. 'Pasch' was formerly far more generally used for 'Easter', and was the name given to someone born at this season. The surnames Pash, Pashe, Paish, Pask, Paske, Pasque, Pascall, Paskell, Pasquill and Pascoe all derive from this source, as may some instances of Pace, Paice, Pays, Payze and Peace. The latter names become confused with Old French *pais* and Latin *pax* 'peace'. Gillian Edwards, in her *Hogmanay and Tiffany*, is convinced that **Peace Sunday** was sometimes used for Pasch Day.

Pascua Florida Day

Observed in Easter Week. *Pascua* is a Spanish word which literally means 'Passover', but it is applied colloquially to any church festival, such as Christmas or Easter, which extends over several days.

Passion Sunday

Traditionally, the Sunday before PALM SUNDAY, two weeks before EASTER DAY. It began the season known as Passion-tide, in which Christ's 'passion' is commemorated. 'Passion' here is from Latin *passionem* 'suffering', and refers to the sufferings of Christ on the Cross. The second part of Passion-tide, immediately preceding Easter, was known as Passion Week (also as Holy Week). This seems to have led to the assumption that Passion Sunday must be the Sunday which introduces Passion Week, namely Palm Sunday. Since 1970, according to John Silverlight in an *Observer* article (March 23rd, 1986), the Roman Catholic Church has indeed referred to Palm Sunday as Passion Sunday. This appears to leave the fifth Sunday in Lent stranded without a name, but fortunately there is an alternative available – **Judica Sunday**. This derives from the opening words in Latin of the Introit for the day: *Judica me, Deus* 'Vindicate me, O God'. There is also a reference in a Worcestershire document of 1603 to **Patient Sunday**, where probably Passion Sunday is meant. 'Patient' ultimately derives from the same word as 'passion' and had the original meaning of 'able to suffer without complaint'.

Pat Casey Day
Early October. Celebrated in Central City, Colorado, in honour of the Irish miners of the past. There is a parade, an Irish stew dinner, Irish folk dances and so on.

Patient Sunday See PASSION SUNDAY.

Patrickmas Day
March 17th. More usually known as ST PATRICK'S DAY, but in the *Life of Charlotte Brontë* Elizabeth Gaskell remarks that the writer's father, the Reverend Patrick Brontë, 'was born on Patrickmas day, 1777.'

Patriots' Day
The third Monday in April. Observed in the states of Maine and Massachusetts in commemoration of those who fought at the Battles of Lexington and Concord in 1775. These two battles took place on April 19th, and marked the first bloodshed of the American Revolution.

Patron Day
The feast day of a patron saint, especially in Ireland. See also PATTERN DAY.

Pattern Day
The festival of a patron saint's day in Ireland. The word 'pattern' was transferred to the festivities, especially the dancing, that occurred on such a day. By the late nineteenth century, 'pattern' was being used of a dance on any occasion. 'Pattern' and 'patron' derive from the same word, French *patron*, itself ultimately derived from Latin *pater* 'father'. The 'patron' was originally someone who acted like a father, affording protection. A father was also supposed to offer a 'pattern', an example meant to be copied.

Paul Pitcher Day
January 24th. The eve of ST PAUL'S DAY, celebrated formerly by the Cornish tin-miners by setting up a pitcher in a public place, then throwing stones at it in order to destroy it. The miners would then buy a replacement pitcher and fill it with beer. This would be replenished throughout the day as the miners drank from it. Tony Deane and Tony Shaw, in *The Folk-Lore of Cornwall*, see in all this a rebellion against the rule that only water was to be drunk during working-time. They also make the point that the miners worked in extremely hazardous conditions, and that they understandably invented reasons for celebrations and holidays.

Pay Day
The regular weekly or monthly day on which wages, or other payments, are due to be made. The *Christian World* was glad to report a remark by Lord Bramwell in 1884, to the effect that 'Saturday was pay-day, drink-day and crime-day'. The short story *Savannah River Payday*, by Erskine Caldwell, is certainly concerned with drinking and criminal activities to a horrifying degree. There is an altogether gentler account of pay day in *Village School*, by 'Miss Read'. 'The last day of the month has a beauty of its own, for it is pay-day.' Cheques for the school-staff arrive on this day, which the schoolmistress distributes. There is a humorous account of the ways in which they

remind her of what day it is, though inevitably they have 'forgotten all about it being pay-day'. One of the early Chaplin films was also called *Pay Day*.

Peace Day
A day celebrating the Treaty of Versailles (1919), which embodied the result of the Paris Peace Conference. There is a fine personal recollection of the day in *Cider with Rosie*, by Laurie Lee:

> The first big festival I can remember was Peace Day in 1919. It was a day of magical transformation, of tears and dusty sunlight, of bands, processions, and buns by the cartload; and I was so young I thought it normal.

Peace Sunday See PASCH DAY.

Penn Day See PROCLAMATION DAYS.

Pentecost
A name used for the Jewish holiday Shabuoth and for the Christian WHIT SUNDAY. 'Pentecost' literally means 'fiftieth (day or feast)'. Julia, in *The Two Gentlemen of Verona*, refers to 'Pentecost,/When all our pageants of delight were play'd', and Shakespeare uses the word in other plays, though he does also make references to Whitsun.

Perfect Day
In *The Plague and I*, by Betty Macdonald, this is the instant nickname given to any woman in the hospital ward who is seen embroidering 'When you come to the end of a perfect day' in bright orange yarn on a maroon velvet pillow. The words of the sentimental song were by Carrie Jacobs Bond (1862–1946).

Picnic Day
The first Monday in August. A holiday in the Northern Territory of Australia. When the word 'picnic' was introduced into English in the eighteenth century, it was often in its French form *pique-nique* and was clearly a borrowing from that language. The

basic meaning was that one 'picked' up some food, then picked up some more. A 'pick-pick' would actually be a more accurate rendering of the French original.

Pig Face Sunday
The Sunday after September 14th at Avening, Gloucestershire. Pork-chop ('pig-face') sandwiches are served in the parish hall and local pubs on this day. It is said that a particularly troublesome wild boar was slain in times past around this time, and that the pork-eating commemorates the fact. At least one other equally vague 'explanation' is related, but no doubt the pleasantness of the sandwiches themselves and the curiosity of the day name are a good substitute for accurate history.

Pinkster Day
Another name for WHIT SUNDAY or PENTECOST. The word derives from a Dutch form of 'Pentecost'.

Pioneer Day
In Idaho, where this day is also known as Idaho Day, the anniversary of the founding of the first white settlement on June 15th, 1860, has been a legal holiday since 1911. In Utah, Pioneer Day is also a legal holiday, celebrated on July 24th. It commemorates the arrival in 1847 of Brigham Young and his followers at the site of what is now Salt Lake City. South Dakota also celebrates a Pioneers Day each October.

Plague Sunday
The last Sunday in August at Eyam, Derbyshire. In 1665–66 the vicar and villagers here voluntarily shut themselves off from the rest of the world in order to avoid spreading the plague. Of the population of 350 people at the time, 260 died.

Play-day
A day exempted from work, a school holiday. An eighteenth-century sermon made the point that 'the soul's play-day is always the devil's working-day'. Writing in 1768, John Wesley said: 'We have no play-

days (the school being taught every day in the year but Sundays).' William Hone, in *The Every-Day Book* (1827) writes:

It appears, from a curious manuscript relating to Eton school, that in the month of September, 'on a certain day', most probably the fourteenth, the scholars there were to have a play-day, in order to go out and gather nuts, a portion of which, when they returned, they were to make presents of to the different masters.

Plot Night

November 5th. An occasional synonym for GUY FAWKES DAY, rare in modern use.

Plough Monday

Also **Plow Monday**. The first Monday after the EPIPHANY, or TWELFTH NIGHT. It marked the commencement of the ploughing season after the Christmas holidays, though on the Monday itself ploughmen and village boys would draw a plough through the village, accompanied by dancers and musicians. Money was collected, originally for a 'plough-light' which would be kept burning in the parish church throughout the year. When this custom was suppressed the money was used instead for eating and drinking. The custom of blessing the plough on this day is still maintained in some areas.

Pocket-money day

Saturday, according to Charles Dickens, in *Nicholas Nickleby*. In the first chapter there is a description of Ralph Nickleby's activities at school, when he lends money to other boys, 'his simple rule of interest being all comprised, in the one golden sentence, 'two-pence for every halfpenny'.' Ralph has another general rule, 'that all sums of principal and interest should be paid on pocket-money day, that is to say, on Saturday.'

Polling Day

A day on which votes are cast at an election. 'Polling' refers to the counting of heads, the basic meaning of 'poll' being 'head'. To poll a person or animal is to crop the hair very

short; to poll a tree or plant is to cut off its head.

Pope Day

November 5th. This was an alternative name for GUY FAWKES DAY until the beginning of the twentieth century. The 'guy' was frequently an effigy of the pope, since a rising of English Roman Catholics was meant to follow the Gunpowder Plot, had it been successful.

Poppy Day

November 11th. Now observed on the second Sunday in November and officially known as REMEMBRANCE DAY or REMEMBRANCE SUNDAY. The red poppies which are worn on this day are sold by the British Legion for the benefit of ex-servicemen. They recall the poppies which were growing in the fields of Flanders during World War I.

Presentation Day

An expression which means much the same as GRADUATION DAY or COMMENCEMENT, when degrees or diplomas are given to candidates. The 'presentation' refers not directly to the giving of the certificates, but to the presentation of the candidates themselves for admission to a degree. 'The next letter in the afternoon mail was from President T. Austin Bull of Kinnikinick, inviting him to be speaker at Presentation Day, in early May' (Sinclair Lewis, *Gideon Planish*).

Presentation day is also the day when prizes are presented in an educational institution. 'Just at the close of his school career,' Frank Harris writes of Oscar Wilde, 'he won the Carpenter Greek Testament Prize, and on presentation day was called up to the dais by Dr Steele'.

Presentation of Our Lord

February 2nd. Also known as **Presentation of Christ in the Temple**, PURIFICATION (OF THE VIRGIN MARY), CANDLEMAS DAY. By Jewish law a child was presented to God in the temple after the ritual purification of the mother, which lasted for forty days after the birth. The presentation of Christ is described in Luke 2:22–40.

Presidential Inauguration Day See INAUGURATION DAY.

Presidents Day
The third Monday in February. See LINCOLN'S BIRTHDAY and WASHINGTON'S BIRTHDAY. Those states which observe Presidents Day (Hawaii, Minnesota, Nebraska, Wisconsin and Wyoming in 1985) are combining these two days.

Press Day
The day on which journalists are admitted to an exhibition or other public event before it opens to the general public. However, Monica Dickens, in *My Turn to Make the Tea*, writes: 'So the week went round, with press day, Wednesday, coming round all too soon and catching you napping because you always thought you had plenty of time to write things up.' Here she is referring to the day on which a weekly newspaper is 'put to bed', or printed.

Primary Election Day
A day set aside for the members of a political party in a particular area to choose the party's candidates for political office, party officials and delegates to the party convention. In Pennsylvania it is a holiday which occurs in late May. 'Primary' is not used in Britain in the same sense.

Primrose Day
April 19th. Benjamin Disraeli, Earl of Beaconsfield, died on this day in 1881. Queen Victoria sent a wreath of primroses to his funeral, referring to them as his favourite flowers. In 1883 the Primrose League was formed. It aimed to support the principles of Conservatism which Disraeli had laid down. The League was at its most influential before World War I, but still has a large membership. In 1898 the *Westminster Gazette* commented: 'Although Sir George Birdwood has never publicly claimed any credit in that direction, we are, we believe,

not very wide of the mark in suggesting that he was the originator of "Primrose Day".'

Proclamation Day
December 28th. A holiday in South Australia, commemorating the foundation of that state. It is observed either on December 28th or the nearest Monday. The equivalent day in Western Australia is known as STATE FOUNDATION DAY.

Proclamation Days
Days devoted to a specific purpose or commemorating a special person or event, by public proclamation of a state governor. In 1913, for instance, the Governor of Missouri proclaimed that August 20th and 21st were **Good Road Days**. In the same year the Governor of Nebraska proclaimed a **State Fire Day**. October 27th, 1923, was **Penn Day** by order of the Governor of Pennsylvania. This no doubt made William Penn turn in his grave, since he was firmly opposed to naming anything after people. The state of Pennsylvania bore his name against his own wishes, and it was Penn who saw to it that streets were either named after trees and plants or received names like First Avenue. Days continue to be proclaimed. The London *Times* reported that President Reagan had signed a proclamation declaring March 20th, 1987, **Afghanistan Day**, to coincide with the Afghan New Year.

Provincial Anniversary
Celebrated in New Zealand at different times of the year in the different provinces. In 1985, for instance, it was observed as follows: January 21st – Wellington; January 28th – Auckland; February 4th – Nelson; March 11th – Taranaki; November 4th – Marlborough; December 1st – Chatham and Westland.

Publication Day
The day on which a book is officially published, or made available to the public; a book's birthday. Used also of the day on

which a weekly or monthly periodical is published.

Pulver Wednesday
An occasional name for ASH WEDNESDAY. Latin *pulver* means 'powder, dust'. The form **Pulvering Day** also occurs.

Punishment Day
The day on which punishment is meted out in an institution. There is a full description of a typical punishment day in *My Autobiography* by Charlie Chaplin. At the age of seven, Chaplin was at the Hanwell School for Orphans and Destitute Children, in west London. Punishment day was every Friday. Boys were laid across a desk with their feet strapped and were either caned or struck with a birch. Chaplin himself was on one occasion caned for setting fire to the lavatory, though all he had done was to go there soon after some other boys had lit pieces of paper on the stone floor. He pleaded guilty, nevertheless, because he had been told that the punishment was likely to be worse if one denied the offence. The seven-year-old Chaplin was duly caned in front of the whole school.

Punkie Night
The last Thursday in October. The children at Hinton St George, Somerset, keep up the tradition of touring the village with candles set in hollowed-out mangolds. It is these candle-lanterns which are the 'punkies', though the origin of the word is obscure. It may derive from 'pumpkin'.

Purification, The
February 2nd. More fully, the **Purification of the Virgin Mary**, now known as the PRESENTATION OF OUR LORD. 'Purification' here refers to the ritual cleansing of a woman after child-birth according to Jewish law. Thomas Hardy implies that references to the Purification were normal in rural soci-eties: 'We were talking about this very family, and 'twas only last Purification Day' (*Far From the Madding Crowd*). The Purific-ation flower is another name for the snowdrop.

Purim
A Jewish festival that is celebrated on the fourteenth day of Adar (in 1986 this fell on March 25th). This is the day of relaxation for Jewish families. As Leo Rosten says in *The Joys of Yiddish* 'it is the closest thing to the carnival in Jewish life'. 'Purim' means 'lots', a reference to the lots cast by a man called Haman to determine the day on which all the Jews in the Persian Empire should be massacred. Haman was prime minister of the empire, and demanded that everyone should bow to him. Everyone complied except Mordecai, the Jew. Haman, in revenge, obtained the king's consent to massacre all the Jews, the king not realizing that his own queen, Esther, was Jewish. Mordecai was Esther's uncle, and told her of Haman's plans. She in turn pleaded with her husband on behalf of her people. The king ordered Haman to be hanged, and decreed that Mordecai should occupy his position. The story is told in the Book of Esther, which is read in synagogues on the eve and morning of Purim. By long-standing tradition, children in the syna-gogue boo and jeer and make other noises every time Haman's name is mentioned during the reading. Purim is also a time for distributing charity to the poor and exchanging gifts of food with friends. A considerably less solemn description of Purim is to be found in Mordecai Richler's comic novel, *Joshua Then and Now*.

Putting-A-Brave-Face-On-It-Day   See
Introduction p. x.

Q

Quadragesima Sunday

The first Sunday in Lent. The name derives from the Latin word for 'fortieth' and refers to the forty days of the Lenten period.

Quarter Day

The four traditional quarter-days in England and Ireland are LADY DAY, MIDSUMMER DAY, MICHAELMAS and CHRISTMAS DAY. In Scotland the quarter-days are CANDLEMAS DAY, WHIT SUNDAY, LAMMAS DAY and MARTINMAS. On such days it was customary to take up the tenancy of a house, or to move out. Payments of rents and other charges also became due, hence the thought of the anonymous poet quoted by Hone in *The Every-Day Book*:

Relentless, undelaying quarter-day!
Cold, though in summer, cheerless, though in Spring,
In Winter, bleak; in Autumn, withering –
No *quarter* dost thou give, not for one day.

In 'Making a Night of it', one of the *Sketches by Boz*, Charles Dickens writes: 'The quarter day arrived at last – we say at last, because quarter days are as eccentric as comets; moving wonderfully quick when you have a good deal to pay, and marvellously slow when you have a little to receive.'

Quasimodo Sunday

The Sunday following EASTER DAY. It is also known as LOW SUNDAY and LOW EASTERDAY. 'Quasimodo' derives from the Latin form of the Introit which is said at mass on this day. The Introit begins: *Quasi modo geniti infantes* . . . ('As newborn babes . . .'). It was on this day that a child was found abandoned and named Quasimodo to commemorate the fact. He became the Hunchback of Notre Dame in Victor Hugo's novel.

Queen's Birthday See KING'S BIRTHDAY.

Queen's Day

November 17th. The anniversary of Queen Elizabeth I's accession to the throne in 1558. Observed as a holiday in government offices from 1570 until the nineteenth century. From the time of the Gunpowder Plot in 1605 it was marked by anti-papal demonstrations, which included the burning of the pope in effigy. This seems to have led to a later merging with GUY FAWKES' DAY. The day was also known as **Queen Elizabeth's Day**.

Quinquagesima Sunday

The Sunday before Lent, also known as **Shrove Sunday**. The name derives from the Latin word for 'fiftieth' and refers to the fifty days between this and EASTER DAY.

R

Race Day
The day on which a particular race, such as the Derby or Grand National, is to be run. The term is also applied to races other than those on the turf. The chapter called 'Racing Days' in Mark Twain's *Life on the Mississippi*, for instance, contains some excellent descriptions of boat races. Various race days lie behind the stories collected by Vincent Orchard and published as *Best Racing Stories*.

Racing Day See VOLTAIRE DAY.

rainy day
The figurative use of this expression, meaning 'a time of need', has been proverbial since the sixteenth century. There is a poem by Longfellow called 'The Rainy Day' which shows the poet in philosophical, if gloomy mood. The last verse is:

Be still, sad heart! and cease repining;
Behind the clouds is the sun still shining;
Thy fate is the common fate of all,
Into each life some rain must fall,
Some days must be dark and dreary.

Raisin Monday
Celebrated at St Andrews University, Scotland, in November. First year students at the university acquire a 'mother' and 'father' from amongst the senior students when they arrive. These student-parents help the newcomers during the first few weeks, showing them around, introducing them to other students and so on. On **Raisin Sunday** the student 'children' visit their academic mother for afternoon tea. In the evening they are taken out for a drink by their academic father. On Raisin Monday, when the first year students (known as bejants or bejantines) used to present their parents with a pound of raisins, but are now more likely to present them with a bottle of wine, the mothers 'dress' their children. Students find themselves dressed as anything from ducks to clowns, commercial products or buildings. On Raisin Monday morning they then pelt one another with flour, eggs and shaving foam. The frolics end at midday, and student volunteers clear up the mess in the quad. The first year students, having been eased through the first traumatic weeks of university life, are able to continue with their studies.

Ramadan
Normally this refers to the ninth month of the Muslim year, during which no food or drink may be taken between sunrise and sunset. Herman Melville uses the word in *Moby Dick* to refer to 'a day of fasting, humiliation and prayer . . . some sort of Lent', undertaken by Queequeg.

Reckoning Day See DAY OF RECKONING.

Recreation Day
The first Monday in November. Observed as a holiday each year in Northern Tasmania, Australia.

Red Friday
July 31st, 1925. A day of victory for British mine-workers. A major strike was averted by the announcement of government subsidies to support wages. The name was also applied to January 31st, 1919. On that day, to quote the obituary in *The Times* (May 9th, 1986) of Lord Shinwell, 'the authorities' panicky handling of a strike led to a clash with the police in the Glasgow streets'.

red-letter day
Originally a day marked in an ecclesiastical calendar in red letters, in order to give it prominence. The literal meaning is therefore 'a saint's day' or other important church festival. By the late eighteenth century the phrase had taken on its modern figurative meaning, 'an important, memorable, particularly happy day'. Coleridge wrote in 1811: 'To sit at the same table with Grattan, who would not think it a memorable honour, a red letter day in the almanac of his life?'

Refection Sunday
Another name for REFRESHMENT SUNDAY. 'Refection' is from a Latin word meaning 'to renew, to remake, to restore'.

Refreshment Sunday
The fourth Sunday in Lent, also called **Refection Sunday**. MID-LENT SUNDAY, MOTHERING SUNDAY. The Gospel for this day in the *Book of Common Prayer* describes the miraculous feeding of the five thousand.

Release Day See INTAKE DAY.

Relic Sunday
The third Sunday after MIDSUMMER DAY. On this Sunday, from at least the sixteenth century, the relics preserved in a church were specially venerated. 'Relics' here refers to parts of the body or clothing, or anything directly connected with the body or clothing, of a saint, martyr or other holy person. In early times such relics were thought to have miraculous healing powers.

Remembrance Day
November 11th. Formerly called ARMISTICE DAY. Now known as **Remembrance Sunday** and observed on the second Sunday of November. In the US it has become VETERANS DAY. There was a moving description in the London *Times* of the first observance of this day, in 1919. Nearly a million British soldiers died in World War I, and those who survived had their grief renewed as the great silence was observed for two minutes at eleven o'clock:

> The best tribute to the genuineness of the moments was to be seen in the bowed heads and streaming eyes of all too many men. And even those who kept the tears back cleared their throats, coughed, and seemed very uneasy when the traffic again began to move and hats were replaced.

Rent Day
The day on which rent becomes due to the owner of property or other items. 'Rent' in this sense is derived from a basic idea of 'rendering' money to someone in exchange for something. In London in the nineteenth century there was a *Rent-Day Tavern*. It is possible that the local rent-collector installed himself there.

Republic Day
May 31st. A public holiday in South Africa. The electorate voted by a narrow majority in 1960 for South Africa to become a republic. The Afrikaners mainly supported the idea while the English-speaking minority did not. South Africa left the British Commonwealth in 1961.

Repudiation Day
November 23rd. Commemorated in Frederick County, Maryland. The court

there repudiated the Stamp Act of 1765, when the English parliament attempted to make it necessary for all publications and legal documents to bear a stamp. The Act was repealed in 1766 after forceful protests.

Restday See TAP DAY.

Restoration Day
May 29th. Also called ROYAL OAK DAY, OAK APPLE DAY, etc. The reference is to the restoration of the monarchy in Britain, when Charles II came to the throne in 1660. This ended the Puritan Commonwealth, introduced in 1649.

Resurrection Day
This is sometimes used as a synonym for JUDGEMENT DAY, referring to the rising again of men at that time. 'Shall you cut her on the Resurrection Day?' asks a character in *Those Delightful Americans* by Sara Jeannette Duncan.

Revel Day
The day on which a parish festival or feast was celebrated. This was the term used in the south-west counties of England, where 'feast' or 'wakes' was used elsewhere. 'Revel' is ultimately from Latin *rebellare*, which also gave us the verb 'to rebel'. The latter word is based on the idea of making war again (Latin *bellum* 'war'), a noisy business. The change to 'revel', keeping this notion of tumult but also associating the word with celebration, occurred in French, where the word was thought to link with *réveillon* 'Christmas Eve or New Year's Eve dinner'.

Ringing Day
November 5th. Also any day when it is appointed that church bells should be rung. November 5th was at one time such a day by order of parliament, to mark the deliverance of the king and his government at the exposure of the Gunpowder Plot.

Robert E. Lee Day
January 19th. The celebrated Confederate general Robert Edward Lee was born on this day in 1807. He was a man of remarkable character and was idolized by the American South. He is one of the great American heroes, and it is perhaps surprising that so few states observe the anniversary of his birth as a holiday. In 1985 a day was devoted to him in Florida, Louisiana, Mississippi and North Carolina. In Alabama he shared the honours of a named day with Martin Luther King Jr, and Virginia celebrated **Lee-Jackson-King Day**. In Texas this day has become CONFEDERATE HEROES DAY,

Rock Day
January 7th. 'Rock' is another word for 'distaff', not connected with rock in the sense 'mass of stone'. See more at DISTAFF'S DAY.

Rogation Days
The Monday, Tuesday and Wednesday preceding ASCENSION DAY. Also known as GANG DAYS. **Rogation Sunday** is the Sunday which precedes Ascension Day. The word 'rogation' is from a Latin word meaning 'to ask', but it has the sense of 'supplication'. In the Roman Catholic Church the litany of the saints is chanted by priests and parishioners during a procession. The old custom was to carry garlands of milkworts at such times, hence the other name of the milkwort, the Rogation flower. 'From our seats in the choir,' writes Laurie Lee, in *Cider with Rosie*, 'we watched the year turn: Christmas, Easter and Whitsun, Rogation Sunday and prayers for rain, the Church following the plough very close.'

Roman Holiday
The famous allusion by Lord Byron in *Childe Harolde* to the death of a gladiator:

He reck'd not of the life he lost nor prize
But where his rude hut by the Danube lay,
There were his young barbarians all at play,

There was their Dacian mother – he, their sire,
Butcher'd to make a Roman holiday.

Rood Day

September 14th. Also known as HOLY ROOD DAY, HOLY CROSS DAY, **Exaltation of the (Holy) Cross**. Rood Day was also used at one time to refer to another church festival, the Invention of the Cross, May 3rd. 'Rood' refers to the wood of which the cross was made. It is connected with 'rod' in some of its senses.

Roodmas

Also **Roodsmas**, **Roodmas Day**. Variants of ROOD DAY, September 14th.

Roosevelt Day See FRANKLIN D. ROOSEVELT DAY.

Rope-yarn Sunday

Formerly, in nautical slang, this meant either a Sunday free of work or the half-day holiday usually granted on a Thursday. 'Rope-yarn' refers to one of the threads of a strand of rope.

Rose Bowl Day

January 1st. The Rose Bowl is a sports stadium at Pasadena, California, named for the Tournament of Roses celebrated since 1890. The tournament was inspired by the Battle of Flowers at Nice, in France. Since 1916 the winning teams of the major leagues of US college football have met for a post-season match. The occasion has become 'a great American spectacular', as Jack B. Ludwig has described it, one which manages to thrive in spite of intense commercial exploitation, parody and denigration. The British equivalent is CUP FINAL DAY.

Rose Day See ALEXANDRA ROSE DAY.

Rose Sunday

The fourth Sunday in Lent. The term is familiar to Roman Catholics, and derives from the custom of blessing the golden rose on this day. The golden rose is an ornament of wrought gold, imitating a spray of roses. After being blessed by the pope it was formerly sent each year to a person, or to a city or church which had given distinguished service to the Church. One was sent to Henry VIII, others to Napoleon III and Isabella II of Spain.

Rosh Hashanah

The Jewish New Year, observed on the first of Tishri (and by Orthodox and Conservative Jews on the second of Tishri as well). 'Rosh Hashanah' literally means 'beginning of the year' in Hebrew. In 1985 the Jewish New Year fell on September 16th and 17th. Since Jews believe that the New Year is a Day of Judgement, when God determines the future course of events for everyone, it tends to be a solemn festival rather than the boisterous celebration that occurs on the Christian New Year's Day. At the morning service the shofar is blown, and the Torah refers to the day as Yom Teruah, the Day of Blowing the Shofar. The blowing of the ram's horn trumpet proclaims God's mastery of the world and has various other symbolic meanings. In the prayers for the day, Rosh Hashanah is called Yom Hazikaron, the Day of Remembrance. It introduces a ten-day period of penance, the Yomim Noraim, or Days of Awe, which ends with Yom Kippur, the Day of Atonement. During this period the judgement which was written down on Rosh Hashanah may still be changed, it only becomes 'sealed' in the last moments of Yom Kippur. This point is marked once again by the blowing of the shofar – a single, long, plain sound.

The above description is, as it were, the official version of the story. In his satirical novel *Joshua Then and Now*, Mordecai Richler gives his own unique version:

'You know what these days are?'
'Cold.'
'No, no. Anybody knows that. If you're Jewish, but.'
'Colder.'

'Oh, very funny. Ha ha.'

'What then, Daddy?'

'These are the Days of Awe. Tomorrow is Rosh Hashonna, our new year, and like a week later it's Yom Kippur, when if you shit on anybody during the year you got a legal right to repent. And God forgives you.'

Rousseau Day See VOLTAIRE DAY.

Royal Oak Day

May 29th. Also known as RESTORATION DAY, OAK APPLE DAY, OAK BALL DAY, NETTLE DAY, YAK BOB DAY, BOBBY ACK DAY, SHICK-SHACK DAY. The local names reflect different traditions still observed by English children, especially in the northern counties. Those children who forget to wear an oak leaf or oak apple on this day are reminded of the omission by being pushed into a bed of nettles or otherwise punished. After his defeat in battle by the English Parliamentarians, Charles II hid in an oak tree to escape his pursuers in September, 1651. He was restored to the throne in 1660, much to the relief of most English people. Charles II was certainly one of the most popular English monarchs and is still remembered for many good deeds. The old soldiers at the Royal Hospital, Chelsea, parade in his honour on FOUNDER'S DAY, each of them wearing their sprig of oak leaves. Apart from the celebrations on the day itself, there is a reminder of the incident in the oak tree in nearly every English town or village, *The Royal Oak* being one of the commonest English pub names.

Roy Hobbs Day See *Introduction* p. x.

Rubenstein Day See *Introduction* p. x.

Rude Day A Scottish form of ROOD DAY.

S

Sabbaday

'Sabbaday for Sabbath day has reached the dignity of an archaism', writes H. L. Mencken in *The American Language*. The term certainly does not appear to be in modern use.

Sabbath Day

Originally the seventh day of the week, Saturday, the day of rest ordained by the Jewish religion. The word 'sabbath' is ultimately from a Hebrew word meaning 'to rest'. By the seventeenth century, 'Sabbath day' had also become synonymous for Sunday, the Lord's Day, the Christian day of rest. Shakespeare uses the word twice, once (in *The Merchant of Venice*) to signify the Jewish sabbath, once (in *Richard III*) to signify Sunday. The ancient Jews named the Sabbath, then numbered the other days in relation to it.

In modern times, the expression 'Sabbath day', like 'Lord's day', is often used by the Sabbatarians, those who would like to see Sunday observed very strictly as a day of rest. In 1836, Charles Dickens was moved by the attempts of Sir Andrew Agnew to introduce a Sabbath Bill in the House of Commons, to publish a pamphlet, entitled 'Sunday Under Three Heads', giving his views on the matter. He described what a typical Sunday would be like if the Sabbatarians had their way. The general tone of his argument can be judged by a short extract: 'The idea of making a man truly moral through the ministry of constables, and sincerely religious under the influence of penalties, is worthy of the mind which could form such a mass of monstrous absurdity as this bill is composed of.' He ends: 'The Sabbath was made for man, and not man to serve the sabbath.' In *My Lady Ludlow*, by Mrs Gaskell, occurs the following:

> He had kept calling Sunday the Sabbath: and, as her ladyship said, 'The Sabbath is the Sabbath, and that's one thing – it is Saturday; and if I keep it, I'm a Jew, which I'm not. And Sunday is Sunday; and that's another thing; and if I keep it, I'm a Christian, which I humbly trust I am.'

This is merely an indication of Lady Ludlow's character, not of general opinion. She is against change of any kind, but it is clear that those around her, including ministers of the Christian church, freely used 'Sabbath' for Sunday.

Sacrament Sunday

The Sunday on which Holy Communion could be received. Formerly, in Scotland, on only one or two occasions a year.

Sadie Hawkins Day

November 9th. A day of desperate crisis for bachelors, introduced by Al Capp into his *Li'l Abner* strip cartoon in 1938. On this day the maids and spinsters of Dogpatch could lawfully pursue the unmarried males. Any such man who was caught by a girl was obliged to marry her. In modern times it is normally a day on which a college dance is held, with the girls issuing invitations to the boys.

St Agnes' Eve

January 20th. Agnes was martyred early in the fourth century, when she was still only twelve or thirteen years old. She had refused to marry, having consecrated herself to Christ. She was subsequently made the patron saint of young virgins, and many superstitious beliefs arose about her. In particular it was thought that on the eve of her feast day (some sources say on the day itself, January 21st). young girls would dream of their husbands-to-be if 'ceremonies due they did aright', as John Keats expressed it. His poem 'The Eve of St Agnes' tells of Madeline, who dreams of her lover Porphyro and wakes to find him at her bedside: 'Into her dream he melted, as the rose/Blendeth its odour with the violet – /Solution sweet.' The couple then elope together. Lord Tennyson's poem 'St Agnes' Eve' describes a nun in her convent garden, thinking of the 'heavenly bridegroom' who awaits her.

St All-Fools Morn

April 1st. An eighteenth-century variant of APRIL FOOLS' DAY.

St Andrew's Day

November 30th. St Andrew is regarded as the patron saint of Scotland. Many Scots continue the custom of wearing a St Andrew's Cross on that day. It consists of blue and white ribands shaped like the letter X. The day was formerly also known as **St Andrew-Mass**. The day before, **St Andrew's Eve**, features in John Steinbeck's *Tortilla Flat*: 'This was the night when all buried treasure sent up a faint phosphorescent glow through the ground.' There is a full description of the superstition that ghosts return that evening to see that their buried treasure remains undisturbed.

St Anne's Day

July 26th. St Anne is traditionally the mother of the Virgin Mary, though nothing is known about her or her husband Joachim. For superstitious young ladies in former times, this was the day when one found a peasecod containing nine peas and put it on the floor near the front door. The written message 'Come in, my dear, and do not fear' had to accompany it. The first man to cross the threshold after that would become the girl's husband.

St Barnabas' Day

June 11th. Also known as BARNABY DAY, **Barnaby Bright**, **Long Barnaby** because it was considered, by Old Style reckoning, to be the longest day of the year. St Barnabas was a Cypriot Jew, mainly remembered for his close association with the work of St Paul. The saint's symbol is a rake, and his feast day traditionally marked the beginning of hay-making.

St Bartholomew's Day See BARTHOLOMEW DAY.

St Blaise's Day

February 3rd. St Blaise is thought to have been an Armenian bishop but little is known about him. Many miraculous deeds were attributed to him, including his saving from imminent death a boy who was choking on a fishbone. The Blessing of St Blaise asks for God's protection against afflictions of the throat. The saint was possibly tortured by having his flesh torn with the iron combs used in the wool trade. One of his emblems is such a comb, and he is the patron saint of wool-combers. His feast day was therefore much celebrated in towns connected with the woollen industry, the celebrations including the lighting of bonfires, a punning comment on his name. This certainly has nothing to do with blazing bonfires, but is something of a mystery. It has been linked with Latin *blaesus* 'deformed, stuttering' and with the name Basil, which means 'kingly'. Blaise is also found in various records at Blase, Blaze, Blazey, etc.

St Catherine's Day

November 25th. Catherine of Alexandria probably did not exist except in the imagination of an early writer, but the story of the wheel on which she was tortured is still remembered in the Catherine wheels of BONFIRE NIGHT. See CATHERN DAY, another name for the day, for customs related to it.

St Cecilia's Day

November 22nd. By tradition Cecilia was a Roman virgin from a noble family who was put to death for her Christian beliefs. She has been the patron saint of musicians since the sixteenth century, possibly because she is said to have sung to God in her heart. She is also credited with having invented the organ. A musical society was formed in London in 1683, especially for the celebration of St Cecilia's Day. A festival was held each year in Stationers' Hall at which a special ode was sung. In 1687, and again in 1697, John Dryden composed the ode. The second of these, 'Alexander's Feast', contains the well-known line: 'None but the brave deserves the fair'. Alexander Pope also wrote an ode in her honour, as did Thomas Hood. Hood acknowledges that

> O music! praises thou hast had,
> From Dryden and from Pope,
> For thy good notes, yet none I hope,
> But I, e'er praised the bad

and gives advice that modern musicians might find useful:

> Folks that are called the hardest names
> Are music's most respectables.
> Ev'ry woman, ev'ry man,
> Look as foreign as you can,
> Don't cut your hair, or wash your skin,
> Make ugly faces and begin.
> ('Ode for St Cecilia's Eve')

St Clement's Day

November 23rd. St Clement is said to have been a Roman who was converted to Christianity by St Peter or St Paul. He became Pope in the first century. His emblem is an anchor because he is reported to have been tied to an anchor and thrown into the sea. The story goes on to say that angels built a shrine for him beneath the waves. He is the patron saint of many different trades, and is the subject of many church dedications. One of these, via the traditional rhyme 'Oranges and lemons, say the bells of St Clement's', has led to his name becoming that of a popular drink, a mixture of orange and lemon juice in equal proportions. A letter in the British newspaper *The Independent* (November 1986) suggested that this fact could lead to St Clement's Day becoming an annual No Alcohol Day, following the model of NATIONAL NO SMOKING DAY.

St Crispin's Day

October 25th. The feast day of two brothers, Crispin and Crispinian, patron saints of shoe-makers and other workers in leather. It was on this day that the battle of Agincourt was fought in 1415, a fact that cannot escape readers of Shakespeare's *Henry* V. The day is variously referred to as Crispian, the feast of Crispian, St Crispian, Crispin's day, Crispin Crispian, St Crispin's day and the day of Crispin Crispianus. In a famous passage the king addresses his army before the battle:

> This day is call'd the feast of Crispian.
> He that outlives this day, and comes safe
> home,
> Will stand a tip-toe when this day is nam'd,
> And rouse him at the name of Crispian.
> He that shall live this day, and see old age,
> Will yearly on the vigil feast his
> neighbours,
> And say 'Tomorrow is Saint Crispian'.
> Then will he strip his sleeve and show his
> scars,
> And say 'These wounds I had on
> Crispian's day'.

The speech ends:

And gentlemen in England now a-bed
Shall think themselves accurs'd they were
not here,
And hold their manhoods cheap whiles any
speaks
That fought with us upon Saint Crispin's
day.

The association of the day with the battle is so strong that writers sometimes use 'St Crispin's Day' to mean 'a time of battle'. Leigh Howard's novel about World War II, for instance, is called *Crispin's Day*, and in *Joshua Then and Now*, by Mordecai Richler, there is the passing remark: 'When our St Crispin's Day came'. The context makes it clear that the sense is 'when it came to our turn to fight'.

St David's Day

March 1st. The patron saint of Wales was called Dewi. David is taken to be approximately the same name. He was an abbot-bishop of the sixth century, his principal monastery being at what is now called St David's, in Dyfed. The association of leeks with St David (and with Wales) is traditionally explained as a reference to a battle fought in the seventh century between Welshmen and Saxons. St David suggested that the Welsh wear a leek in their caps so that they might know one another. Until that time they had been in danger of killing their own men. Another explanation was offered by Drayton in his 'Polyolbion' (1612). He says 'that reverend British saint to contemplation lived, and did so truly fast',

As he did only drink what crystal Hodney
yields,
And fed upon the leeks he gathered in the
fields.
In memory of whom, in each revolving
year,
The Welshmen, on his day, that sacred
herb do wear'.

In a famous passage in Shakespeare's *Henry V*, IV.vii, Fluellen refers to the Black Prince and the Battle of Poitiers:

> if your Majesties is remembered of it, the Welshmen did good service in a garden where leeks did grow, wearing leeks in their Monmouth caps; which your Majesty knows to this hour is an honourable badge of the service; and I do believe your Majesty takes no scorn to wear the leek upon St Tavy's Day.

Earlier in the play (IV.i), Pistol says of Fluellen: 'Tell him I'll knock his leek about his pate Upon St Davy's Day.' He has cause to regret this, since Fluellen eventually makes him eat the leek.

St Distaff's Day See DISTAFF'S DAY.

St Felix's Day

In *The Eighth Day*, by Thornton Wilder, there is the passing remark that Félicité Marjolaine Depuy Lansing received her first name because 'she was born on St Felix's Day'. The problem with that is that nearly seventy different saints named Felix are mentioned in the Roman Martyrology. One of the best-known is Felix of Nola, who is commemorated on January 14th.

St Geoffrey's Day

Never. According to Eric Partridge, in his *Dictionary of Historical Slang*, the expression was in colloquial use between 1786 and 1850, though the *Oxford English Dictionary* cites an instance of 1665. The phrase presumably arose in the mistaken belief that St Geoffrey does not exist; in fact several saints bear this name. See also ST TIB'S EVE.

St George's Day

April 23rd. Little is known of St George, the patron saint of England, though many legends about him have come down to us, including his famous fight with the dragon in order to rescue a maiden. This story was actually a late addition by some fanciful writer, but does not necessarily mean that St George did not exist. He has been associated with England since the reign of Edward

III in the fourteenth century, and his name was commonly invoked in former times as a battle cry. Shakespeare reminds us of this on several occasions, notably in the speech by Henry V which begins 'Once more unto the breach, dear friends'. It ends: 'Cry 'God for Harry, England, and Saint George!' ' In *Henry VI*, *Part One*, I.i., Bedford refers to the bonfire he is to make in France 'To keep our great Saint George's feast withal'.

Edward III had founded the Order of the Knights of the Garter and put it under the patronage of St George. It was perhaps this which caused fashionable gentlemen to wear blue coats on St George's Day, in imitation of the blue mantle worn by the Knights. In modern times a rose is the equivalent token of the leek, shamrock or thistle that Englishmen can wear to mark their national day. But though the same day is traditionally that of SHAKESPEARE'S BIRTHDAY, it goes largely unnoticed. It is, however, a holiday in Newfoundland.

St Grouse's Day

August 12th. Also **Feast of St Grouse**. Ironical names for the TWELFTH or the GLORIOUS TWELFTH, when grouse-shooting officially begins.

St Hilary's Day

January 13th in the English calendar, January 14th for Roman Catholics. St Hilary was a French bishop and theologian of the fourth century. He gave his name to the 'Hilary term' at Oxford and Dublin, formerly also used to denote a term or session of the High Court of Justice in England. January 13th was proverbially said to be the coldest day of the year.

St Hugh's Holiday

An attempt is made in Thomas Dekker's *Shoemaker's Holiday* (1599) to make this an alternative name for SHROVE TUESDAY. The latter was a very special day in the calendar for London apprentices, including apprentice shoemakers. In Dekker's play a journeyman shoemaker named Firk says:

When the pancake bell rings, we are as free as my Lord Mayor; we may shut up our shops, and make holiday. I'll have it called St Hugh's Holiday'.

All   Agreed, agreed! St Hugh's Holiday!

Hodge And this shall continue for ever.

For more on the 'pancake bell', see PANCAKE DAY. The significance of St Hugh in this context is that according to legend he was befriended at one time by journeymen shoemakers and even became one himself. He is said to have described members of the profession as Gentlemen of the Gentle Craft. St Hugh had no worldly goods to give to others, but he bequeathed his bones to his friends, the shoemakers. After his death some of them are said to have used his bones to make a set of shoemaker's tools. This legend certainly led to the slang expression 'St Hugh's bones' being used until well into the mid-eighteenth century to describe shoemaker's tools. On the other hand, there is no evidence to suggest that Dekker managed to establish the expression St Hugh's Holiday as a synonym for Shrove Tuesday.

St James's Day

July 25th. For the customs relating to St James's Day, Old Style (August 5th) see GROTTO DAY and OYSTER DAY.

St John's Day

June 24th. The feast day of St John the Baptist is also MIDSUMMER DAY. Some of the pagan rites associated with Midsummer were transferred to **St John's Eve** or **St John's Night**; thus the traditional bonfires of these nights were called St John fires. In medieval and Tudor times there were great torchlight processions on St John's day. In a similar way villagers would go through the fields in procession to ensure a good harvest. Later they would leap across the embers of the bonfires in order to protect themselves from diseases, or ensure the arrival of children. Stow, in his *Survey of London*, remarks that on this day wealthy people would have tables outside their house and would offer food and drink to passers-by. The day would no doubt have been an important one no matter when St John was born, but his birth near the summer solstice made it convenient for old-established ceremonies to be linked with him. It was on St John's Day that Browning's Pied Piper of Hamlin led away the children because he had not been paid.

St Lambert's Day
September 17th. St Lambert was an eighth-century Flemish bishop and martyr. Shakespeare seems to have thought that reference to the saint would immediately inform his audience of the date that was meant. *Richard II* contains the lines:

Be ready, as your lives shall answer it,
At Coventry, upon Saint Lambert's day.
There shall your swords and lances
                                    arbitrate
The swelling difference of your settled hate
                                    (I.i)

The reference is to the dispute between Henry Bolingbroke, Duke of Hereford, and Thomas Mowbray, Duke of Norfolk. Bolingbroke later became Henry IV.

St Lubbock's Day
The August bank holiday in England, formerly the first Monday in the month. In some cases, when the term was being used at the end of the nineteenth century, the reference may be to any of the other bank holidays. The allusion is to Sir John Lubbock, who introduced an Act of Parliament in 1871 which made provision for bank holidays.

St Lucy's Day
December 13th. A virgin martyr of the fourth century, St Lucy was popularly invoked against diseases of the eye, probably because her name derived from Latin *lux* 'light'. It is on the Sunday following her feast day that one of the four Ember Weeks of the year begins (see GOLDEN FRIDAY). John Donne wrote a 'Nocturnal Upon St Lucie's Day', but for him this was December 21st, also the shortest day of the year. His poem therefore begins: ' 'Tis the year's midnight, and 'tis the day's, Lucie's who scarce seven hours herself unmasks'. St Lucy's Day is especially important in Sweden, and is commemorated by Americans of Swedish descent.

St Luke's Day
October 18th. This, according to tradition, is a lucky day for a maid to choose a husband. Maiden readers may also care to consider the following, from *Advice to Young Wenches* by Mother Bunch:

'On St Luke's Day, says Mother Bunch, take marigold flowers, a sprig of marjoram, thyme and a little wormwood; dry them before the fire, rub them to powder, then sift it through a fine piece of lawn, and simmer it over a slow fire, adding a small quantity of virgin honey and vinegar. Anoint yourself with this when you go to bed, saying the following lines three times:

St Luke, St Luke, be kind to me,
In dreams let me my true love see.'

St Luke is the patron saint of artists rather than unmarried girls. He is said to have painted a portrait of the Virgin Mary. It was this which caused D. G. Rossetti to write a poem in the saint's honour. It begins: 'Give honour unto Luke Evangelist; For he it was (the aged legends say) Who first taught Art to fold her hands and pray'.

St Mark's Day
April 25th. This was formerly an important fair day in the West of England. The previous evening, **St Mark's Eve**, was also an interesting date in the calendar for the superstitious, who were constantly attempting to divine the future. If a watch was kept on the church porch between eleven o'clock at night and one o'clock in the morning, it was said that the ghosts of those who were due to die in the ensuing year would be seen walking up the path and entering the church. Young ladies also believed that if they left a flower at the

church porch during the day and returned for it at midnight, they would see a wedding procession as they walked home, including the ghostly form of their future husband. One imagines that they also frequently met the less-than-ghostly forms of local young men, taking advantage of the situation.

St Martin's Day
November 11th. See MARTINMAS, the more usual term.

St Michael and All Angels' Day
September 29th. Normally referred to as MICHAELMAS.

St Monday See MONDAY.

St Nicholas's Day
December 6th. Little is known about this fourth-century bishop, though the many legends about him made him one of the most popular saints of the Christian world. He is the patron of children, sailors, merchants, pawnbrokers (who borrowed his emblem of three balls as a sign of their trade), and many others. In some European countries, such as Germany, presents are given to children on his feast day. In the English-speaking countries this custom is transferred to Christmas Eve, but the saint still gets the credit for delivering them. 'Santa Claus' is ultimately a form of 'St Nicholas', via a Dutch dialect form of the name, Sinte Klaas.

St Partridge's Day See PARTRIDGE DAY.

St Patrick's Day
March 17th. St Patrick lived in the fifth century and was responsible for converting many Irishmen to Christianity, though he was not Irish himself. He subsequently became the patron saint of the Irish, and his feast day is celebrated by Irishmen everywhere. The wearing of the shamrock on his day commemorates the saint's use of this plant to demonstrate the Trinity. There are passing references in literature to St Patrick's Day parades and the like, but the main literary reference occurs in Richard Brinsley Sheridan's play, first produced in 1775 and called *St Patrick's Day*. It is a farce in which an Irish lieutenant adopts various disguises as he attempts to win the hand of Lauretta.

St Paul's Day
January 25th. This was one of the days in the year when, according to folkloric tradition, it was possible to make a prediction about the weather for the coming year. If the sun shone on St Paul's Day, then it would be a good year. If there was rain or snow, the year would be an indifferent one. Mist during the day indicated that there would be a shortage of food during the year because the weather would destroy the crops. If there was thunder or a great wind on the day, then many people were doomed to die.

St Philibert's Day
August 20th. The nuts which ripened on or about this day became known in French as *noix de filbert*. The 'filbert' was borrowed into English and is now used for the nut of the cultivated hazel.

St Piran's Day
March 5th. Little or nothing is known about this saint, but he was regarded by the tin-miners of Cornwall as their patron saint. His feast day was therefore a time of celebration.

St Pumpkin's Day
Also **St Pompon's Day**. Derisive terms used by early churchmen for THANKSGIVING DAY, which the Puritans introduced as an alternative to CHRISTMAS. Pumpkin pie has been an important part of the Thanksgiving celebration since the seventeenth century. 'Pumpkin' itself is an altered form of 'pumpion', 'pompion', 'pompon'. Ultimately the derivation is from a Greek word meaning a large melon.

St Roch's Day

August 16th. The name of this saint is also found as Rock, Roche, Roque. He was a Frenchman who went on a pilgrimage to Rome in the fourteenth century. The plague began while he was there and he is said to have gone from place to place, healing those afflicted by miraculous means. He eventually became a victim of the plague himself, and was aided by a dog, normally shown with him when artists represent him. As the patron saint of those afflicted with the plague he was formerly far better known than he is today. His feast day usually coincided with the Harvest Home festival. In literature he has been celebrated to most effect by Gabriel Chevallier in *Clochemerle*, a book probably as popular in its English version as in the original French. The Clochemerle Fête takes place on St Roch's Day, and 'as this falls on 16th August, the day after the Feast of the Assumption, during the time when there is nothing to do but quietly await the ripening of the grapes, it is normally an occasion for several days of feasting and merriment.' Chevalier gives his own satirical version of St Roch's life.

Saint's Day

The day on which the anniversary of a particular saint is commemorated. Occasionally used for NAME DAY, as when Graham Greene writes, in *Our Man in Havana*:

> She attended Mass not only on Sundays and the special feasts of the church, but also on her saint's day. Milly was her home name: her given name was Seraphina – in Cuba 'a double of the second class'.

St Stephen's Day

December 26th. The Opies report in *The Lore and Language of Schoolchildren* that the custom of 'hunting the wren', formerly known in Wales, south-west England and the Isle of Man, is still practised in southern Ireland on this day. At one time a wren was killed, hung on a pole and carried around in procession. Everyone who gave money to help bury the wren was presented with a feather, which was considered to be lucky. In modern times Irish children blacken their faces and carry a decorated wren-bush which may, or may not, contain the body of a wren. Householders are asked to contribute money and usually pay up quickly to get noisy children off their doorsteps. The traditional rhymes chanted on the day all refer to St Stephen's Day rather than BOXING DAY, the normal term in England.

In Mary McCarthy's novel *The Group*, the day is also significant:

> The nativity had been accomplished. Glory be, on the Feast of St Stephen, the day after Christmas, Priss had been brought to bed with a seven-and-a-half pound son .... The child was to be called Stephen, after the first martyr.

It was on 'the feast of Stephen', as every English child knows, that good King Wencelas went out to perform his good deeds. The Christmas carol is less popular in North America.

St Swithin's Day

July 15th. This saint was a ninth-century English bishop. He is said to have wished to be buried in the churchyard so that 'the sweet rain of heaven might fall upon his grave'. When he was made a saint, some over-zealous monks decided to move his body inside the cathedral. It is said to have rained for forty days when they did this, occasioning the traditional belief that if it rains on St Swithin's Day it will rain for forty days. By contrast, is is said that if it is fair on St Swithin's Day, there will be no rain for forty days. Thomas Hood had his own inimitable comments to make on the Saint of the Soakers, as he described him in his 'Ode to St Swithin'. The day becomes 'the Jubilee of Show'rs', and the street scene is punningly captured:

A dripping Pauper crawls along the way,
The only willing out-of-doorer,

And says, or seems to say,
'Well, I am poor enough – but here's a
pourer'!

St Tavy's Day
March 1st. See ST DAVID'S DAY.

St Thomas's Day
December 21st. There are many saints of
this name but the reference here is to the
Apostle. The day is also referred to as
Thomastide, as the SHORTEST DAY because
it is the winter solstice, and in some areas
as DOLEING DAY because of the licensed
collection of alms. See also TOMMY DAY.

St Tib's Eve
Never. Sometimes explained as 'the eve of
the Day of Judgement' and said to be an
Irish expression. 'Tib' was a common pet
form of Isabel in the sixteenth century. In
The Bivouac, by William H. Maxwell, occurs
the passage: 'He would return and claim
her hand on 'Tib's Eve', an Irish festival
which is stated to occur 'neither before or
after Christmas'. This novel was published
in 1837, but the expression was already
glossed in Grose's *Dictionary of the Vulgar
Tongue* in 1785. See also ST GEOFFREY'S DAY.

St Valentine's Day
February 14th. It was anciently believed
that birds chose their mates on this day.
This practice was taken over by young
people, who would write the names of possible 'mates' on slips of paper and then draw
them by lot. The sweethearts selected in this
way could be changed a year later. By the
early nineteenth century the custom of
sending anonymous messages or cards to
those one admired was well established. An
English official commented in 1822 on the
extra postal sorters who were needed to cope
with the volume of mail on this day.
Towards the end of the nineteenth century
the cards and messages, according to a daily
newspaper report, had become rather more
satirical than sentimental in nature. Both
kinds of card continue to be sent – in some
cases one of each kind is sent by the same

person to the same recipient. The ano-
nymity is not always preserved, which is
a pity. The intriguing mystery of a truly
anonymous card can maintain a young
person in a state of excitement for a full
week. In recent years the sending of cards
has to some extent been replaced by the
placing of announcements in newspapers on
February 14th. Certain British newspapers
are suddenly invaded by pages of intimate
little messages between couples who conceal
their identities from the general public by
means of 'love names'. Thus Piglet assures
Bunny (the names are frequently drawn
from nursery tales) of his or her undying
affection, or Snookums tells Bogfrog that all
is forgiven.

All such amorous activity, absurd in
public though normal in private, has
nothing to do with the saint or saints whose
feast day happens to be observed on
February 14th. The day could presumably
have become St Maro's Day, since that saint
also is commemorated on this day, but
Valentine was rather better known. As
Valentine's Day it seems set to stay, though
we appear to have lost **St Valentine's Eve**,
or **Valentine's E'en** as it was known in
Scotland. It was formerly the custom to
have parties or otherwise celebrate the
approach of Valentine's Day. Of the many
literary references to the day, the essay by
Charles Lamb devoted to it is especially
worthy of note. He has many amusing
comments to make about 'the Immortal Go-
Between'. In Hardy's *Far From the Madding
Crowd*, the Valentine sent by Bathsheba
Everdene to Boldwood has important conse-
quences. In Trollope's *The Small House at
Allington*, Lilian Dale's ex-lover gets married
on this day, causing her some anguish.
Finally, there is a place in Texas which is
called Valentine, but for no very romantic
reason. The first train to arrive there
happened to do so on February 14th.

salad days
The days of youth, when one is inexperi-
enced, or 'green'. The phrase was used by
Shakespeare in *Antony and Cleopatra*. It is

Cleopatra who refers to 'My salad days,/ When I was green in judgement, cold in blood' (I.v). 'Green' had been used to mean 'immature' since the fourteenth century. *Salad Days* was the title of a highly successful musical in the 1960s.

San Jacinto Day

April 21st. A holiday observed in Texas. It commemorates the battle of San Jacinto, fought on the banks of that river some 17 miles south-east of Houston. It was this battle, fought on April 21st, 1836, which decided the Texan independence issue. The Texans under San Houston defeated a superior force of Mexicans under Santa Anna.

Santa Claus Day

'Next day, 25 December, was Santa Claus Day; no holiday in the department of Euthanasia, which was an essential service' (Evelyn Waugh, *Love Among the Ruins*).

Saturday

The seventh day of the week. The word half-translates the Latin *Saturni dies* 'day of the planet Saturn'. Thomas Burke celebrated a Saturday of his childhood in his essay 'An Uncle of a Day'.

> Saturday was the Day of my week, the day to which all other days pointed and led. It was not a white-stone day in the high key of Christmas, with all its coloured treasure; or of Easter, with its hot-cross buns and chocolate eggs; or the Fifth of November, with its night of golden rain. But it certainly was a day of mild carnival. For one thing, it was a holiday. For another, it was pocket-money day. And again it had a quality and colour and personality of its own – a Saturday quality, a Saturday personality, genial and expansive. It was an Uncle of a day where the other days were thin, querulous Aunts.

Mr Burke talks of the decisions he had to make on a particular Saturday, when he had five halfpence to spend, and goes on to describe Saturday Night, when most of the shops in the High Street stayed open until midnight. The essay was published in 1945, shortly after Mr Burke's death, and gives a vivid description of a Saturday in London fifty years earlier. See also BLACK SATURDAY, EGG SATURDAY, NEGRO DAY, POCKET-MONEY DAY, STRAW BEAR DAY.

Saturnalia

December 17th. In the religion of ancient Rome this was a festival in honour of Saturn, the Roman god of agriculture. It was the time when crops were sown, but also a time of unrestrained celebration, even for slaves. It is often said to have been the prototype, or origin, of the Christian Christmas celebrations. References to the Saturnalia in English literature occasionally have a figurative meaning, not necessarily indicating the December festivities but any period of high celebration. In his fine essay about childhood at the turn of the century, 'An Uncle of a Day', Thomas Burke cleverly linked the word with Saturday:

> I had no notion of saving part of my five halfpennies for Monday or Wednesday. Whatever my Saturday money, whether a halfpenny or a penny or even what it was on that rare occasion, my way was always to dash it in one Saturnalia.

Sauerkraut Day

Celebrated in mid-October in Wishek, North Dakota. The German heritage of many local inhabitants is recalled in music, food, etc. 'Sauerkraut' literally means 'sour cabbage' in German.

Seal Day

The day on which official papers receive the seal at a meeting of the State Council in Guernsey. There is a similar reference to a **Sealing Day** in *The Affair* by C. P. Snow. In that instance the sealing of a conveyance at the College is meant.

Second Day

Monday. An expression used by those people, such as Quakers, who wish to avoid the reference to moon-worship inherent in the word 'Monday'. It has a different meaning in the following sentence, which occurs in Thackeray's *Vanity Fair*: 'So she invites her father and sister to a second day's dinner (if those sides, or *ontrys*, as she calls 'em, weren't served yesterday, I'm d——d).' This appears to be nonce usage, rather than a normal expression, for 'leftovers'.

Secretaries' Day
April 24th. An attempt to launch this day was made in the 1970s (by secretaries, gift-shop owners, etc) but it does not appear to have become generally accepted.

Septuagesima Sunday
The third Sunday before Lent. The name refers to the 'seventieth day' before Easter, though this is not an accurate description of the day.

Settlement Day
Also known as **Settling Day**. See ACCOUNT DAY.

Settlers' Day
Formerly a public holiday in South Africa, usually in September. It commemorated the arrival in 1820 of British settlers.

Settling Day
The day on which accounts at the London Stock Exchange are due to be settled. Also known as **Settlement Day**. See ACCOUNT DAY.

Seventeenth of Ireland, The
A humorous reference to ST PATRICK'S DAY.

Seventh Day
Saturday. This term is used by the Society of Friends (Quakers). It is also used by the Seventh Day Adventists and the Seventh Day Baptists. The former adopted in 1846 the observance of their Sabbath from sunset on Friday to sunset on Saturday. The latter were also known as Traskites, John Trask having advocated the adoption by Christ-

ians of certain Jewish practices in the seventeenth century.

Seward's Day
March 30th. Observed on or near this day in Alaska. It commemorates William H. Seward (1801–72), who negotiated the purchase of Alaska from Russia. He signed the treaty on March 30th, 1867. This act was popularly known as Seward's Folly until gold was discovered in the territory. The day is loosely referred to in speech as **Seward Day**.

Sexagesima Sunday
The second Sunday before Lent. The name literally means 'sixtieth day' (before Easter), which is not an accurate description.

Shakespeare's Birthday
April 23rd. The date of Shakespeare's birth is not actually known for certain. He was baptized on April 26th. He certainly died on April 23rd, which also happens to be ST GEORGE'S DAY, and perhaps because it seems fitting to celebrate the birth of England's greatest dramatist on the feast day of England's patron saint, that has become the traditional day for commemorating his birth. The day is mainly celebrated in Stratford-upon-Avon, Shakespeare's birthplace, where there is a procession with music and dancing. Elsewhere the day is marked according to local enthusiasm and is not the national celebration which many think it should be.

Charles Dickens comments on this day in passing, while sniping as usual at his 'boyhood's home':

An Immortal Somebody was wanted in Dullborough [i.e. Rochester, Kent], to dimple for a day the stagnant face of the waters; he was rather wanted by Dullborough generally, and much wanted by the principal hotel-keeper. The County history was looked up for a locally Immortal Somebody, but the registered Dullborough worthies were all Nobodies.

In this state of things, it is hardly necessary to record that Dullborough did what every man does when he wants to write a book or deliver a lecture, and is provided with all the materials except a subject. It fell back upon Shakespeare. No sooner was it resolved to celebrate Shakespeare's birthday in Dullborough, than the popularity of the immortal bard became surprising. You might have supposed the first edition of his works to have been published last week, and enthusiastic Dullborough to have half got through them. (I doubt, by the way, whether it had ever done half that, but this is a private opinion).
('Birthday Celebrations', in *The Uncommercial Traveller*)

Sharp Tuesday

A local name in Somerset for SHROVE TUESDAY. The name is associated with the privilege claimed by boys to throw stones against people's front doors on this day. 'Sharp' may refer to the rapid departure from the scene which the boys need to make when enraged householders appear.

Shaving-Day

'Though it was shaving-day, head and beard, yet I was out early to see Lord Bolingbroke, and talk over affairs with him.' So wrote Jonathan Swift to Stella in March, 1712. She was used to hearing about his 'shaving-days' in letters; he mentioned them quite often. 'Although it was shaving-day, I walked to Chelsea, and was there by nine this morning' (July 14th, 1711).

Sheelah's Day

March 18th. The observance of this day, which follows ST PATRICK'S DAY, was reported by William Hone in the eighteenth century. It is by no means clear who 'Sheelah' was. Hone remarks that those who observe the day 'are not so anxious to determine who 'Sheelah' was, as they are earnest in her celebration.' Some claim that she was either the wife or the mother of St Patrick. 'All agree', Hone says, 'that her immortal memory is to be maintained by potations of whiskey.'

Sheer Thursday

Another name for MAUNDY THURSDAY, the day before GOOD FRIDAY. Also found as **Skire Thursday**. 'Sheer' in this context means 'bright, pure' and is thought to allude to the purification of the soul by confession. It was also the tradition to wash the altar on this day. An early folk-etymologist, however, explained the term as if it were Shear Thursday, the day on which men sheared their heads and beards in honour of the following day.

Sheffield Wednesday

The name of an English football club. This name originally distinguished it from Sheffield United, in the same city. Games were played on a Wednesday at that time. In modern times Sheffield Wednesday usually plays its games on Saturdays.

Shick-Shack Day

May 29th. This name appears in many different spellings, such as SHIK-SHAK DAY, SHICSACK DAY, SHITSACK DAY, SHIG-SHAG DAY, etc. The *Oxford English Dictionary* is no doubt right to suggest that 'Shit-sack' is the original form. This was used as a term of abuse for Nonconformists. It was applied on May 29th to anyone who did not wear an oak leaf or oak apple in memory of Charles II (see ROYAL OAK DAY). In some areas, the origin of the phrase having been forgotten, 'shick-shack' now means the sprig of oak itself.

Shilling Day

A day when a shilling was charged for admission to London Zoo in the 1880s. ' "Let's go to the Zoo," they had said to each other; "it'll be great fun!" It was a shilling day; and there would not be all those horrid common people.'
(John Galsworthy, *The Man of Property*)

shoemaker's holiday

A Monday taken as an unofficial holiday, especially because of excessive drinking on the Sunday. The phrase was used as the title of a play by Thomas Dekker, written in 1599 and first performed in 1600. One of the shoemaker apprentices in the play says at one point: 'Mum, here comes my dame and my master. She'll scold, on my life, for loitering this Monday; but all's one, let them all say what they can, Monday's our holiday.' One explanation that was offered for the habit of 'resting' on Mondays in the shoemaking profession was that all members of the gentle craft were keen to observe St Crispin's Day as a holiday. No-one was quite sure on which day his feast day occurred, though it was thought to be on a Monday. To be safe, the shoemakers decided to observe all Mondays as feast days. For another equally unlikely explanation see COBBLERS' MONDAY.

According to the *Oxford English Dictionary*, 'shoemaker's holiday' was occasionally used in a more general way to mean any day's holiday or outing in the country. In Dekker's play it could also be taken to mean SHROVE TUESDAY. This was a particular day of celebration for all London apprentices, including journeymen shoemakers. The last scenes of the play specifically take place on Shrove Tuesday.

Shortest Day

December 21st. The day of the winter solstice. John Donne equated it with ST LUCY'S DAY, whose feast day is on December 13th, New Style. His 'Nocturnal Upon St Lucie's Day' begins:

'Tis the year's midnight, and 'tis the day's,
Lucie's who scarce seven hours herself
                                    unmasks;
The Sun is spent, and now his flasks
Send forth light squibs, no constant rays;
The whole world's sap is sunk.

The Pilgrim Fathers landed in New England on this day in 1620.

Shrove Tuesday

The Tuesday immediately preceding ASH WEDNESDAY. It is popularly known as PANCAKE DAY, pancakes being the traditional dish of the day. At one time apple fritters were also eaten, and the day was associated with cock-fighting and various ball games. Shrove Tuesday is one of the three days of Shrove-tide, the other two days being **Shrove Sunday** and **Shrove Monday**, which come before it. 'Shrove' refers to the practice of being shriven, that is, going to confession and doing penance for one's sins. In Shakespeare's *All's Well that Ends Well*, II.ii we find:

Countess Will your answer serve fit to all questions?
Clown As fit as ten groats is for the hand of an attorney, as your French crown for your taffety punk, as Tib's rush for Tom's forefinger, as a pancake for Shrove Tuesday, a morris for Mayday, as the nail to his hole, the cuckold to his horn, as a scolding quean to a wrangling knave, as the nun's lip to the friar's mouth; nay, as the pudding to the skin.

Shuttlecock Day

Another name for SHROVE TUESDAY in Leicester and parts of Yorkshire in former times, because the game of battledore and shuttlecock was traditionally played in the streets on this day.

Sidereal day See DAY.

Silent Days

The last three days of Holy Week, when church bells remain silent. In Old English they were known as the Swidages, from a word meaning 'to be silent'.

Silver Jubilee

The twenty-fifth anniversary of a particular event, such as a monarch's accession to the throne. In *South Riding*, by Winifred Holtby, there is a comment on the Silver Jubilee celebrations which occurred on May 6th, 1935, marking twenty-five years of the reign of George V. It was 'an opportunity for a general beano, a moment of sunlight between storms . . . a demonstration of national unity – of common fortune.' In 1935 'Silver Jubilee' also became the name of a train service between London and Newcastle, hauled by the first streamlined locomotives to be seen in Britain. The latter had an exterior finish of silver-grey and bore appropriate names — *Silver Link*, *Quicksilver*, *Silver King* and *Silver Fox*. A rose was also named 'Silver Jubilee' to commemorate the event. See also JUBILEE.

Simnel Sunday

Another name for MID-LENT SUNDAY or MOTHERING SUNDAY. The name derives from the rich currant cake which it was once the custom to eat on this day. 'Simnel' itself is from a French word that ultimately derives from Latin *simila* 'fine flour'. The seventeenth-century poet Robert Herrick wrote:

> I'll to thee a simnel bring,
> 'Gainst thou go'st a-mothering;
> So that if she blesseth thee,
> Half that blessing thou'lt give me.

Sixth Day

Friday. A term that avoids the pagan reference to the goddess Frigg, or Freya, in the word 'Friday', and is consequently favoured by the Society of Friends (Quakers).

Sixth of June, The

A novel by Lionel Shapiro about World War II. June 6th, 1944 was D-DAY.

Skire Thursday

An obsolete alternative form of SHEER THURSDAY.

Solar day See DAY.

Soma-holiday

A drug-induced 'trip' described by Aldous Huxley in his *Brave New World* (1932).

Lenina felt herself entitled, after this day of queerness and horror, to a complete and absolute holiday. As soon as they got back to the rest-house, she swallowed six half-gramme tablets of *soma*, lay down on her bed, and within ten minutes had embarked for lunar eternity.

'Miss Crowne's gone on *soma*-holiday,' says one of her friends. 'Soma' looks like a jokey link with 'summer', but there is a soma plant which yields a juice, from which a highly intoxicating drink is made. This plays an important part in Vedic religious rituals.

Someday

An unspecified day in the future; the optimist's favourite day.

Song days

Popular songs sometimes focus on a particular day of the week. Monday recalls 'Monday Monday', first heard in 1966 and revived in 1971, the theme song of The Mamas and Papas. 'I Don't Like Mondays' was a success for the Boomtown Rats, as was 'Manic Monday' for the Bangles. Monday gets rather a bad press where songwriters are concerned: 'Rainy Days and Mondays' (1971) and 'Blue Monday' (1957) are other typical references. Saturday is a day of celebration, by contrast, and in 1919 a popular song in the US mournfully anticipated Prohibition: 'What'll We Do on a Saturday Night When the Town Goes Dry?'. 'Juke Box Saturday Night' (1942) was a foretaste of the later 'Saturday Night Fever'. For those without a partner, however, 'Saturday Night is the Loneliest Night of the Week' (1944). The mid-week days attract little attention, but see also GLOOMY SUNDAY.

Sovereign's Official Birthday

The second Saturday in June, though it can be moved to the first or third Saturday in June if the British sovereign has other commitments. The idea of an 'official' birthday was introduced by Queen Victoria, whose own birthday was May 24th. She preferred to celebrate this quietly. A day in June was therefore chosen for a more public celebration. The custom was continued by Edward VII, whose real birthday was November 9th. When George V came to the throne it was possible for his real birthday, June 3rd, to be used for both private and public celebrations. George VI was born on December 14th, and a summer 'official' birthday once again became desirable. Queen Elizabeth II was born on April 21st, 1926. In June she presides at the Trooping the Colour ceremony. The June date for the official celebration of the sovereign's birthday was chosen simply because the weather was more likely to be favourable at that time.

Speech Day

The day, normally at the end of the school-year, when prizes are distributed for high achievement in academic work or sport. The occasion is usually marked by at least one speech from a guest speaker. At public schools it is a day when parental visits are made. In Thackeray's *Vanity Fair* Mr Osborne thinks back on the schooldays of his son, on the evening that he removes his name from the family bible: 'Anything that money could buy had been his son's. He used to go down on speech-days with four horses and new liveries, and scatter new shillings among the boys at the school where George was.'

Spinning Wheels Day

Late July. Celebrated at Warminster Heights, Pennsylvania. The main feature of the day is a parade for people of all ages in or on any kind of wheeled vehicle.

Sports Day

A day near the end of the school year, in summer, set aside for sports events, both serious and light-hearted. The Sports Day described in *Village School*, by 'Miss Read', for instance, describes such activities as a sack race, potato race and flower-pot race. There is also an unscheduled 'chase the goat' race when one appears. In *Scenes from Provincial Life*, by William Cooper, the main Sports Day prize is stolen before it can be awarded. V. S. Naipaul also explores the significance of Sports Day in his novel *The Mimic Men*.

Sprat Day

November 9th. Henry Mayhew, in *London Labour and the London Poor*, writes: 'Sprats . . . are generally introduced about the 9th November. Indeed, 'Lord Mayor's Day' is sometimes called "sprat day".' The sprat is a fish like a herring, only much smaller. It has never been held in high esteem. Shakespeare, for instance, uses the word only once, as a term of contempt for a small person in *All's Well that Ends Well*.

Spy Wednesday

The Wednesday before EASTER DAY. The term is said to be Irish, and alludes to Judas, though he is never described in Matthew 26 as a 'spy'. 'She spakes like a French spy', says a character in Samuel Lover's *Handy Andy*, 'and she was missin', I remember, all last Spy Wednesday.'

State Foundation Day

June 1st. A holiday in Western Australia commemorating the foundation of that state.

Statehood Day

A variant of ADMISSION DAY, used especially in Kentucky and Tennessee. **State Day** is also found.

Stepfather's Day See DOTTY DAY.

Sterrendei

In the mythological works of J. R. R. Tolkien, this was the first day of the week for the Hobbits. Its later form was **Sterday**, and it was the equivalent of Saturday. It was followed by **Sunnendei**, **Monendei**, **Trewesdei** (later **Trewsday**), **Hevenesdei** (later **Hevensday**, **Hensday**), **Meresdei**, **Highdei**. The last-named, the equivalent of Friday, was the most important day of the week for the Hobbits. Elsewhere in

Tolkien's works the days are referred to by other names, such as Elenya, Anarya, Isilya, Aldúya, Menelya, Valanya in a six-day week. Tolkien also named specific days of the year, such as **Loëndë** (Midsummer's Day), **Mettarë** (New Year's Eve), **Yáviérë**, a holiday falling near the Autumnal equinox. There can be few authors who have so extensively named the days.

Still Days
A variant of SILENT DAYS, when church bells are not rung (between MAUNDY THURSDAY and the Easter Vigil mass).

Stir-up Sunday
The Sunday before ADVENT SUNDAY, i.e. five weeks before Christmas. In the *Book of Common Prayer* the collect for the day begins: 'Stir up, we beseech thee, O Lord, the wills of thy faithful people. . . .' It has long been the custom, however, to associate the 'stir-ring up' with the Christmas mincemeat or pudding. In some families each member of the family gives the Christmas pudding a stir on this day. It is thought to bring luck during the following year.

Straw Bear Day
The Saturday before PLOUGH MONDAY at Whittlesey, Cambridgeshire. This is a revival of a custom formerly associated with Plough Monday itself, when a man disguised entirely in straw collected money through the streets. In the past the money would have been spent on liquid refreshment for the ploughmen, which led to the suppression of the straw-bear man at the beginning of the century. In modern times the money goes to reputable charities.

Suez Sunday
November 4th, 1956. The day on which a mass rally in Trafalgar Square, London, called for the resignation of Sir Anthony Eden as Prime Minister because of his policy on the Suez Canal issue. In the *New Statesman* some years later, Paul Johnson wrote: 'On Suez Sunday we all thronged to a monster rally in Trafalgar Square, where

Nye Bevan made one of the most sparkling speeches of his life.'

Summer Bank Holiday See AUGUST BANK HOLIDAY.

Summer solstice
June 21st–22nd (Northern hemisphere), December 21st–22nd (Southern hemisphere). One of the two occasions in the year when the sun is at its furthest point from the equator. The word 'solstice' reflects the fact that the sun appears to 'stand still' at such a time – Latin *sol* 'sun', *stitium*, from *sistere* 'to stand still'. This is the longest day of the year, a fact pleasantly turned on its head in a poem by Edith Thomas:

In the month of June, when the world is
green,
When the dew beads thick on the clover
spray,
And the noons are rife with the scent of
hay,
And the brook hides under a willow screen;
When the rose is queen, in Love's demesne,
Then the time is too sweet and too light to
stay;
Whatever the sun and the dial say,
This is the shortest day!

Sunday
The first day of the week. It is sometimes called the SABBATH DAY or THE LORD'S DAY by those who wish to remind themselves and others that it is meant to be a day of worship as well as rest for Christians. FIRST DAY is traditionally used by members of the Society of Friends, or Quakers, who wish to avoid the reference to pagan worship of the sun. The normal name of the day translates late Latin *dies solis* 'day of the sun.'

Dr Johnson set himself eight tasks for Sunday observance: 1) to rise early, 2) to spend morning at devotion, 3) to look back over the last week from a religious point of view, 4) to read the Scripture, 5) to go to church twice, 6) to read books of divinity, 7) to instruct his family, 8) to wear off by meditation any worldly soil contracted in the week. In Oliver Goldsmith's *The Vicar of Wakefield*, the vicar is distressed by the habit of his wife and daughters of making Sunday 'a day of finery'. They dress in 'laces, ribbons, bugles and catgut', while his wife is especially fond of 'crimson padasuoy'. This habit of dressing in one's best clothes on Sunday lingers on, perhaps because it provides something to do on what John Updike calls 'that dog of a day' in *Rabbit Redux*. One popular activity in summer led to the ice-cream sundae, where 'sundae' simply respells the name of the day.

The argument as to whether Sunday should be made to encourage devotional rather than leisure activities, by the simple expedient of banning the latter by law, has raged for a long time. Charles Dickens was moved to present his views on the matter in 'Sunday Under Three Heads'. He demolishes scornfully the arguments of those who want to force everyone to go to church and pleads for a day which will allow working people to relax as fully as possible in whatever ways they wish.

A minor literary curiosity connected with Sunday occurs in Arnold Bennett's *Clayhanger*, where a character called Charlie Orgreave is 'invariably called "the Sunday" – not "Sunday", but "the Sunday".' Bennett rather disappointingly tells us that 'nobody could authoritatively explain how he had come by the nickname'. Many Sundays in the year have individual names. See for instance ADVENT SUNDAY, BLACK SUNDAY, BRAGGOT SUNDAY, BROTHERHOOD SUNDAY, CANTATE SUNDAY, CARE SUNDAY, CARLING SUNDAY, CLOSE SUNDAY, EASTER SUNDAY, FIG SUNDAY, GOOD THIEF SUNDAY, JUBILATE SUNDAY, LAETARE SUNDAY, PALM SUNDAY, PASSION SUNDAY, PIG FACE SUNDAY, QUADREGESIMA SUNDAY, QUASIMODO SUNDAY, QUINQUAGESIMA SUNDAY, REFECTION SUNDAY, REFRESHMENT SUNDAY, RELIC SUNDAY, ROPE-YARN SUNDAY, ROSE SUNDAY, SACRAMENT SUNDAY, SEPTUAGESIMA SUNDAY, SEXAGESIMA SUNDAY, SIMNEL SUNDAY, STIR UP SUNDAY, TRINITY SUNDAY, WAKES SUNDAY, WALKING SUNDAY.

Sunflower Daze
Late September. Normally a one-day celebration in spite of the implication of the name. Groton, South Dakota, which describes itself as the 'sunflower capital', indulges in outdoor feasting and other activities in honour of the flower.

Sunnendei See STERRENDEI.

Super Flush Sunday
January 25th, 1987. The much-publicized name given to the day on which the Super Bowl American football game was played. Harvey W. Schultz, New York's Commissioner of Environmental Protection, bestowed the name. He pointed out that millions of New Yorkers would be watching the game on television, and if they all went to the bathroom at half-time or at the end of the game and simultaneously flushed their toilets, there would be a serious, if temporary, drop in water pressure. He did not suggest, but perhaps should have thought of doing so, that supporters of the New York Giants should do their flushing in the first half of the game, while those of the Denver Broncos should make use of the second half.

Superstitious Man's Idol Day
A seventeenth-century Puritan description of CHRISTMAS DAY.

Susan B. Anthony's Birthday
February 15th. The birthday of Susan Brownell Anthony is observed only in Florida. Daughter of a Quaker Abolitionist, Miss Anthony was born in 1820 and died in 1906, having devoted most of her life to the fight against slavery and the women's suffrage movement. It is said that her work did much to bring about the Nineteenth Amendment to the Constitution, which in 1920 finally gave women the right to vote

Swallow Day
The day on which the swallows are reputed to arrive, proverbially heralding the summer. A nineteenth-century English writer dated it as April 15th. **Swallows Day** in California is said to be March 19th, when the birds return to San Juan Capistrano Mission.

Sweet Thursday
The title of one of John Steinbeck's Cannery Row stories. Thursday itself is a 'magic day', one on which 'Miss Winch, who took pride in her foul disposition before noon, said good morning to the postman.' It is a day when city businessmen invent a reason for driving into the country, a day when 'old people sit looking off into the distance and remember inaccurately that the days of their youth were all like that.' Steinbeck contrasts it with '**Lousy Wednesday**', his version of a DISMAL DAY. 'Some days are born ugly. From the very first light they are no damn good whatever the weather, and everybody knows it.' He also offers some interesting comments on '**Waiting Friday**:

Not everyone believes that Friday is unlucky, but nearly everybody agrees it is a waiting day. In business, the week is really over. In school, Friday is the half-open gate to freedom. Friday is neither a holiday nor a work-day, but a time of wondering what Saturday will bring.

T

Tag day

A day when money is solicited for charitable purposes, small tags being given in return. In Britain this would be called a FLAG DAY. The London *Times* reported in December 1908: 'A new system of street collecting for public charities by means of tags or labels [was] tried at San Francisco recently on behalf of the Children's Hospital . . . The advent of 'tag day' is well advertised.' This was probably the first time this idea had been tried. It was taken up in Britain soon afterwards – see LIFEBOAT DAY.

Taily Day

April 2nd. This appears to be confined to Kirkcaldy, Fife. Children pin 'tails' to other people's backs with cheerful little messages on them, such as 'Kick me hard for I am soft'. It was reported in the 1950s that the custom had been extended to April 3rd, when extra long tails were pinned onto victims and set on fire. The cry of 'Taily, taily' would then warn the victim of what was happening.

Tap Day

'Could I help it,' says a character in Scott Fitzgerald's *Tender is the Night*, 'that Pete Livingstone sat in the locker-room Tap Day when everybody looked all over hell for him.' The reference is to the day when election to membership of an American student fraternity was announced, by tapping those elected on the shoulder. The custom still continues in some colleges.

In 1972 the British newspaper *The Daily Mirror* reported that Professor Geza Vajda, formerly a teacher of Space Physics in California, wanted to redesign our time system. His proposed new week would have consisted of five days: **Actday**, **Tapday**, **Middleday**, **Endday**, **Restday**. The significance of Tapday in this context was not explained.

Tax Saturday

The last Saturday before the end of the financial year, which in Britain ends on April 5th. 'It's Tax Saturday, isn't it? They're all getting married,' says a character in *Border Country* by Raymond Williams. Those so doing would obtain tax relief for the whole of the financial year, being taxed at the lower 'married' rate rather than the 'single' rate.

Teacher for a Day Day

Described by Bel Kaufman, in *Up the Down Staircase*, as 'the day kids turn the tables on us. It always takes place just before Xmas; it's the occasion for certain responsible seniors to run the school for one day.' The day at Calvin Coolidge High School, New York, is not too chaotic, though it deteriorates as it progresses. One of the student teachers sees to it that the mathematics teacher gets a zero in his subject by setting him a fiendishly difficult question, suggested by someone in the Graduate Math Department at Berkeley.

Tennant Creek Show Day See HOBART REGATTA DAY.

Tenth of April
'The name of this day', says Chambers in *The Book of Days*, 'is almost the only one applied in England as a denomination for an event.' He was writing in 1863, when the phrase 'the Tenth of April' still reminded many people of the English Revolution that might have taken place on that day in 1848. The Chartists, mostly working men, had arranged to petition parliament in huge numbers to demonstrate their strength. The government, fearing violence, brought in the troops, swore in citizens as special constables and displayed cannon near Westminster Bridge as a deterrent. These measures succeeded, so that 'the *Tenth of April* remained only a memory of an apprehended danger judiciously met and averted.' The Chartist movement itself collapsed after this anti-climax, and the *People's Charter*, drawn up in 1838, was allowed to lapse.

Tenth of September, The
The title of a novel by A. R. and R. K. Weekes, published in 1934. The story hinges on the fact that the heroine, Annette Damerel, will inherit a considerable sum of money on her twenty-third birthday, which occurs on September 10th.

Term Day
A Scottish expression for a day in the year fixed for a specific purpose, such as the payment of rent, hiring of servants, etc. The two main term days of the year were traditionally WHIT SUNDAY and MARTINMAS, though the other QUARTER DAYS, CANDLEMAS DAY and LAMMAS DAY were also term days. In the nineteenth century, 'term days' were also those on which scientific observations were systematically made, for example in the study of the weather.

Texas Independence Day
March 2nd. This was the birthday of Sam Houston (1793–1863), who led the Texans to victory over the Mexicans at the Battle of San Jacinto and thus assured Texan independence. Texas remained an independent republic from 1836 until 1845, when it was annexed to the United States. The day was especially important in 1986, as Texas celebrated its sesquicentennial.

Thamesday
Early September. A celebration on and alongside the River Thames between the Westminster and Waterloo bridges. Various events begin at noon and end at night with a grand fireworks display. The purpose seems to be to remind Londoners that the city can be a place of fun as well as business.

Thanksgiving Day
The last Thursday in November in the USA; the second Monday in October in Canada. In 1621 the settlers of the Plymouth colony celebrated their first harvest home with a day of thanksgiving to God for his bounty. The day was primarily a religious one, but inevitably it was also a day of family and social enjoyment. The observance of an annual day of thanksgiving first became general throughout New England. After the Revolution it spread to the Middle States, then to the West. It reached the Southern states after the Civil War. It has been observed nationally in the US since 1863 by presidential proclamation.

In modern times the day is associated with family reunions and family traditions. Americans who spend Thanksgiving Day with another family will say that they ate all the usual food and did all the usual things, but not in quite the correct order – the order in which they do things in their own home. For countless Americans meticulous attention to detail where traditions are concerned is very important indeed. O. Henry comments on this aspect of American life in his short story *Two Thanksgiving Day Gentlemen*. Louisa M. Alcott also comments on it in *Little Men*. She describes the 'good old-fashioned way' of observing the day, and refers to the 'popular belief that Thanksgiving must be kept by coming as near apoplexy as possible, and escaping with merely a fit of indigestion or a head-ache.' For Whittier it was the day 'When the gray-haired New Englander sees round his board/ The old broken links of affection restored.' Nowadays a morning visit to church may precede the meal, or perhaps a sortie to see one of the parades which take place on this day. New Yorkers are especially fond of Macy's Parade, and will be out on the often freezing streets at an early hour, waiting to see the giant floats pass by. One has only to be amongst the crowd of onlookers, preferably near the starting point of the parade, listening to the affectionate remarks of young and old as each float begins its journey, to realize just how much such traditional events mean to Americans.

Erica Jong was well aware of these senti-mental associations of the day when she began *How To Save Your Own Life* with the bleak sentence: 'I left my husband on Thanksgiving Day.' An English writer would probably have had to say: 'I murdered my mother on Christmas Day' to achieve the same effect. Mark Twain's comment on the day actually hints at the wholesale slaughter (of turkeys) which accompanies it, but as usual displays his wit. In *Pudd'nhead Wilson's Calendar* he writes: 'Thanksgiving Day. Let all give humble, hearty, and sincere thanks now, but the turkeys. In the island of Fiji they do not use turkeys: they use plumbers. It does not become you or me to sneer at Fiji.'

Thanksgobble Day

A humorous reference to THANKSGIVING DAY, which is noted for the consumption of turkeys.

These Were the Days

An autobiographical work by the American writer Clarence Day. See DAY.

Thinking Day

February 22nd. The birthday, in 1857, of Lord Baden-Powell, founder of the Boy Scout movement. Scouts and Guides are encouraged on this day to think about Lord and Lady Baden-Powell and fellow scouts throughout the world.

Third Day

Tuesday. An expression used by the Society of Friends (Quakers).

Thirtieth of January

'We must neither play cards, nor read, nor sew on the fifth of November and on the thirtieth of January, but must go to church, and meditate all the rest of the day'. This is the narrator, Margaret Dawson, describing life at the house of her kins-woman, Lady Ludlow, in the short novel by Mrs Gaskell, *My Lady Ludlow*. The 'fifth of November' reference is to the Gunpowder Plot (see GUY FAWKES DAY); the 'thirtieth of January' refers to Charles I, who was executed on that day in 1649. The king was beheaded by the supporters of Cromwell after many indignities had been thrust upon him, and was buried the same night in St George's Chapel, Windsor. The execution is referred to briefly in a poem by Andrew Marvell (1621–78):

He nothing common did or mean
Upon that memorable scene,
But with his keener eye
The axe's edge did try:
Nor called the gods, with vulgar spite,
To vindicate his helpless right,
But bowed his comely head
Down, as upon a bed.
('Horatian Ode upon Cromwell's Return from Ireland')

Charles I is one of a lengthy list of royal personages bearing that name to have suffered great misfortune, causing the superstitious to regard Charles as an unlucky name for royalty.

Three Dog Night

A bitterly cold night. This has become a common expression in the US and is said to derive from the Eskimo habit of describing cold nights in terms of the number of dogs needed as bed-companions.

Three Kings' Day

January 6th. Another name for the EPIPHANY, or TWELFTH DAY. On this day the infant Christ was shown to the Magi, the three 'wise men' or 'kings' from the East.

Three-Quarter Day

An expression used in Jamaica to indicate 9.00 a.m. At that time three-quarters of the working day remain.

Thump-the-door Night

Formerly a name in the Isle of Man for HALLOWE'EN.

> The turnip, of course, played a most prominent part in the Manx version of Hallowe'en ceremonies, and indeed All Saints' Eve was known in some districts as 'Thump-the-door Night'. Parties of the 'mob-beg' would gather outside the houses of people who were not specially respected, and bombard the door with turnips. A group of lads who were prosecuted at Ramsey some years ago for persecuting some old cottager whom they thought eccentric pleaded in excuse that they were only honouring a good old custom.

The good old custom mentioned by this correspondent to the *Isle of Man Weekly Times* in November, 1933 (known locally as the 'Hop-tu-naa' custom), was originally a kind of 'trick or treat'. The boys who took part in it would pound the front doors with turnips, cabbages and the like until they were given some money to go away.

Thunderday

A term which has been used for THURSDAY. The following, from Leonard Digges's *Prognostication Everlasting of right good Effect* (1556), is also of interest:

> Some write (their ground I see not) that Sunday's thunder should bring the death of learned men, judges and others; Monday's thunder the death of women; Tuesday's thunder plenty of grain; Wednesday's thunder the death of harlots; Thursday's thunder plenty of sheep and corn; Friday's thunder the slaughter of a great man, and other horrible murders; Saturday's thunder a general plague and great dearth.

Thursday

The fifth day of the week. In late Latin it was *dies Jovs* 'the day of Jove'. This was turned in Old English into 'Thor's day', since Thor, like Jove, was a god of thunder. **Thunderday** was used occasionally as a synonym for Thursday by writers familiar with mythologies. 'Thursday' seems to have appealed to writers of fiction as a name for a character, perhaps under the influence of Defoe's Man Friday. In Chesterton's novel *The Man Who Was Thursday* (1908), the poet-detective Gabriel Syme is known as 'Thursday'. Noel Streatfeild later created Margaret Thursday, who was found on the steps of a church porch on that day at the end of the nineteenth century. Michael Bond invented a mouse called Thursday. Special Thursdays in each year include BOUNDS THURSDAY, CARNIVAL THURSDAY, GREEN THURSDAY, HOLY THURSDAY, MAUNDY THURSDAY, SHEER THURSDAY. See also SWEET THURSDAY.

Tib's Eve See ST TIB'S EVE.

Toast 'n Jelly Day

An annual celebration in Lake Wobegon, Minnesota, according to Garrison Keillor, in *Lake Wobegon Days*. He also mentions 'the Germans' quadrennial Gestuffa [i.e. 'Boozing'] Days and 'Krazy Daze'.

today
The present day, or by extension, the present time or age. 'To' here has the meaning 'at, on, during/a period of time', as it has also in the words 'tonight' and 'tomorrow'.

Today Day
A Jamaican expression meaning 'this very day'.

Tommy Day
The day on which a tommy shop was open. 'Tommy' in this sense refers to the groceries and other goods which workmen received in lieu of wages by the so-called truck-system. Men received vouchers which could only be exchanged at the employer's truck or tommy shop. The system was much abused in the nineteenth century by employers who set high prices on the goods they exchanged for the vouchers. It has been pointed out that the loaves of bread distributed in charity on St Thomas's Day became known as 'Tommy'. This may account for the later use of the word for food and provisions other than bread. Benjamin Disraeli's novel *Sybil* contains a full account of the truck system in operation and describes a 'grand Tommy-day'. The shop-keeper maliciously keeps his customers waiting and insults them. Some of them take their revenge on him later.

tomorrow
The day following today. The original meaning of the word was 'the morn'. 'Tomorrow is a new day' was a Greek proverb. Montaigne has an essay of that title in which he relates that it came about when a tyrant whose name was Archias received a letter one evening when he was at dinner. He deferred opening it, saying 'Tomorrow is a new day'. The letter actually contained details of a plot to kill him, and the delay proved to be a fatal one. The anecdote would please those who think that 'tomorrowing', or procrastinating, is 'the thief of time'. For optimists, however, 'tomorrow is another day' are words of perpetual hope. In literature they are most notably the final words of Margaret Mitchell's *Gone With The Wind*.

Town Meeting Day
An annual event in Vermont. See ADMISSION DAY.

Trafalgar Day
October 21st. The Battle of Trafalgar was fought on October 21st, 1805, off Cape Trafalgar, southern Spain. The British fleet under Nelson were victorious over the French-Spanish fleet of Villeneuve, Gravina and Alava, though it cost Nelson his life. The name of the battle is familiar to all Englishmen, mainly because of Trafalgar Square in the heart of London, but there are no longer general celebrations to mark the day, other than in naval circles. Thornton Wilder, in his novel *The Eighth Day*, writes:

> Eustacia's father, Alexander Sims, was every inch an Englishman. He not only observed the royal birthdays, but on October 21 he raised the flag at dawn to commemorate the glorious victory at Trafalgar and later lowered it to half mast to mark the death of Lord Nelson.

There is a delightful essay by Kenneth Graham called 'The Twenty-First of October' in his *Dream Days*. It describes how a child decides to mark Trafalgar Day, a day about which 'nobody cares', as she says, by means of a bonfire:

> It was another sort of smoke that the inner eye of Selina was looking upon – a smoke that hung in sullen banks round the masts and the hulls of the fighting ships; a smoke from beneath which came thunder and the crash and the splinter-rip, the shout of the boarding party, the choking sob of the gunner stretched by his gun.

Transfiguration
August 6th. A Church festival commemorating the transfiguration of Christ on the mountain. The event is described by Matthew 17:2 as follows:

And after six days Jesus took with him Peter and James and John his brother, and led them up a high mountain apart. And he was transfigured before them, and his face shone like the sun, and his garments became white as light.

There is a very similar description in Mark 9:2.

Trewesdei See STERRENDEI.

Trick or Treat Night
A children's name for HALLOWE'EN, especially in North America. The custom of children touring the neighbourhood and asking householders for a 'treat' has spread in recent years to Britain. There has been some comment that the threat to play a trick on anyone who does not give money or sweets amounts to a juvenile form of blackmail, especially where old people are concerned. Others have remarked that on this night children are allowed or encouraged to do what is forbidden normally – namely, to approach strangers at night.

Trinity Sunday
The Sunday after WHIT SUNDAY. It honours the Trinity, the three persons of the Godhead – the Father, Son and Holy Spirit. This Sunday is sometimes known simply as **The Trinity**. The following day is also referred to as **Trinity Monday**.

Tuesday
The third day of the week, which commemorates in its name an ancient Teutonic deity, Tiw, or Tiu, a younger brother of Thor. He was identified with Mars, the Roman god of war, and Old English 'Tiwesdaeg' was thus a translation of late Latin *dies Martis*, 'day of Mars'. Modern French *mardi* 'Tuesday' refers to the same god. The Tuesday Club was founded by Lord Keynes and brings together economists and Treasury officials at occasional Tuesday meetings in London. Special Tuesdays include APPLE TUESDAY, BINDING TUESDAY, BLACK TUESDAY, FAT TUESDAY, SHARP TUESDAY, SHROVE TUESDAY. See also BECKET'S DAY, MAYBE TUESDAY.

Turkey Day
A common colloquial reference to THANKSGIVING DAY.

Tutti Day
The second Tuesday after Easter. A 'tutti' (or 'tutty', 'tuttay', 'tuttey', 'totty') is a dialectical word for a nosegay, or beribboned bunch of spring flowers. At Hungerford, in Berkshire, two 'Tutti-men' make their rounds to collect the nominal one-penny payments from local house-holders which are paid for certain grazing and fishing rights. The Tutti-men carry, as symbols of their authority, tutti-poles (or tutty-poles) wreathed with flowers and ribbons. They collect both the monetary payments and a kiss from each lady within the house, offering an orange in exchange. Tutti Day is also HOCK TUESDAY, traditionally a day for the collection of dues.

Twelfth, The
Normally a reference to August 12th, the GLORIOUS TWELFTH, when grouse-shooting legally begins. Occasionally the 12th of July is intended, more commonly known as ORANGE DAY.

Twelfth Day of August
William Hone published a letter written by 'Twelfth Day of August' in the first volume of *The Every-Day Book* (1827). The day, a lady, had written to say that she was mistreated sadly. Although King George IV was born on August 12th, 1762, April 23rd was known as the King's Birthday,

upon some shallow pretence that, being St George's Day, she must needs be King-George's Day also. All Saints' Day we have heard of, and All Souls' Day we are willing to admit; but does it follow that this foolish Twenty-third of April must be All George's Day, and enjoy a monopoly of the whole name . . .?

Twelfth Night
There is some dispute about when Twelfth Night occurs. **Twelfth Day** is undoubtedly January 6th. In former times Twelfth Night appears to have been used where Twelfth Eve might be used today, referring to the evening of January 5th. In modern times most people would consider Twelfth Night to be the night of January 6th, but several respectable reference books, such as the *Oxford English Dictionary*, Brewer's *Dictionary of Phrase and Fable*, etc, insist that it is the night of the fifth. Some dictionaries say that it is either one or the other, which seems to say that 'twelfth' can sometimes mean 'eleventh' or 'thirteenth'. Shakespeare seems to have known a thing or two when he called his play *Twelfth Night, or What You Will*. The play is probably best known for some of its minor characters, such as Sir Toby Belch, Sir Andrew Aguecheek, Malvolio, Maria and Feste, the clown. The main plot concerns Sebastian and Viola, twin brother and sister, and what occurs when Viola disguises herself as a man and is mistaken for Sebastian.

Twenty-Sixth Day of October 1812, The
This was the name of a British schooner which was captured in 1814 by an American privateer. Don Kennedy, in his *Ship Names*, speculates about the reason for the name – 'launch date, a birth date, a marriage date. Perhaps the date a previous vessel was lost, a loss the new vessel was to avenge?'

Tynwald Day
In the Isle of Man, the day on which the laws which have been enacted during the year are proclaimed to the people at an annual gathering. 'Tynwald' means 'Thing-field', where 'thing' refers to a council or parliament.

U

unbirthday

A day when it is not your birthday. In Lewis Carroll's *Through the Looking Glass*, Humpty Dumpty tells Alice about his un-birthday present. 'What *is* an un-birthday present?' she asks him. 'A present given when it isn't your birthday, of course.'

Uncle of a Day, An See SATURDAY.

Union Day

May 31st. The former name in South Africa of REPUBLIC DAY, referring to the Union of South Africa.

United Nations Day

October 24th. The anniversary of the adoption of the Charter of the United Nations Organization by its member countries was designated United Nations Day in 1947. Its purpose was to inform everyone of the UN's aims and to be a day of world peace. It appears to have little impact in modern times.

Up-Helly-A

Also referred to as **Uphelya, Up-Helly-Day, Uphalie Day, Uphalimass, Uphalliday**, etc. In Lerwick, Shetland, this refers to the last Tuesday in January, when a model of a Viking longship is paraded through the streets, then burned. The ceremony is said to commemorate the decision of many invading Vikings to remain in Shetland. 'Uphaliday' originally meant January 6th, the EPIPHANY. It was the day when the Christmas or Yuletide holidays came to an end, or were 'up'. **Up-halli(Day) Even** was used for TWELFTH NIGHT, which in former times was the evening of January 5th. The change of date for Up-Helly-A probably reflects the confusion caused by the change from the Julian to the Gregorian calendar in 1752.

V

Valentine's Day Also **Valentine Day**. See ST VALENTINE'S DAY.

Valium Picnic
A slow day on the New York Stock Exchange is known by this slang term in the American financial world, according to Philip Howard, writing in *The Times* (August 7th, 1987).

Veast Day
'On "veast day" and the day after, in our village, you might see strapping healthy young men and women from all parts of the country going round from house to house in their best clothes.' So writes Thomas Hughes, in *Tom Brown's Schooldays*, describing how young people returned home for the feast day celebrations. See FEAST SUNDAY.

VE-Day
May 8th, 1945. 'Victory in Europe' Day, after the unconditional surrender of Germany at the end of World War II.

Vernal equinox See EQUINOX.

Veterans Day
November 11th. This was originally ARMISTICE DAY, honouring the dead of World War I. Later it became REMEMBRANCE DAY, and was associated as well with World War II.

In the US, it has been Veterans Day since 1954, and now honours all those who fought for their country, regardless of the war they fought in. In Britain and Canada the term Remembrance Day is still used. J. D. Salinger writes, in *The Catcher in the Rye*: 'They have this day, Veterans' Day, that all the jerks that graduated from Pency around 1776 come back and walk all over the place, with their wives and children and everybody.'

Victoria Day
The Monday closest to May 24th. A national holiday in Canada since 1903. Elsewhere in the Commonwealth the day was for some fifty years observed as EMPIRE DAY, then COMMONWEALTH DAY. May 24th was Queen Victoria's birthday.

Victory Day
The second Monday in August in Rhode Island. The 'victory' referred to was that over the Japanese in World War II. See also VJ-DAY.

visiting day
The day on which a person of rank remains at home to receive visitors, hence the alternative name AT-HOME DAY. Also the day when visitors come to an institution which is normally not open to the public. 'How well I remember,' writes Charlie Chaplin in

My Autobiography, 'the poignant sadness of that first visiting day: the shock of seeing Mother enter the visiting-room garbed in workhouse clothes.' Betty Macdonald, in *The Plague and I*, has described the importance of visiting day from the point of view of a patient in a sanatorium:

> I have always liked any special day, be it Mother's Day, Groundhog Day or Bastille Day and the big full-bodied holidays like Christmas, Thanksgiving and Easter fill me so full of feeling and spirit that I can get tears in my eyes just looking at a fruitcake. Lying in bed at The Pines day after day, week after week, month after month . . . should have increased this feeling for holidays about a billionfold. It didn't. The days were all so exactly alike and followed each other with such monotonous regularity that I lost all interest in holidays as such. I knew them only as 'gas' day, bath day, fluoroscope day, visiting day, supply day or store day. It was in part infiltration into Sanatorium life, divorce from normal living. It was also in part the childish self-centred attitude of an invalid.

VJ-Day

August 15th, 1945. 'Victory in Japan' Day, after the unconditional surrender of Japan at the end of World War II. Norman Mailer writes, in *An American Dream*: 'A hero in mid-'44, a hero for all of '45, surviving even VJ-Day, I had my pick of opportunities and used them.' *V-J Day* is the title of a novel by Alan Fields, concerning a man who intends to blow up a hotel in New York as crowds gather to celebrate the victory.

Voltaire Day

Auguste Comte (1798–1857) was the founder of Positivism. As part of his 'religion of humanity' he proposed dedicating days to those who had furthered the progress of human beings. George Meredith refers to this in his novel *The Egoist*:

> 'There's a French philosopher who's for naming the days of the year after the birthdays of French men of letters, Voltaire-day, Rousseau-day, Racine-day, and so on. Perhaps Vernon will inform us who takes April 1st.' . . . 'No, but, my dear good Vernon, it's nonsensical,' said Sir Willoughby; 'why be bawling every day the name of men of letters!'
> 'Philosophers.'
> 'Well, philosophers.'
> 'Of all countries and times. And they are the benefactors of humanity.' . . . 'We might,' said Vernon, 'if you like, give alternative titles to the days, or have alternating days, devoted to our great families that performed meritorious deeds upon such a day.'
> The rebel Clara, delighting in his banter, was heard. 'Can we furnish sufficient?'
> 'A poet or two could help us.'
> 'Perhaps a statesman,' she suggested. 'A pugilist, if wanted.'
> 'For blowy days,' observed Dr Middleton.

W

Waitangi Day

February 6th. A national holiday in New Zealand. Waitangi is a town on the Bay of Islands in Northland. In 1840 the Treaty of Waitangi was signed between the British and the Maoris on this day agreeing to peaceful coexistence.

Waiting Friday See SWEET THURSDAY.

Wakes Sunday

Also found as **Wake Sunday**. The local annual festival of an English parish church, originally observed on the feast day of the patron saint but later transferred to a convenient Sunday during the summer. It is often followed by several other days of celebration, constituting a Wakes Week. The origin of the expression appears to derive from an original **Wake Day**, when a religious wake would be observed. On the eve of certain important feast days the early Church demanded that an all-night vigil be undertaken, the night being spent in prayer and meditation. The word 'wake' then seems to have become associated with the less solemn activities which frequently took place on the eve of a feast day. These could include the superstitious rites practised by young ladies on the EVE OF ST AGNES, for instance. Later still, the activities of the evening preceding a festival became part of the festival itself. The 'Wakes' became the

days of celebration, or the celebrations themselves. Shakespeare uses the word in the latter sense in *The Winter's Tale*, when the clown says: 'He haunts wakes, fairs and bear-baitings' (IV.iii). Particular celebrations on Wakes Sunday could lead to a local name for the day, such as **Bell Belt Day** in Congleton, Cheshire. Since the parish church there was dedicated to St Peter, belts with hand-bells attached to them were worn to represent his chains.

Walking Day

William Hone, in *The Every-Day Book* (1827) wrote:

> During the first few days [of June] you cannot walk the streets without waiting, at every crossing, for the passage of whole regiments of little boys in leather breeches, and little girls in white aprons, going to church to practise their annual anthem-singing, preparatory to that particular Thursday in this month, which is known all over the world of charity-schools by the name of 'Walking Day'; when their little voices, ten thousand strong, are to utter forth sounds that shall dwell for ever in the the hearts of their hearers.

The Opies (*The Lore and Language of School-children*) refer to a Walking Day at Warrington, Lancashire 'when hundreds of

Sunday School children process through the streets'. The latter custom continued at least until World War II, and occurred early in July. It was probably not connected with the day mentioned by Hone, when the children walked from their schools to St Paul's Cathedral for a thanksgiving service.

Walking Sunday

End of August. The name given to the Sunday before the start of the Donnybrook Fair, in Ireland. In *Fair Day*, Patrick Logan advances the theory that 'walking' is in this case a corruption of 'wake' (see WAKES SUNDAY). In the eighteenth century it was a day on which much fighting and drinking occurred, causing great scandal. Mr Logan adds that at the fair itself, in addition to these two activities, there was a great deal of dancing, love-making, pocket-pinching, thimble-rigging, cheating and horse-dealing, 'but these went on at hundreds of other fairs, and at any other such assembly in Ireland.'

Walpurgis Night

April 30th. This is the Eve of MAY DAY. According to German superstitious beliefs, it is the night when witches ride on broomsticks and he-goats and engage in revels with their master, the Devil. They are thought to do this especially on the Brocken, the highest point of the Harz Mountains. The legend of Walpurgis Night has been made known, especially, by Goethe's *Faust*. The name derives from an innocent English nun who became an abbess in Germany and died there in the eighth century. Her name was probably Walburga rather than Walpurga, and her feast day is February 25th, not May 1st as stated by Brewer. Her bodily remains were transferred to Eichstätt from Heidenheim on the eve of May 1st, which led to this day being called *Walpurgisnacht* in German. The existing pagan rites and beliefs then became associated with her name. Her name actually suited her occupation as abbess very well, since it meant 'ruler of the refuge'. The shrine of the abbess became a popular place of pilgrimage because of a kind of oil which exuded from the rocks at Eichstätt. The oil was reputed to have miraclous curative powers.

wash day

Also **washing day**. The day of the week when the dirty clothes, etc., of the household are washed. Often a Monday. There is a story of a low-church vicar writing to his bishop, heading the sheet 'St Timothy's Day'. The sarcastic reply was headed 'Wash Day'. A. A. Milne makes the following perceptive remark in his *Bachelor Days*:

> Of course, it is quite possible to marry for love, but I suspect that a good many bachelors marry so that they may not have to bother about the washing any more. That, anyhow, will be one of the reasons with me. 'I offer you,' I shall say, 'my hand and heart – *and* the washing.'

The *Oxford English Dictionary* quotes some advice given to nineteenth-century clergymen: 'Don't attempt to pay a pastoral visit on washing-day; you had better make it your day off.' Samuel Pepys, in his *Diary* (April 4th, 1666), noted: 'Home, and being washing day, dined upon cold meat.'

Washington-Lincoln Day

The third Monday in February, Ohio. See also LINCOLN'S BIRTHDAY, WASHINGTON'S BIRTHDAY.

Washington's Birthday

February 22nd; observed on the third Monday in February as a legal holiday in most states of the US. Because of the proximity of LINCOLN'S BIRTHDAY, some states observe PRESIDENTS DAY (e.g. Hawaii, Minnesota, Nebraska, Wisconsin, Wyoming in 1985). Other states which combined the two events in 1985 were Ohio (WASHINGTON-LINCOLN DAY) and South Dakota (LINCOLN-WASHINGTON DAY). George Washington (1732–99) naturally holds a unique position in the history of the USA. He was commander-in-chief of the Continental Army during the American Revolution and became the first president of the country in 1789. He looms large in American literature and legend, the most famous legend concerning the chopping down of a cherry tree and his subsequent 'I cannot tell a lie' remark to his father. This was invented by 'Parson' Weems. Less fictional was the great common sense, charm and graciousness of Washington's wife, Martha(1731–1802).

Wassail Eve

This was formerly a Northern English dialect term applied to TWELFTH NIGHT. 'Wassail' represents an Old English expression which meant 'Be in good health!' or 'Be hale and hearty!' This was said to a guest as he was handed a drink or as one drank his health. 'Wassail' was later applied to the drink itself, whatever was being used to drink someone's health, such as spiced ale. On Twelfth Night (also on Christmas Eve) it was the custom for the assembled company to toast one another from the wassail bowl, a sort of punch bowl or loving-cup. By this roundabout route Twelfth Night received its alternative name, which would roughly translate into modern English as 'Cheers Day'.

Watch Night

December 31st. The night on which a service is held by Methodists and others. A five-minute period of silence is observed leading up to midnight, when a hymn of praise is sung.

Waterloo Day

In military slang at the end of the nineteenth century this expression was used for PAY DAY. The Battle of Waterloo, which saw the final, decisive defeat of Napoleon, was fought outside the village of Waterloo, near Brussels, on June 18th, 1815. Although 'Waterloo' immediately became a significant name in English history, and gave rise to the expression 'to meet one's Waterloo', meaning 'to meet defeat', it is surprising that Waterloo Day never seems to have been commemorated, other than in the casual way mentioned above. There is

a rather more dignified reference to the battle in *Vanity Fair* by William Thackeray: 'The old grandfather pompously presented the child as the Son of Captain Osborne of the —th, who died gloriously on the glorious eighteenth.' In *Clayhanger*, by Arnold Bennett, a character laments his poor knowledge of history: 'The one fact engraved on his memory about the battle of Waterloo was that it was fought on a Sunday.'

Watermelon Day

A common name for a day of celebration in such American states as Iowa, usually in mid-July. A similar day in Sanborn, Minnesota, includes a melon-seed spitting contest, the world record for this activity being some forty-five feet, established in 1973. Mark Twain celebrated the watermelon itself, or its 'true Southern' variety, at least, in *Pudd'nhead Wilson's Calendar*:

> It is chief of this world's luxuries, king by the grace of God over all the fruits of the earth. When one has tasted it, he knows what the angels eat. It was not a Southern watermelon that Eve took: we know it because she repented.

Wattle Day

August 1st or September 1st. This is not a holiday in Australia, but a day on which 'national sentiment' is encouraged, focussing on the symbol of the wattle flower. The wattle is a species of acacia, of which seven hundred different kinds are found in Australia. In Europe the wattle has long been popularly known as a mimosa. The long pliant branches of certain acacia trees were used in Australia to make wattled fences or wattle-and-daub buildings, hence the name. 'Wattle-and-daub' refers to a method of construction using twigs plastered with clay or mud. The origin of 'wattle' in this sense is obscure.

Wedding Anniversary

The annual commemoration of a couple's wedding day. The twenty-fifth anniversary is commonly celebrated as the silver wedding anniversary, while the fiftieth is the golden celebration. The diamond wedding anniversary should be the seventy-fifth, but is normally taken to be the sixtieth. Names have been given to the celebrations of other years, but are rarely taken seriously. They are as follows:

1st cotton	11th steel
2nd paper	12th silk or fine
3rd leather	linen
4th flower or fruit	13th lace
5th wooden	14th ivory
6th iron or sugar-	15th crystal
candy	20th china
7th woollen	30th pearl
8th bronze or	35th coral
electrical appliance	40th ruby
9th copper or pottery	45th sapphire
10th tin	55th emerald.

Wedding anniversaries are often commented on in literature. There are two, for example, in *Our Mutual Friend* by Charles Dickens. There is a hypocritical celebration of the Lammles' first anniversary, that amiable pair having married in the mistaken belief that the other partner was rich. Dickens is at his funniest when he describes the anniversary of the Wilfers a few chapters later, 'kept morally, rather as a Fast than a Feast'. Mrs Wilfer tends to be sombre on such occasions. Her attitude is 'one compounded of heroic endurance and heroic forgiveness. Lurid indications of the better marriages she might have made shone athwart the awful gloom of her composure.'

Wedding Day

The day on which a marriage is celebrated, or the anniversary of that day. The verb 'wed', which contains the idea of plighting one's troth, has been replaced in normal English usage by 'marry', but 'wedding' remains the usual word for the ceremony itself. In *Romeo and Juliet*, IV.v, Capulet tells Paris 'O son, the night before thy wedding day/Hath Death lain with thy wife,' though in the same play (V.iii) there is a reference

to 'marriage-day'. Shakespeare also uses such poetic expressions as 'nuptial day' and 'bridal day'.

Wednesday

The fourth day of the week; mid-week. In late Latin this day was known as *Mercurii dies* (Mercury's day), a name still recalled in modern French *mercredi*, Spanish *miercoles*, Italian *mercoledi*. This became in Old English 'Woden's day', Woden (or Odin) being identified with Mercury, both gods of war. The modern pronunciation of Wednesday probably shows that a process known as metathesis (whereby the order of letters is transposed) has taken place, leading to an intermediate form *Wendesday*. The most important Wednesday in the year is ASH WEDNESDAY. See also SPY WEDNESDAY. John Steinbeck's 'Lousy Wednesday' is dealt with under SWEET THURSDAY.

weekday

A day of the week other than Saturday or Sunday. Until the nineteenth century the normal meaning would have been a day of the week other than Sunday. As Alexander Pope wrote in 1732: 'One solid dish his weekday meal affords,/An added pudding solemniz'd the Lord's' (Epistle to Bathurst').

welladay

This was formerly an exclamation of sorrow, similar to 'Alas!' or 'Lack-a-day!' It was the latter expression which caused it to be altered by analogy from 'wellaway', the original form, though 'wellaway' also survived until the nineteenth century.

West Virginia Day

The anniversary of West Virginia's admission to the American Union, June 20th, 1863. See also ADMISSION DAY.

Wet night

An evening when a great deal of drinking is done. 'As he knew he should have a wet night, it was agreed that he might gallop back again in time for Church on Sunday morning,' writes William Thackeray in *Vanity Fair*. In Horace Vachell's *The Hill* we find: 'Some of us had a wet night of it, last night'. Eric Partridge says this expression was frequently used, and gives other examples of 'wet' being connected with much drinking. He quotes Coleridge: 'Some men are like musical glasses; – to produce their finest tones, you must keep them wet.'

White Stone Day
A particularly happy or fortunate day. The Romans used a piece of white stone or chalk to mark such days in their calendar. Unlucky days were black days, marked with charcoal. See quotation at SATURDAY.

Whit Sunday
The seventh Sunday after EASTER DAY, also known at PENTECOST. In the Christian Church it commemorates the descent of the Holy Spirit. The name means 'white Sunday', thought to be an allusion to the white baptismal garments once worn on this day. The following day, **Whit Monday**, is a holiday in Britain, now known to officialdom as the **Late May Bank Holiday**. The whole period, beginning with the Saturday before Whit Sunday and extending until the following Saturday, is known as Whitsuntide, or in modern times more simply as Whitsun. In Scotland, Whit Sunday became **Whitsunday** or **Whitsun Day**, one of the quarter days. It was fixed for all time in 1693 as May 15th, the term day relating to it being May 28th. As Gillian Edwards pointed out in her *Hogmanay and Tiffany*, this fixing of Whit Sunday on a specific date means in effect that in Scotland it is possible for one Sunday of the year to occur on any day of the week.

Winter Friday
This description was applied in nineteenth-century English dialect to a person, one who looked cold and wretched. In the colloquial speech of the city at this time people said: 'He's like a winter's day', i.e. short and dirty. Presumably the next stage would have been to say: 'He *is* a winter's day',

converting a general description into a specific term. The same halfway stage between the general and specific is seen in a sentence like the following, from Thomas Hardy's *Far from the Madding Crowd*: 'He had made a toilet of a nicely-adjusted kind – of a nature between the carefully neat and the carelessly ornate – of a degree between fine-market-day and wet-Sunday selection.'

Winter solstice
December 21st–22nd. See SUMMER SOLSTICE for explanation of 'solstice'. This is the shortest day of the year in the Northern hemisphere.

Witches' Sabbath
See BLACK SABBATH. There is a novel by Paula Allardyce called *Witches' Sabbath*.

workaday
A work day as opposed to a holiday. The form 'workaday' is presumably by analogy with 'nowadays', or it may be a reduction phonetically of the earlier 'workyday', itself by analogy with 'holy day'. This sense of 'Workaday' is now obsolete, but Charles Dickens was still able to write, in *The Old Curiosity Shop* of someone 'in the very clothes that he wore on work-a-days'. He also used the expression in its modern meaning of 'ordinary, everyday' in *Nicholas Nickleby*: 'The less of real, hard, struggling work-a-day life there is in that romance, the better.'

work day
A day on which work is normally performed, a week day. **Working day** is sometimes used in the same sense, though the latter also refers to the portion of the day used for working, e.g. 'an eight-hour working-day'.

Wrong Days
Celebrated at Wright, Minnesota, in mid-July. There are the usual local festival activities.

Wry-Neck Day
A slang expression in the eighteenth and nineteenth centuries for a day on which a hanging occurred. 'Wry' here means 'awry, twisted, out of shape'.

X

Xmas Day

The abbreviated form of CHRISTMAS DAY has been in use since at least the fourteenth century, though it is now somewhat frowned upon. The 'X' represents the Greek letter *chi*, the first letter of *Christos* 'Christ'. 'Xp' was often used as the abbreviation for 'Christ' in various compound words, or standing alone, 'p' representing the Greek letter *rho*. Later this tended to become 'Xt', perhaps influenced by the common 'St' for 'saint'.

Y

Yak Bob Day
May 29th A local name in Westmorland for ROYAL OAK DAY. 'Yak' is a dialectal form of 'oak'. 'Bob' refers to the knob-like oak-apple. At Ulverston the day is known as BOBBY ACK DAY for a similar reason.

Yáviérë See STERRENDEI.

Year Day
This is sometimes a form of NEW YEAR'S DAY, especially when written as **Year's Day**. It is otherwise a variant of MIND DAY.

yesterday
The day immediately preceding the present day. It may seem strange, but it is clear that 'yesterday' at one time could also mean 'tomorrow'. The basic sense was 'a day other than today'. The need to distinguish clearly between the past and the future was felt at an early stage, and by the tenth century yesterday had taken on its modern meaning (though the *Oxford English Dictionary* quotes an isolated sixteenth-century instance where it means 'tomorrow'). 'Yester–' can also be affixed to words other than 'day' to refer to time in the past. **Yesternight** was formerly common, **yester-evening**, **yestermorn** or **yester-morning**, **yester-afternoon**, etc., were found, and **yester-year** was used as it still

is. 'Yester-evening' tended to become **yestreen**, especially in poetry (and in Scotland). A rare modern use of the word occurs in Mary McCarthy's *The Group*: 'Washington's Birthday Report. Yestreen I saw Kay Strong Petersen's new husband in Norine Schmittlapp Blake's arms.'

'Yesterday' itself is a word that tends to arouse philosophical thoughts in the minds of poets, whether it be expressed as in the Beatles' song or Fitzgerald's translation of the *Rubaiyat* by Omar Khayyam:

Ah, fill the cup: – what boots it to repeat
How time is slipping underneath our feet:
Unborn Tomorrow, and dead Yesterday,
Why fret about them if Today be sweet!

yestreen See YESTERDAY.

Yom Hazikaron
Hebrew for **Day of Remembrance**. See DAY OF BLOWING THE SHOFAR.

Yom Kippur
A Jewish day of fasting and prayer observed on the tenth day of Tishri, the first month of the Jewish year. The Hebrew words mean **Day of Atonement**, and this name is sometimes used. In *The Adding-Machine*, a play by Elmer Rice, a non-Jewish character has difficulty with the Hebrew expression,

which he renders as 'Young Kipper'. Perhaps he can be forgiven, since Leo Rosten, in *The Joys of Yiddish*, gives the pronunciation as *yum*-KIP-*per*, 'to rhyme with 'hum dipper'). Mr Rosten also gives interesting notes about the significance of the day to Jewish families.

Yom Teruah See DAY OF BLOWING THE SHOFAR.

Yule Day
A mainly Scottish expression for CHRISTMAS DAY. Similarly **Yule-Even** is used for CHRISTMAS EVE. 'Yule' is a form of Old Norse *jól*, the name of a pre-Christian festival which lasted for twelve days, somewhere near the time of the WINTER SOLSTICE.

CALENDAR

Many of the days mentioned in this book cannot be linked with a specific date. Those connected with Easter, for example, are all moveable feasts and occur at different times each year. Many other days are like Thanksgiving, which has a fixed formula 'fourth Thursday in November' (in the US), but where the actual date still varies from year to year. Then there are the days which are observed on a convenient day close to the actual date, rather than on the day itself.

In the following pages there is a list of specifically-dated days. It will be seen that many dates have no named day associated with them. Readers may wish to add to the calendar days of personal importance, such as birthdays, anniversaries, and so on. Some dates can be named in several different ways. March 25th, for example, is either Lady Day or the Annunciation in Church circles. In the US it is also both Maryland Day and Greek Independence Day.

In an orderly world, perhaps, every day of the year would be named in one way or another, and duplications would be avoided. Reality is not so tidy. The days listed here have become special at the random whim of history, which partly explains why they are so interesting.

January

1

New Year's Day · Ne'erday · Circumcision · Rose Bowl Day · Dismal Day

2

3

4

5

Wassail Eve

6

Twelfth Night · Epiphany · Three King's Day

7

Distaff's Day · Rock Day

8

Jackson Day · Old Hickory's Day · Battle of New Orleans Day

9

10

League of Nations Day

11

12

13

St Hilary's Day

14

Mallard

15

Martin Luther King's Birthday

16

17

Franklin's Birthday

18

Four an' Twenty Day

19

Robert E. Lee Day · Confederate Heroes Day

20

St Agnes's Eve

21

22

23

24
Paul Pitcher Day

25
St Paul's Day · Burns Night · Super Flush Sunday · Dismal Day

26
Australia Day

27

28

29
Carnation Day

30
Franklin D. Roosevelt Day · Thirtieth of January

31

NOTE
Also in January: Handsel Monday · Inauguration Day · Plough Monday

February

1

2
Candlemas Day · Groundhog Day · Presentation of Our Lord

3
St Blaise's Day

4
Dismal Day

5

6
Waitangi Day

7

8

9

10

11

12
Lincoln's Birthday

13

14
St Valentine's Day

15
Decimal Day · Lupercalia · Battleship Day · Susan B. Anthony's Birthday

16

17

18

19

20

21

22
Washington's Birthday · Thinking Day

23
Hobart Regatta Day

24

25

26
Dismal Day

27
Majuba Day

28

29
Leap Day · Bachelors' Day

NOTE

Also in February: Meal Monday · Presidents Day · Washington-Lincoln Day

March

1

St David's Day · Dismal Day

2

Texas Independence Day

3

4

Town Meeting Day

5

Mother-in-law Day · St Piran's Day

6

Alamo Day

7

8

International Women's Day

9

March the Ninth

10

11

12

Girl Scout Day

13

14

15

16

17

St Patrick's Day · Evacuation Day

18

Sheelah's Day

19

20

21

Back Badge Day · Vernal equinox · Earth Day

22

23

24

25

Lady Day · Annunciation · Maryland Day · Greek Independence Day

26

27

28

Dismal Day

29

30

Seward's Day

31

NOTE

Also in March: Commonwealth Day · Friday in Lide · International Women's Day · Lifeboat Day

April

1

All Fools' Day · April Fools' Day

2

Taily Day

3

4

5

6

7

8

9

10

Dismal Day · Tenth of April

11

12

Halifax Day

13

14

Pan-American Day

15

Swallow Day

16

17

18

19

Primrose Day

20

Dismal Day

21

San Jacinto Day

22

Arbor Day

23

St George's Day · Shakespeare's Birthday

24

Secretaries' Day

25

Anzac Day · St Mark's Day

26

27

28

29

30

Walpurgis Night

NOTE

Also in April: Geranium Day · Patriots' Day

May

1

May Day · Labour Day · Beltane Day · Lei Day

2

3

Crouchmas · Dismal Day

4

5

6

7

8

Furry Day · Harry S Truman's Birthday · VE-Day

9

Liberation Day

10

11

12

Hospital Day

13

14

15

16

17

18

19

20

Mecklenburg Declaration of Independence Day

21

22

23

24

Commonwealth Day · Empire Day

25

Flitting Day · Dismal Day

26

27

28

29

Royal Oak Day · Oak Apple Day · Restoration Day · Shick-Shack Day

30

Memorial Day · Decoration Day

31

Republic Day

NOTE

*Also in May: Armed Forces' Day · Cup Final Day · Fishin' Day · Early May Bank Holiday · Late
May Bank Holiday · Mother's Day · Victoria Day*

June

1

Corpus Christi · State Foundation Day

2

3

Jefferson Davis' Birthday · King's Birthday

4

Fourth of June

5

6

D Day

7

8

9

10

Dismal Day

11

Long Barnaby · St Barnabas' Day · King Kamehameha Day

12

146

13

14
Flag Day

15
Pioneer Day

16
Bloomsday · Dismal Day

17
Bunker Hill Day

18
Waterloo Day

19
Emancipation Day

20
West Virginia Day

21
Longest Day · Mumping Day · Summer solstice

22

23
Midsummer Eve

24
Midsummer Day · St John's Day

25

26

27

28

29

30

NOTE

Also in June: Alexandra Rose Day · Ascot Sunday · Father's Day · Lanimer Day · Sovereign's Official Birthday

July

1
Canada Day · Dominion Day

2

3

4
Independence Day · Fourth of July · Old Midsummer Eve

5
Tynwald Day

6

7

8

9

10

11

12
Orange Day

13
Dismal Day

14
Bastille Day

15
St Swithin's Day

16

17

18

19

20

21

22
Dismal Day

23

24

25
St James's Day

26
St Anne's Day

27

28

29

30

31

NOTE

Also in July: Diamond Day · Spinning Wheels Day · Watermelon Day · Wrong Days

August

1
Lammas Day · Colorado Day · Gule of August · Dismal Day

2

3

4

5
Oyster Day · Grotto Day

6
Transfiguration · Hiroshima Day

7

8

9

10

11

12
Glorious Twelfth · St Grouse's Day · Twelfth Day of August

13

14

15
Assumption · VJ-Day

16
Bennington Battle Day · St Roch's Day

17

18

19

20
St Philibert's Day

21

22

23

24
Bartholomew Day

25

26

27
Lyndon B. Johnson's Birthday

28

29

30
Huey P. Long Day · Dismal Day

31

NOTE

Also in August: Belgian–American Day · Lou Bunch Day · Nut Monday · Picnic Day · Plague Sunday ·
St Lubbock's Day · Victory Day · Walking Sunday

September

1
Partridge Day · The First

2

3
Cromwell's Day · Dismal Day

4

5

6

7

8

9
Admission Day

10
Air Force Day · *The Tenth of September*

11

12
Defenders' Day

13

14
Holy Cross Day · Holy Rood Day

15

16

17
Citizenship Day · St Lambert's Day

18

19

20

21
Dismal Day

22

23
Autumnal equinox

24

25

26

27

28

29
Michaelmas · Ganging Day

30

NOTE
Also in September: Kids' Day · Labor Day · Pig Face Sunday · Sunflower Daze · Thamesday

October

1

2
Old Man's Day

3
Dismal Day

5

6
German Day · Ivy Day

7

8

9

10
Kruger Day

11

12
Columbus Day · October the Twelfth

13

14
The Fourteenth of October

15

16

17

18
Alaska Day · Lukesmas · St Luke's Day

19

20

21
Trafalgar Day

22
Dismal Day

23

24
United Nations Day · Pioneer Day

25
St Crispin's Day

26

27
Big Bang Day · Day of Peace

28

29

30
Devil's Night

31
Hallowe'en · Nevada Day

NOTE

Also in October: Apple Tuesday · Fall Harvest Day · Fraternal Day · Good Thief Sunday · Punkie Night

November

1
All Saints' Day · All Hallow's Day · Hallowmas

2
All Souls' Day · Day of the Dead

3

4
Mischief Night

5
Guy Fawkes Day · Bonfire Night · Ringing Day · Dismal Day

6

7

8

9
Lord Mayor's Day · Sadie Hawkins' Day · Sprat Day

10

11
St Martin's Day · Martinmas · Remembrance Day

12

13

14

15

16

17
Queen's Day

18

19

20

21

22
St Cecilia's Day

23
Repudiation Day · St Clement's Day

24

25
Cathern Day · St Catherine's Day

26

27

28
Dismal Day

29

30
St Andrew's Day

NOTE

Also in November: Grey Cup Day · Melbourne Cup Day · Raisin Monday · Recreation Day ·
Thanksgiving Day

December

1

2

3

4

5

6
St Nicholas's Day

7
Dismal Day

8

9

10

11
Indiana Day

12

13
St Lucy's Day

14
December the Fourteenth

15

16
Day of the Covenant · Day of the Vow

17
Aviation Day · Saturnalia

18

19

20

21
Forefather's Day · St Thomas's Day · Gooding Day · Winter solstice · Shortest Day

22
Dismal Day

23

24
Christmas Eve

25
Christmas Day

26
Boxing Day · St Stephen's Day · Feast of Stephen · Day of Good Will

27

28
Childermas Day · Holy Innocents' Day · Proclamation Day

29

30

31
New Year's Eve · Hogmanay

NOTE
Also in December: Advent Sunday